Visit Autocity at www.motor.org.uk/careers
to find out more about the exciting
career opportunities on offer in today's
motor industry.

- ☑ Navigate through the cityscape to find your ideal career

- ☑ Look for roles available across the retail automotive industry

- ☑ Watch interactive video clips of real people in real jobs

- ☑ Read up on the qualifications you'll need

- ☑ Link through to employers' and automotive recruitment
  agencies' websites

WWW.MOTOR.ORG.UK/CAREERS

THE INSTITUTE OF THE MOTOR INDUSTRY

Turning your passion into a profession

Employing more than 800,000 people and with a £51 billion turnover, the automotive sector is critical to the health of the UK economy but the motor industry of tomorrow will depend on getting bright young people to join today who want a career that they can enjoy and progress in. When times are tough, businesses need people who are talented enough to bring them through it and the automotive sector is looking for the right people with the right skills.

There are loads of great career opportunities available in the retail motor industry, not to mention excellent career prospects. A career in the retail motor industry is as exciting and as interesting as you choose to make it. So if you want a career that's dynamic, fast moving and exciting, then it could be just right for you.

Vehicle manufacturers continue to push back the boundaries of technology, resulting in cars, trucks and motorcycles of increasingly high quality, reliability and performance. A successful future for the UK motor industry will depend on the recruitment and training of high calibre young people to develop skilled technicians in a range of hi-tech disciplines, using state-of-the-art specialist equipment. But it's not just a career for the technically minded. The motor industry needs professional staff in sales, management, marketing, human resources, finance and administration, who have the skills to work with people.

If you have the drive, confidence and ability to perform in this challenging and dynamic sector, the rewards can be very attractive.

What next after school?

THE TIMES

What next after school?

All you need to know about work, travel and study

9th edition

Elizabeth Holmes

KoganPage

LONDON PHILADELPHIA NEW DELHI

This book is dedicated to Jessica Greatwood.

Publisher's note

Every possible effort has been made to ensure that the information contained in this book is accurate at the time of going to press, and the publisher and author cannot accept responsibility for any errors or omissions, however caused. No responsibility for loss or damage occasioned to any person acting, or refraining from action, as a result of the material in this publication can be accepted by the editor, the publisher or the author.

The views expressed in this book are those of the author, and are not necessarily the same as those of Times Newspapers Ltd.

First published in Great Britain in 1996 as *The School-leaver's Handbook*
Second edition 1999
First published as *What Next?* in 2001
Second edition 2003
Third edition entitled *What Next after School?* 2004
Fourth edition 2006
Fifth edition 2007
Sixth edition 2008
Seventh edition 2009
Eighth edition 2009
Ninth edition 2010

Kogan Page Limited
120 Pentonville Road
London N1 9JN
United Kingdom
www.koganpage.com

© Joanna Grigg, 1996, 1999, 2001, 2003
© Elizabeth Holmes, 2004, 2006, 2007, 2008, 2009, 2010

The right of Elizabeth Holmes to be identified as the author of this work has been asserted by her in accordance with the Copyright, Designs and Patents Act 1988.

British Library Cataloguing in Publication Data

A CIP record for this book is available from the British Library.

ISBN 978 0 7494 5972 7
E-ISBN 978 0 7494 5973 4

Typeset by Saxon Graphics Ltd, Derby
Printed and bound in Great Britain by MPG Books Ltd, Bodmin, Cornwall

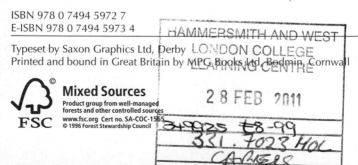

Organisations like the Institute of the Motor Industry (IMI) are working hard with manufacturers and retailers to encourage talented young people to consider a career within it. Of course, it's not just about cars. If it's motorcycles or trucks that you are interested in, then there's plenty of qualifications to choose from as well.

What you should remember is that qualifications DO MATTER in today's business. Whether you choose to do an apprenticeship, where you get paid during your training as an employed member of staff, or you prefer to do a full-time college course or a university degree in automotive engineering or even management, for example, it's important that you show your commitment and ability.

For young people with the right qualifications under their belt, the automotive industry offers almost boundless opportunities. Of course you need the right qualifications, but you also need to show that you're serious about doing right by the industry. Employers and customers want the reassurance of dealing with people who are respected for their professional attitude and know what they're talking about.

The IMI's careers website can help you find out more about the hundreds of different jobs in the motor industry.

Autocity brings to life the diverse roles available within the industry by using video case studies of real people in real jobs. Visitors to the site can also find out about qualifications, salary guidelines, job descriptions and lots more. Using the concept of a city, the site features a series of retail automotive businesses which the user can explore.

To visit Autocity go to **www.motor.org.uk/careers**

YOUTH IN ACTION

The Youth in Action programme is funded by the European Commission and provides young people with a variety of opportunities for non-formal and informal learning with a European dimension.

Programmes include:

- Group Youth Exchanges
- European Voluntary Service
- Youth Initiatives
- Training and Support for youth workers

Visit our website:

www.**british council**.org/**youthinaction**

BRITISH COUNCIL

Youth

Education and Culture

Contents

Youth in Action programme

Youth

The Youth in Action programme (2007-2013) is funded by the European Commission and provides young people with a variety of opportunities for non-formal and informal learning with a European dimension. It builds on the experience of the previous YOUTH programme (2000-2006).

The programme's general objectives are: the promotion and development of young people's active citizenship; solidarity and social cohesion; as well as the development and promotion of quality support systems and European-wide cooperation. Specific programme priorities are: European Citizenship; participation of young people; intercultural dialogue; and the inclusion of young people with fewer opportunities. The programme is divided into 5 Actions:

- Action 1 – Youth for Europe
- Action 2 – European Voluntary Service
- Action 3 – Youth in the World
- Action 4 – Youth Support Systems
- Action 5 – Support for European Cooperation

The Youth in Action programme is particularly looking for new applicants to the following programmes:

Action 1.1 - Youth Exchanges

Youth Exchanges offer an opportunity for groups of young people from different countries to meet and learn about each other's cultures. The groups plan together their Youth Exchange around a theme of mutual interest.

Action 1.2 - Youth Initiatives

Youth Initiatives support group projects designed at local, regional and national level. They also support the networking of similar projects between different countries, in order to strengthen their European aspect and to enhance cooperation and exchanges of experiences between young people.

Action 1.3 - Youth Democracy Projects

Youth Democracy Projects support young people's participation in the democratic life of their local, regional or national community, and at international level.

To find out more please contact:

Youth in Action Programme
British Council
10 Spring Gardens
London
SW1A 2BN
Tel: +44 (0)20 7389 4030

 BRITISH COUNCIL
 Education and Culture
Youth in action

Emai: youthinaction@britishcouncil.org
Internet: www.brititishcouncil.org/youthinaction

What is a Taxation Technician?

All businesses and individuals earning over a certain amount of money must file tax returns – Tax Technicians provide the technical expertise. Taxation Technicians are qualified professionals who prepare tax returns for businesses, or for individual taxpayers. Tax Technicians also work for the Government in HM Revenue and Customs. Members of the Association have passed their examinations and have gained relevant experience - their qualification is recognised by use of the title of "Taxation Technician" and the designatory letters ATT.

Why should you think about ATT and a career in tax?

Tax won't disappear – there will always be a need for tax professionals regardless of the state of the economy

Jobs are in every sector and industry – Tax Technicians are employed by professional services firms, accounting firms, tax specialist firms, in businesses, banks, by charities and in the public sector

Choice of which kind of tax you want to focus on – personal tax, business / corporation tax, inheritance and estate tax, environmental tax and VAT

Flexible study and exams – many trainees work part-time or full-time and modular exams are available twice a year

Career progression – studying for the ATT and becoming a member provides the opportunity to progress from a tax trainee, then tax manager, to a tax senior with corresponding increases in salary and responsibility. Many ATT's go on to run their own businesses

Broaden options for the future – open the doors to other qualifications - ATT membership provides credit towards other finance qualifications, e.g. CTA (The Chartered Tax Adviser qualification) and ACCA.

Become part of something – you'll join a network and a membership body of like-minded students and members to support you, your job, your technical learning and your professional development

Prestige – with a membership of over 6,500, the Association of Taxation Technicians (ATT) is the leading professional body for those providing tax compliance services and related activities in the UK.

Do you want to know more?
Visit our website on **www.att.org.uk**
Or ring us on **0844 251 0830** or **020 7340 0551**

If you've enjoyed the challenge of dance or drama throughout secondary school, it might be worth considering a future in Performing Arts. Whether you want to act on stage, television, or the latest West End musicals, a good qualification from an established institution is the best, if not the only way forward.

Arts Educational Schools London is an industry leader in Performing Arts training and the leading institution for Musical Theatre training in the UK. Now in our 90th year, we strive to continuously produce the most talented and successful names in theatre, film and TV. Over the years graduates from the School have gone straight into major West End and National

theatre productions and musicals, with past students appearing in almost every staged production across the UK. More and more of our graduates can also be seen regularly in quality dramas on BBC, ITV and Channel 4, and in British and International feature films.

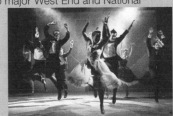

You will already know many of our former students: Julie Andrews, Darcy Bussell, Sarah Brightman, Martin Clunes, Gillian Lynne, Michaela Strachan, Will Young and Catherine Zeta-Jones are just a few of our esteemed alumni. And with Andrew Lloyd Webber as our newly appointed president, you know you're in good company.

Our mission is clear: We want everyone to succeed, with a firm belief in the power of education, creativity and innovation.

Arts Educational Schools offer a range of choices for school leavers at A-Level and degree level:

The sixth form is currently the highest ranked performing arts school in the country and suits those who want to continue their academic studies, while following their passion as a performer. We offer A-Levels in Drama and Theatre studies, Dance, Music, and Photography, alongside more traditional subjects such as Maths, History, Philosophy, and English to name a few. Classes are small and careful assessment ensures that each student maximises their ability and achieves at the highest possible level.

This year we will also be introducing a BTEC extended diploma in Musical Theatre. This two year course, which provides students with a qualification equivalent to three A-levels, is perfect for those wishing to pursue a career in Musical Theatre. The course is assessed continuously, with students undertaking classes in Acting, Jazz Dance, Ballet and Singing.

For those who have finished sixth form and are thinking about pursuing a degree in performing arts, ArtsEd offer two 3 year courses: BA (Hons) Musical Theatre and BA (Hons) Acting focusing on film and television. Both options train students to work in a contemporary, industry-relevant environment. Students are provided with the opportunity to work alongside prominent industry figures, including directors, musical directors and choreographers such as Ché Walker, Steve Marmion, and Stephen Mear. We ensure all of our students build the skills to become confident performers ready for the professional industry and further education.

The newly re-developed BA (Hons) Acting focusing on film and television draws on the strengths of our film department to provide unparalleled training. This is an unprecedented step that puts ArtsEd at the forefront of film and television training. The course concludes with the graduate film screening which is now an annual fixture at BAFTA.

For further information on all our courses please visit **www.artsed.co.uk**

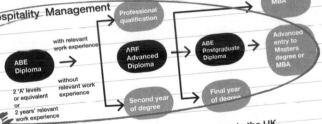
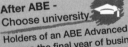

The Association of Business Executives (ABE) is a professional awarding body providing business & management qualifications around the world. We are an exam board, but more than that - you are a member of ABE as soon as you register to study our qualifications.

ABE qualifications are recognised by universities and employers worldwide. After studying with us you could top up your professional qualification by going straight on to the third year of a university degree programme, or directly on to an MBA programme. Many of our members also go straight on to work within the field they have studied.

Being a member means you get access to heaps of benefits including an associate NUS card packed full of discounts, access to our online social networking page and you'll receive our members' magazine 'Student Focus' four times a year which is filled with success stories, study tips and business articles.

Our qualifications cover Business Management, Business Information Systems, Financial Management, Human Resource Management, Marketing and Travel, Tourism & Hospitality Management. They are available from Certificate to Advanced Diploma level and Postgraduate Diploma level in the case of Business Management.

If you hold two A levels or equivalent you could enter directly at Diploma level and entry to our Certificate level is open to all.

Choosing where to study is simple, find a college near you by visiting www.abeuk.com/colleges/collegesearch.

Visit www.abeuk.com/registration/onlineregistration to register online now. If you would like to request an information pack or have any questions, you can contact Lauren or Chloe at marketing@abeuk.com or 0208 329 2936. You can also get connected with ABE students around the world on the ABE Facebook group or hear ABE tweets at: http://twitter.com/abetalk.

We look forward to hearing from you!

Preface

At a time when the world is changing rapidly, when words like 'recession' and even 'depression' are regularly in the news and job losses are widely reported on, the decisions that young people take when facing a new phase of life certainly have an added significance. Yes, there are many new possibilities to consider, but there are costs associated too, and being able to plan for an uncertain future – using solid knowledge of the options open to you – is a skill that all adults need.

For this reason, this latest edition of *What Next After School?* includes plenty of advice on how to make great decisions that will support you most effectively, how to plan for times ahead, how to navigate disappointment and how to give yourself the best chance of turning dreams into reality. There's also all the usual up-to-date information on the many options facing 16- and 18-year-old school leavers.

Acknowledgements

Throughout the course of writing this book I visited many schools and colleges to get ideas about the kind of information and advice that school leavers really need. Although they are too numerous to mention individually by name, I would like to thank all of the teachers, lecturers, students and careers advisers who willingly gave their time and thoughts; your help was very much appreciated. In particular, thanks must go to Callum Stannard, whose thoughtful insights have contributed greatly to this book.

I would also like to thank Charlotte Howard of the Fox & Howard Literary Agency, Jon Finch, Ian Hallsworth and the Kogan Page team.

The information in this book is correct at the time of going to print, but be aware that some of the detail will be subject to change on a regular basis. Where this might be an issue, relevant website addresses have been included so that you can find updated information if necessary.

BRITISH SUGAR

EARN WHILE YOU LEARN

MODERN PRODUCTION
ENGINEERING APPRENTICESHIPS

A great salary from the moment you start

Locations: Bury St Edmunds, Cantley (near Norwich),
Newark (near Nottingham) & Wissington (near King's Lynn)

Join us, and over the next four years we'll give
you all the support you need to achieve a
recognised professional qualification, as well
as first-hand experience at our state-of-the-art
production plants. What's more, at the end of
the apprenticeship you could find yourself
earning c30k as one of our Process Technicians.

If you have or are expecting at least 5 GCSEs or
equivalent (grade c or higher), including Maths,
English and a Science subject, then visit our
website to find out more.

www.notjustsugar.com

BRITISH SUGAR

Modern Production Engineering Apprenticeships

Factory Locations: Bury St Edmunds, Cantley (near Norwich), Newark (near Nottingham), Wissington (near Kings Lynn)

Every year, we give talented people the chance to earn as they learn, at the heart of our varied business. It's certainly an education. You get on-the-job training, college study and valuable qualifications to show for it – plus the chance to make friendships that could last a lifetime.

The Apprenticeship scheme is a four-year course that begins with full-time college study. During vacations, you'll join us for a factory-based training scheme. That will prepare you for years two, three and four, which you'll spend on site, with day release to college. During the scheme, you'll be part of a business that's every bit as complex as the oil, chemical and power industries.

We process the UK's entire crop of beet – that's over 7 million tonnes – and turn it into 7,500 tonnes of sugar per day. It's a 24/7 operation that demands the highest levels of technical expertise. With the guidance of our experts, you'll soon begin to learn the ropes. In fact, we'll give you your own personal mentor; a highly experienced member

of our team, who'll watch your progress and offer support. Feel free to call on them whenever you need to.

Through business-specific courses and on-the-job learning, you'll build

 excellent all-round knowledge of our whole operation – including our sophisticated processing plants. Just as importantly, you'll gain qualifications: first NVQ Level 2 Engineering Foundation and then NVQ Level 3 in Engineering Maintenance. By the time you've finished, you'll have a BTEC HNC in Engineering, plus loads of practical experience. After that we'll appoint you as a factory-based technician and help you develop over the following two years. If you're ambitious and keen, there's no telling how far you'll go.

Got what it takes to join us? You must be 16 or over with at least five GCSEs (or equivalent), at grade C or higher. These will include English, Maths and Science. If you can add team spirit, imagination, determination and plenty of get-up-and-go, we'd definitely like to hear from you.

There's a very big team aspect to it, you feel part of one team and there's always some support there for you with the training, with the job - with everything, pretty much."

Shaun Jermy, Technician, Cantley Factory

"I think it's very satisfying when you come in and something's not working, and you need to get it working, you've got the tools and the equipment there."

Matthew Goodrum, Technician, Cantley Factory

Skills for Care & Development
Sgiliau Gofal a Datblygu

Caring careers

social work, social care, early years and child care

Care is one of the fastest growing areas of employment in the UK. Never before have there been so many great career opportunities.

A career in care offers great job prospects, good job security, training opportunities, and a career ladder for people with the right skills and motivation

For more information visit **www.caringcareers.org.uk**

Skills for Care & Development is the sector skills council for social care, children, early years and young people's workforces in the UK.

Couldn't care less?

Almost everybody comes into contact with the social care system at some point in their lives. Whether they need to use care services themselves or because a friend or family member needs help.

We can all expect to face problems due to old age, family circumstances, illness and sometimes disability. What happens when people find they can't cope and friends and family can't help? They look to our well trained, committed care workers.

Social care services help older people to continue to live in their own homes, or foster care for children and young people in residential care, enable adults with long term illnesses and disabilities to enjoy a wider range of opportunities in life.

Or couldn't care more?

There are currently around 2.5 million people in the UK who receive social care services. With people working harder and living longer, we need highly motivated and committed staff to provide support to the people who need them most.

A career in care offers great job prospects, good job security, training opportunities and a career ladder for people with the right skills and motivation. With over 1½ million jobs in our sector - this could be the career for you!

Visit www.caringcareers.org.uk for more information.

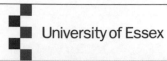
University of Essex

Thinking about your future?

If you are thinking about higher education, why not visit our open days in September and October 2010?

To find out more and to book your place visit:
www.essex.ac.uk/ads/times

University of Essex

Why not see what the University of Essex can offer?

Academically excellent

Essex is a leading academic institution for the quality of its research and teaching. Departments span the humanities, social sciences, science and engineering, and law and management.

Friendly and supportive undergraduate experience

Programmes are designed to equip students with the skills demanded by today's employers in the highly competitive world of work.

Exceptional recourses and facilities

First-class facilities and support services enable students to make the most of their studies.

www.essex.ac.uk/ads/times

Introduction

It doesn't matter how much you may be looking forward to leaving school and moving on to your next challenge, this can still be a nerve-racking time. Many people of your age find themselves thinking: How do I know what I want to do? What options are open to me? Have I made the right decision? What should I do next?

On top of any uncertainty you might be feeling, you are probably really pushed for time. If you are in the middle of your GCSEs, you will be up to your eyes in coursework, studying, revising and exams, and finding time even to start thinking about your next steps in life can be impossible.

It's tough that so much seems to happen all at once. Just as you are ploughing through the most demanding period of your school life so far, you are expected to search out new courses that you would like to take, think about where you want to work, even consider leaving home. This means gathering information and application forms, writing CVs and creating personal statements that reveal who you are and why you would be great for the course/job/voluntary position (delete as appropriate). It also means thinking just as much about the past as about the future. What have you done so far in your life that you have enjoyed? What have you learned from the experiences you have had? What have part-time jobs you have had taught you?

That's where this book comes in to help you out. Packed with information on the kinds of choices that you face right now, as well as information on options you may not even have thought of, this book helps you to take a good look at where you have been, where you are now, where you want to be in the future and how you can get there. It helps you to take a good look at yourself, to see yourself as clearly as possible and to think about life goals that you know will give you that kick.

This book will not tell you what will earn you the most money, or what qualifications you need to do certain jobs. There are other sources for this information that your school or local library can help you find out. Instead, when you have gone through all that this book has to offer, you can expect to know where it is you want to head for in life and what you might find when you get there.

You may not always feel totally in control of your life; growing up and being at school has to be like that. But with the help of this book, you will see what opportunities lie ahead of you and can start to direct the next scenes of your life. Good luck!

Who this book is for

If you are looking ahead to when you leave school, then this book has been written for you. However, it will also be invaluable for teachers and parents who are supporting teenagers through the decision-making processes linked to leaving school at either 16 or 18 years old.

How to use this book

Now that you have picked this book up and started reading it, don't feel that you have to continue from this point and plough your way through to the very end. *What Next After School?* has been written in a way that allows you to dip in for specific chunks of information or, alternatively, treat it like a cover-to-cover read. Either way, I hope you get what you need from it.

Features of this book

Each part of *What Next After School?* has been broken down into parts to enable you to find the information you need as quickly as possible. At the start of each chapter is a list of what you will find within it and at the end of each there is a summary.

Action features

Action features are questions for you to consider or activities for you to do. They have been designed not as essential tasks that you must do, but as interesting 'thought-provokers' that will help you to clarify your thinking. Do what you think will help you and leave out what you don't feel you need to do. Your responses are for your eyes only. Don't feel that you need to share them with anyone if you don't want to.

Information points

Here you will find website addresses, e-mail addresses and telephone numbers where you can find further information about what you have just read.

'View from...' boxes

Many young people, teachers, lecturers and parents gave their views, experiences and opinions to me when I was writing this book. You will find these throughout in 'View from...' boxes (for example, 'Perfectionism... View from Amy'). Although the names have been changed, and sometimes some of the ideas have been merged, the views are of real people.

Glossary

There may be words or abbreviations in this book that you have not come across before. If this is the case, take a look at the glossary in the Appendix, page 323, where you should find an explanation. It might be a good idea to read through this section anyway, so that you know what is covered there. If you can think of anything that should be included in the glossary in future editions of this book, you can e-mail your suggestions to eh@ elizabethholmes.info.

The internet

Just about everything you need to know about the options you have can be found on the internet but it can be hard tracking down just where to look. To save you the trouble of trawling through what search engines churn up for you, I have included details of useful websites that you might like to visit. These appear in the main text of the book as well as in the directory of useful information in the Appendix.

Step up, Step forward

For a career in podiatry

If you are looking for a flexible and rewarding career with great earnings potential, step this way.

- 87% graduate employment rate
- Earnings up to £100k plus
- Tuition fees paid for UK & EU students
- NHS bursaries available
- HPC approved courses

Would you like to run a successful business, work as an NHS or private consultant, work part time, train as a podiatric surgeon, get a management position, work with children, become a medical researcher, work abroad or with a professional sports team?

A career in Podiatry can offer you all of these possibilities and more.

Podiatrists are healthcare practitioners responsible for assessing, diagnosing and treating problems relating to the lower limb.

Podiatrists work with a huge range of patients to relieve symptoms, treat conditions and maintain their quality of life. The scope of practice includes musculoskeletal assessment, administering local anaesthetics, wound care, vascular/tissue viability and neurological assessment, skin, nail and bone surgery, care planning and health promotion.

Podiatrists can work in many settings including private practice, NHS GP surgery, a hospital, a visiting practice or a sports club. Other opportunities include becoming a medical researcher, teaching in higher education, training as a podiatric surgeon and establishing your own private clinic or working alongside the police in forensics.

A new graduate in podiatry would have a starting salary of approximately 22k in the NHS but the earning potential could be in excess of 100k.

To qualify you have to complete a BSc (Hons) degree in Podiatry at one of the 13 universities across the UK. Courses are NHS funded and for UK and EU students there are no tuition fees. Additionally you may be eligible for a bursary to help with other costs.

For further information on podiatry log on to **www.feetforlife.org**

For those in Scotland, Wales and Northern Ireland

There are some significant differences between the countries that make up the United Kingdom regarding education. Since devolution, Wales and Northern Ireland have been developing their own (but similar) education systems, and the education system in Scotland has long had significant differences when compared with the English education system. For example, Scottish readers should be aware that in order to simplify the text I refer only to NVQs in this book. In nearly every respect, these are the same as their Scottish equivalent, SVQs. You can find out more about the education systems in Wales, Scotland and Northern Ireland from the following websites:

Wales: www.wales.gov.uk
Scotland: www.scotland.gov.uk
Northern Ireland: www.niassembly.gov.uk
England: www.bis.gov.uk (Department for Business, Innovation and Skills), www.education.gov.uk (Department for Education)

A word about change

The world of education is in the process of change, and, in particular, the education choices of 14- to 19-year-olds. This may mean that you need to do some additional research on the choices that you have in front of you. The best place to start looking for further information on the changes for 14- to 19-year-olds is www.education.gov.uk.

Other useful websites for information on choices for 14–19 year olds include:

- www.need2know.co.uk
- www.direct.gov.uk/en/Parents/index.htm
- www.direct.gov.uk/en/YoungPeople/index.htm
- www.connexions-direct.com

Why Physiotherapy?

**'Words fail to describe the feeling of first seeing a patient
make improvements because of my time with them'**
Nick Southorn, 26, physiotherapy graduate

We've all hurt ourselves at some time through playing sport or an accident, and though we may first visit our family doctor, or need an operation, we often need to see a physiotherapist to ensure that our body movements return as near to normal as is possible, and our recovery is complete.

Physiotherapists help and treat people of all ages (from children to the elderly), from all walks of life (from professional sports people to those with permanent disabilities), and practise in a variety of locations (from hospitals to sports clubs). No two days are the same for physiotherapists.

Qualification for this hugely rewarding career is through a 3-year degree course. Find out more about entry requirements and university locations at www.csp.org.uk/careers. Or if you'd prefer a chat, call us on 020 7306 6666.

advertisement feature

Part One
Career planning

1
Being your own life coach

This chapter looks at:

- where you are now;
- life coaching as a concept;
- how to become your own life coach.

So, you're about to make the move into the next phase of your life. Your compulsory school career is over and the next steps are for you to decide. How does it feel? Is it a relief to be free and in charge of your life? Or is it all a daunting responsibility?

You're probably sick of hearing people telling you that 'you're at an important stage of your life' and that 'the choices you make now will affect you for the rest of your life' and so on. As if you might have missed that fact! Most teenagers know exactly how crucial their decisions are likely to be, but what is the best way of making them?

If anyone passes on any gems of advice to you, they almost certainly mean well. But it can be incredibly confusing when you are bombarded with opinions from others who simply want to make sure that you don't make the same 'mistakes' that they think they made. It's at times like these that you need to be able to trust in your own decision-making abilities (see Chapter 2), based on sound advice from people in the know. And knowing who and where to go to for that advice is essential. Basically, to find your way round the potential pitfalls so that success is yours, not just at this stage of your life but beyond into the future, you need to become your own life coach.

Life coaching... what does it mean?

Life coaching is just what the name implies. It has become very popular, particularly among those who are keen to make changes in their lives, or who envisage combining several careers throughout their working lives. There are many reasons for this, probably to do with the fact that people increasingly have a variety of careers rather than just one, as used to be the case. Life coaching helps you to seek out and create the kind of opportunities you need in order to get where you want to go, instead of merely reacting to opportunities that may present themselves to you during the course of your life. A life coach typically talks you through what you hope to achieve, what resources you have to help you achieve it, and what next steps you can take to set you on the right course. It should be a really positive process, although it may sometimes involve facing up to self-sabotaging habits.

Making decisions... View from Lee

I don't think I ever thought about what I wanted to do that much. I just took whatever next step was in front of me. I didn't really ever plan anything. But then I started to think that I should have some idea of my goals and what I want to achieve. It boosted my confidence because I started to see that planning and making goals are important steps to achieving what you want to achieve. That sounds really obvious now, but I don't remember ever being told that, or being told how to do it effectively. I think it's about seeing your life as something that you can create, rather than something you are stuck with and can't do anything about.

Becoming your own life coach

You are bound to have the support of others around you, whether at school or college or at home, to help you sort out what your next moves might be, and you may even have the benefit of a mentor who works closely with you, but it is important not to forget what a great resource you are!

There are some key ways to help you become your own life coach. And it's always going to be worth doing that, rather than risking unintentionally standing in your own way. As you read through this book, which contains stacks of information on decision making, goal setting, studying, taking time out, travelling, moving away from home, money management and much more, keep in mind these key life-coaching ideas:

- **Stay confident** – As soon as you start to doubt your skills and abilities, or to doubt your value as a person, your confidence will nosedive. Clearly, there's a balance between healthy confidence and excessive confidence, but severe self-doubt is rarely, if ever, useful or constructive. Talk to a trusted friend, teacher, tutor or family member if you think your confidence may be sliding downwards. There are many reasons for this happening, and nearly everyone experiences it from time to time, but it is important to talk to someone about how you are feeling, sooner rather than later.
- **Build up a support network** – It can be easy to feel isolated and as though you must tackle everything alone, but that isn't the case. There will always be someone you can turn to for advice, so make sure that your inner life coach remembers that. In each section of this book there are contact details for organisations and other sources that will be able to help you through any problem you may come across.
- **Follow your interests** – It can really make life easier if you pursue the things you are naturally interested in (and it's amazing how many people find themselves in jobs or on courses that they aren't really that keen on). Aim to nurture your natural talents and interests, and whatever you choose to do is bound to be more achievable.
- **Aim to anticipate obstacles** – You're likely to hit potential problems along the way, whatever path you choose to follow after the age of 16, but there will be a way over them (or under, round or through them). Obstacles are always easier to deal with, though, if you have seen them coming, rather than crashing into them blindly. Arm yourself with information and knowledge about your choices as this will help you to anticipate all the potential difficulties that may arise. And 'difficulties' aren't always what they seem. Sometimes they are 'blessings in disguise', leading us to better, unanticipated outcomes.
- **Be positive about your next steps** – The more positive you can be about the possible directions your life can take, the more likely you

are to make a go of it. If you can really look forward to your new job or your move to college or university, you'll get the most out of it. It's natural to feel some nerves, but if you are dreading it, or feel a sense of doom about the whole thing, then the chances are that you may need to rethink your plans. Being positive can only help, but if it's impossible to muster positive thinking, talk to someone you trust, sooner rather than later.

- **Keep an eye on your money** – The chances are you'll be budgeting through your next steps, whatever they are, and while it's important not to completely deprive yourself, it's essential not to overspend and pretend it didn't happen (something many people seem to do). Keep on top of your money and ask for help sooner rather than later if you think you may be getting into debt or you need help with budgeting. There is plenty of advice on this in Part Six.
- **Don't succumb to peer pressure** – You have to live your life, not your friends. It's easy to feel pressured by those around you, but don't let this affect the decisions you make. What you want to achieve is important.
- **Keep your eyes on the prize** – Know what you want and go for it. And if you don't know what you want, you will by the time you reach the end of this book!

Action

Take a few minutes to think about how you feel about what you have just read. Do you feel able to be your own life coach? Or do you feel in need of talking to someone about how you might best make your next moves? How confident and positive are you at the moment? If at all possible, talk through your thoughts on these questions with someone else, maybe a family member, tutor or mentor. Even if you feel completely on top of things, it can be great talking about that.

Keeping an eye on the bigger picture

When you're focusing on one aspect of your life, such as whether to study or work, where to live or what career to have, it's really important not to lose sight of the bigger picture. This means taking what's known as an holistic view of your life. You are more than what you study or where you work; you are a complete and developing human being. You probably have family relationships with parents or carers, siblings and extended family such as aunts and uncles; friendships and maybe partnerships with a girlfriend or boyfriend; work commitments and goals for the future; study commitments and plans for the future; hobbies; activities to keep you fit and healthy such as taking part in sport and maybe belonging to a team; or perhaps you follow a particular religion or faith. Of course you need to work hard at your job or your course, but there's far more to your life than that. There are many facets to who you are, so remember to keep this in mind as you read through this book and decide on your next steps.

A word about change

Change is one of the few inevitable facts of life and yet it can be difficult to cope with, whatever age you are. Sometimes we can fall into the trap of thinking that change has to be big to be significant. It doesn't. Often it is the smallest changes that can bring about the biggest results. For example, making a commitment to spending just 10 minutes a day studying something we don't understand, or getting fitter, can have an amazing accumulative impact, without causing too much pain! It is always possible to bring about change through small steps, and sometimes that's all that feels comfortable. It doesn't make it less effective, though.

Bringing about change... View from Anna

I was fine when I was deciding what I wanted to study at uni. I looked at all my options but I knew I really wanted to do something textiles related. I found a great course in a town I knew I wanted to live in but I wasn't happy with my weight. I'd got heavier while I was doing my A levels and wanted to get back to how I was before. I knew it would help boost my confidence when I started my course and had to meet new people, but I had friends who had been on crash diets and I knew these didn't work in the long run. So I decided to run for 10 minutes twice a day. I was careful with what I ate, too, but didn't diet. Just making those small changes meant that I lost the weight that I had put on through my exams. It sounds odd, but I hadn't realised what a little effort can do if you stick at it.

---

discover
r1sk
.co.uk

Do you have an ENQUIRING mind?

Have you got an enquiring mind?

Do you ask more questions than you can answer?

Want to know more?

Discover Risk – right here

Risk – it's a word we've seen a lot of this year.

Earthquakes, hurricanes, floods, finance, piracy on the high seas – they're all obvious risks.

Surgery, the World Cup, accounting, acting, singing – perhaps not ones that spring to mind.

The fact is, risk is all around us, every day, and risk professionals help people all over the world who are faced with all manner of tricky situations.

If you're considering a career in risk, you are in good company. One-third of all jobs in financial services are related to risk – that makes risk one of the biggest employers we have. And one of the most successful.

Our profession is the third largest in the world, and the largest in Europe. Not bad for the world's sixth largest economy.

People who work in risk don't just work in large companies in the City of London. They have jobs all over the UK, all over the world, in companies small and big. Some will work in specialist insurance companies, others will work in accountancy firms, local government, health, education, just about anywhere – because risk touches all our lives.

You may not have heard of the specialist roles – loss adjusting, underwriting, broking, risk management, claims management, actuarial – but the support functions of marketing, accounting, finance, HR, IT and general management will be familiar to you. All of these roles are well-paid and offer great opportunities for seeing the world.

Do you have great communication skills, a problem-solving mind, empathy and a gift for negotiation and cutting a deal? Welcome to your new career.

Whether you're thinking of getting a job straight after school, doing an Apprenticeship or going to uni, risk has something for you.

Find out which risk career matches your skills by visiting **www.discoverrisk.co.uk** or emailing **discover@cii.co.uk**, quoting WNAS in the subject line.

Facing problems

Part of being your own life coach involves devising ways of dealing with problems. Everyone develops their own approach to this. The only real rule is that whatever method you use, it shouldn't adversely affect yourself or others.

There is no fail-safe way of avoiding problems. It's impossible to predict every eventuality, and the chances are, the more you try to do in your life, the more issues you will naturally face. But you will become increasingly skilled at dealing with them, predicting them and possibly even avoiding them.

A great way of approaching hurdles positively is to think about how you might turn the situation to your advantage. Look for the benefits and you will definitely find them. Often it helps to learn from others too, and to take their advice and appreciate their concern, particularly if they have direct experience of the kinds of issues you are facing. It's human nature to want to help others, and what you learn, you will then be in a position to pass on. There is more on working with other people in this way in Chapter 18.

As you experience difficulties and find ways around or through them, you are bound to build up a network of support. These people who believe in you and are behind your goals and ambitions may become mentors, and it's a great idea to find people whom you admire and respect. Get into the habit of finding out how other people dealt with their difficulties. Model the behaviour and attitudes that led to their success on your own journey. This is what makes life interesting and fulfilling.

Finally, be aware that there can sometimes be unintended consequences to your problem solving. In other words, you may even create further problems without meaning to. Don't worry about it. This is a chance to learn about how you bounce back and to use that knowledge in the future. Nothing is ever wasted. Learn from the past and move on. You may also want to take a look at Chapter 19 for more advice on dealing with problems.

Problems or opportunities?... View from Matt

I used to get really stressed out every time things didn't go my way. Whenever I hit a problem I'd think that I'd never resolve it and would have to completely change my plans. It has taken me a while to realise that problems can be a great way for us to work out what we really want to achieve. Sometimes they help us to refocus and to be even more determined to go for our goals. If we can see problems as opportunities, we're more likely to succeed.

Summary

The key points from this chapter include the following:

- Life coaching can be a useful tool to help you to make decisions at key points in your life.
- It is possible to be your own life coach if you follow a few basic steps such as aiming to anticipate obstacles and building up a support network.
- Change is inevitable, and it can be achieved through small steps as well as large steps.
- Advice, suggestions and sources of further information for anything you may come across in your decision-making processes are included throughout this book.
- Problems will arise, but the way in which you deal with them can give you valuable lessons, and knowledge about yourself, for the future.

If you're reading this guide there's a good chance you're sitting in the comfort of your home. But have you ever wondered how your home got there in the first place and who is responsible for planning and managing the nation's housing stock?

In fact the UK has nearly 22 million private homes and another five million 'social homes' owned by local authorities and housing.

Working in housing is extremely challenging. But is not just about the credit crunch, eco-towns, house prices, mortgages, banks and estate agents; it is also about helping people with different needs and in different circumstances, especially the millions of people who rely on social housing. The work varies from giving advice to homeless people on how they can go about getting a house, to collecting rents, assessing and carrying out repairs on a house, allocating houses to tenants and even being a chief executive of a multi-million pound organisation responsible for thousands of houses. It is one of the most rewarding careers in a sector vital to the UK's economy and quality of life.

The Chartered Institute of Housing (CIH) – the professional body for people involved in housing and communities – provides a wide range of housing qualifications and works with a number of colleges and universities across the UK. People studying CIH accredited courses receive free membership of CIH for the duration of their course. To find out more please visit www.cih.org

Paula Reynolds, Supported Housing Manager, The Wrekin Housing Trust

My original plan when I left school was to go to college and then university. I was however fortunate to be offered a position as a Housing Trainee. The position was structured in a way that it incorporated gaining experience in housing and going to college once a week to do the BTEC course that I had planned to do anyway. So it seemed a good option for me to follow; studying whilst gaining housing experience.

Over the years I have had a number of posts in the sector including working in housing benefits, lettings, repairs and resident involvement. My current role is that of Supported Housing Manager and I have responsibility for managing support and the property management services of over 30 sheltered housing schemes. Many of the jobs in housing provide the opportunity for getting involved in partnership working to help deliver a joined-up service and many roles are diverse and varied.

I have completed a Degree in Professional Housing Studies at Birmingham City University, which I feel will help support my future progression. I do feel passionate about delivering a high quality housing service and I feel really fortunate to be working in an environment where I feel that the work I do makes a real difference - and that gives me great job satisfaction.

2
Decisions

This chapter looks at:

- how to make decisions;
- where to go for help.

The chances are that if you have picked up this book, you are not entirely certain about what your next step should be. That's not at all unusual. Although some lucky people seem to be born knowing what they want to do, others may take years to find themselves in a job or career that feels right. Yet for others, choosing the right courses to do can prove to be virtually impossible, resulting in a series of false starts.

In some ways it seems that there are far more choices now than there ever have been. In years gone by, career choice was often limited by what sex you were. Females would have followed 'feminine' jobs such as going into service or becoming a dressmaker and males would have done the jobs that men did such as physical labouring or engineering. Sometimes young people would do what their father or mother did. For example, some may have been expected to follow in the footsteps of their father and work for the family business.

It's not like that now, though, and in some ways that's harder, although it is ultimately better that many people have more career freedom. Because of this, you may need to seek career and job advice. In fact, even if you don't feel that you need career advice, it is a good idea to have some just in case options that you had not even considered come up. It is important to take a look at everything that is available to you so that you really can make an informed decision.

Decisions – the issues

Whether you are reading this at the age of 15 or 16 or at 17 or 18, you face choices, which means making decisions. Basically, you could stay in education, go into a work-based training programme or apprenticeship, join the armed forces, get a job or work for yourself. You could also go travelling, work as a volunteer or join the ranks of the unemployed.

What you do can be a tough decision to make. It is likely that many people will want to influence you. But as you read through this book and work through the activities that you feel are relevant to you, you will see that it is possible to know for yourself the direction that you should take. As long as you explore all the options open to you and honestly answer the questions you ask yourself, you will be giving yourself the best possible chance.

Making decisions can be one of the hardest things that humans have to do. So many things can stand in our way. Sometimes we feel that we will not be able to stick to the decisions we make and at other times we think that we are not good enough to follow them through. We may even think that we are too good for something once we start it, or our lack of self-esteem may prevent us from giving it a go. The question is: how can we give ourselves the chance to make sound decisions that stick?

Making decisions... View from Taylor

I don't think I'm good at making decisions. I don't think I've ever given it that much thought. I've always just done what seemed most obvious, but that's not always what's best for you. The thing is, that if you really think about each decision, about all that could happen if you did a certain thing, you'd have to make a lot of effort. I think lots of people don't want to put in that effort. Or perhaps they think they don't have to because they'll just change their minds and do something else if it doesn't work out. I can see now that's not a good idea but the thought of sitting down and actively deciding rather than doing one of the first things that comes to my head is quite frightening. What if I can't follow it through perfectly? What if I fail?

Perfectionism

Wanting to do things perfectly is one of the most common reasons for not having a go at something. Suppose you want to be a singer. Would you want to do this as a hobby or would it have to be your career? Would you be happy to sing to yourself and your mates or would you want to give a proper performance? Would you sing in your local pub or want to be in front of an audience of thousands? Or broadcast your music via a webcam like singer-songwriter Sandi Thom? How much, or little, would you settle for?

Wanting to do things with excellence is fine, but wanting to do things perfectly can be paralysing. It can actually prevent us from taking action and mean that we might never know what we could have achieved. If perfectionism is something you sometimes suffer from, you need to try to take a step back for now and give yourself the chance to follow your dreams.

Action

Are you a perfectionist? Take a moment to answer these questions. If you jot your answers down, you can see how many times you answer 'yes' and how many times you answer 'no'.

- Does making mistakes make you feel self-conscious – over-aware of yourself?
- How do you feel when other people make a mistake? Do you tend to comment and point out their errors?
- Do you get anxious if your appearance is not perfect?
- Do you tend to write rough drafts before completing a neat version?
- Do you give yourself a hard time if you do something embarrassing?
- Are you always neat and tidy in everything you do?
- Do you tend to stick to set routines – for example, when you get ready in the mornings, when you do your homework and so on?
- Do you work extra time to ensure that your homework is just right?
- Do you know exactly how you will spend each day when you wake up in the morning?
- Do you sometimes put off making decisions out of fear that you might do the wrong thing?

How did you do? Did you answer 'yes' to all or most of them? If that is the case, it looks as though you just might have some perfectionist tendencies! Keep this firmly in mind as you go through your decision-making processes and don't give yourself a hard time! Perfectionism doesn't exist, and if you think it does, it will be something you will always strive for and never achieve.

Perfectionism... View from Amy

It took me years to realise that you don't have to think of the decisions that you make about your career as being permanent. Just because you decide to train as a hairdresser, for example, that doesn't mean that you will have to do that for the rest of your life. People are increasingly changing their jobs completely and having several careers in their lives. That can really help the decision-making process if you say to yourself that you will pursue a job or career for as long as it fulfils you rather than looking on it as a life sentence.

How to make decisions that stick

Whenever you face having to make a decision in your life there are certain techniques that you can use to help you. These are described for you below.

Brainstorming

Whether you call them maps, thought showers, spider diagrams or mind blasts, they all, essentially, amount to the same thing: brainstorming. Basically, this means taking a large sheet of paper, putting the issue that needs a decision at the centre of the page and writing the possibilities open to you all around the outside in as much detail as you like. Perhaps there are connections that you can make between the things you write down. Can you find any linking themes?

Make sure that you include things that might seem a bit 'way out there'. The purpose of the exercise is to bring to your awareness all the possibilities that could conceivably be facing you. You don't have to make judgements on these ideas.

Brainstorming can be as organised or as chaotic as you like. As long as it helps you, feel free to develop your own techniques!

Action

Think of a decision that you have to make. Don't choose a massive question such as 'How shall I spend the rest of my life?' Instead, go for something like 'What shall I do on Saturday?'

Now take a large sheet of paper and write your question right in the middle of the page. After that, scatter all the possible ideas you can think of around the outside of your question. Don't stop after just one or two, but keep going. You will probably find that all your really good ideas start to flow after you have already written down about five or so.

Now look at what you have produced. Are you surprised by the quantity of ideas that you have?

Gathering information

In order to make effective decisions, you need to have all the relevant information available to you. This may not involve additional work, but the chances are that you will have to do at least some research in order to make most decisions. For example, suppose you want to go out for the day with your friends. You cannot decide between two possible choices, so what do you do? You find out:

- how much each option will cost you;
- how far you will have to travel for each option;
- whether you will have to take food with you or can buy something when you get there;
- what preference each of your friends has.

Only when you have this information can you make a decision about where you should go for the day.

Whether your decisions are small like the example above, or big like deciding what to study at university, the information-gathering stage will probably be a pretty important part of the whole process.

Pros and cons

Sometimes it can really help to write a list of pros and cons about a particular course of action. In case you have not come across this before, 'pros'
are the good points and 'cons' are the bad points. So, for example, if you
were writing a list of pros and cons about buying a new bike you might
end up with something like the list shown in Table 2.1.

Table 2.1

Pros	Cons
I need a new one as my bike is quite old now and needs some repairs.	I could get my bike repaired and save some money.
I'll be able to get a mountain bike and cycle off-road.	I'd have to ask Dad to put a bike rack on his car so that I could get out to the country.
I've got just enough money saved.	It would leave me with no savings at all.
The local bike store has got a discount on the bike I've chosen.	The bike shop has always got something on offer, so there's no hurry.

Faced with the list of pros and cons in Table 2.1, what would you
choose?

Visualising

Visualisation means imagining, or picturing, something in your mind. If
you were to visualise yourself working in a bakery shop, you would see
yourself, in your mind's eye, standing behind the counter. What have you
got on? You're probably wearing a uniform and there may be something
on your head to keep your hair out of the way. Perhaps you are wearing
gloves and putting some bread or rolls into a bag for a customer. Is there
a queue in the shop? Are there cakes on display? Is it hot or cold in the
shop? What is covering the floor? Are there flies buzzing around? Can you
see yourself there? That's visualisation.

Visualising can be really useful to find out whether you can envisage
yourself following through on a particular decision. For example, if you

decide that you want to travel the world, can you truly see yourself doing it? Can you see yourself packing your bags, getting on planes, seeing new places, staying in different hostels around the place? If you can see yourself doing it, how does it feel? Exciting? Daunting? Does it feel like the right thing to do or do your gut feelings say that you would not really enjoy it?

Using visualisation is a little like daydreaming; but it is daydreaming with a focus and a goal. It is like saying to yourself, 'What if... then what?' Many people find it a good way of making a decision.

Gaining experience

Gaining experience of something is a great way of deciding whether it is what you really want to do. Much like trying on a pair of jeans before you buy them, you would actually be trying the options before making your final decision. Work experience is a great example of this. If you think you might like to be, for example, a personal trainer, shadowing one while he or she works is the perfect way of helping you to finalise your decision.

Gaining experience... View from Charlotte

I always try to get a bit of first-hand experience of anything I think I might want to do. Even when I was looking for a Saturday job I spent a morning shadowing one of the others in the shop to see if I'd like it. I'd hate to get myself into something I couldn't wait to get out of, and this helps me to avoid that.

Facing fears

Sometimes we stop ourselves from even considering something because we have fears about what might happen. Facing up to those fears can really help to show us that we actually have more options than we once thought. For example, if you'd like to work for the European Parliament but are afraid of travelling overseas, you could either settle for a job that is unlikely to take you out of the United Kingdom or do something about your fear to enable you to choose from a far wider range of jobs.

There are many ways of getting help for your fears. Sometimes just talking to someone else and verbalising what you have been holding inside is enough to make the fear less powerful. At other times, professional counselling may be more appropriate. Hypnotherapy can help, too.

If you think that you might have some fears that are stopping you from making certain decisions, talk to your family or trusted friends. Your teachers or tutors at school or college may be able to help, and so can your doctor.

Info

Pretending that you are someone looking on

What if you were someone else watching you as you are now going through the anguish of making a decision? From your position on the outside, what advice would you give yourself? Imagining this can be a really effective way of helping us to see a course of action, especially when we feel paralysed by the choice. Imagine stepping outside your situation and looking on with a clear mind, and the right course of action just might come into your head.

A word of warning

Sometimes we just need to give ourselves a nudge to actually take the plunge and make that decision. If you think this might apply to you, don't let procrastination (purposely delaying action) get in your way. If it does, you may drift along, avoiding the decision-making process, and thereby missing opportunities all along the way.

If you are guilty of procrastinating, you are not alone by any means! Most people know that they are prone to procrastination at some stage of their lives, but recognising it and not allowing it to take hold are important. Do not delay decision making endlessly. If you think it would help, give yourself a deadline and aim not to go over it. This does not mean you have to rush at the decision, but there comes a point when you just do not need to think about something any longer!

Choosing your next steps

A lot can be made of the idea of choosing a path for your life to follow, but the fact is that we can only ever decide on what our very next step is going to be. We cannot map out our entire lives, nor should we try to. Things happen; we grow and develop in unexpected ways, and we often change our minds about the directions we wish to take. Be flexible! That's the best way to approach change, and it's those who are happy with the concept of change who are most able to deal with what life presents them with.

A great way of approaching your decision on your next step is to think about what really gives you a sense of meaning and purpose. What do you really enjoy? What are you passionate about? What are you curious about? What do you dream of doing, being, becoming? What brings out your determination and enthusiasm? It is through answering questions such as these, just for yourself, that you'll start to understand what really gets you motivated, and that's what's worth pursuing. And remember, what you don't *like*, you can set about *changing* – and that applies to anything in life.

Where to go for help

If you feel that you need outside help with any decisions you have to make in your life right now, remember that the following people in particular may be a great source of advice.

Your parents

Your parents or other adults who are like parents to you are likely to know you better than anyone else and may be able to point out a few 'home truths' as well as being there to bounce ideas off. They have watched you through your life so far and will probably have followed your changing likes and dislikes, preferences and desires, more closely than their own. You may not feel that you always want to ask for the help of your parents when you are making decisions but they will have a perspective that is at least worth considering, if not fully taking on board!

Your brothers and sisters

Your brothers and sisters, especially if they are older than you, may well have been through experiences that you can learn from. What did they choose to do? What advice have they got for you? How about your younger siblings? How do they see you? Do they have any wise observations to make about, for example, the kind of career they see you doing well in? Maybe they have an opinion that can help you.

Your extended family

Do you have cousins, aunts, uncles, grandparents, godparents, even friends of the family? How close are you to them? Can you talk to them about the decisions that you face? What can you learn from their experiences? What perceptions of you do they have?

Your teachers

Like your parents, your teachers will have tracked your development over a period of time. Are there any who you get on with particularly well? What have they said to you over the years? Have any of them been particularly inspiring? Are any really easy to talk to about the things that are concerning you? Most students at school or college can think of at least one teacher whom they could turn to in moments of indecision. Who is this for you?

Connexions

Connexions is the place to go for everything to do with education, careers and much, much more for everyone between the ages of 13 and 19.

Connexions Direct offers a whole range of advice and support for young people through an easy-to-navigate website. You can speak to a Connexions Direct adviser on the telephone or through web chat, e-mail or text.

Connexions Service is a network of Connexions offices that you can drop into for information, advice and practical help about pretty much anything and everything from relationships to careers, drugs to jobs. You can do this anonymously if that will make you feel more comfortable, so you do not need to give your name and address. The people at Connexions do not share what you tell them with anyone unless they think that you may be in danger.

Info
- *The main website for Connexions is www.connexions.gov.uk.*
- *You can telephone to speak to a Connexions adviser on 080 800 13 2 19.*
- *You can text Connexions on 07766 4 13 2 19.*
- *You can e-mail Connexions anonymously via the website.*
- *To find your local Connexions Service, look in your* Yellow Pages *or search for the details on the website.*

Above all else, never feel that you have to make choices and decisions in your life alone; you don't. There are people out there who can help you, whether they are from within your family or not. You are not alone.

Summary

The key points from this chapter include the following:

- If you are reading this book, it is likely that you are facing a turning point in your life. What will you do next?
- Making decisions can be difficult for all sorts of reasons, particularly if you tend to be a perfectionist.
- There are tools that you can use to help you to make effective decisions that you can stick to. These tools include brainstorming, gathering information, writing a list of pros and cons, visualisation, gaining direct experience and facing your fears.
- There are many sources of help for you when you face important decisions, including your parents, your siblings, your extended family and friends, your teachers, and Connexions.

3

Career planning

This chapter looks at:

- planning your career and next steps;
- tracking progress.

While you cannot possibly know at the moment exactly how things are going to turn out for you as the years go by, it is important to have some idea of the direction you would like your life to take. These plans that we make for ourselves cannot be set in stone. We have to be willing and able to change our minds and direction as new opportunities present themselves. But without any plan at all, we could risk drifting without purpose, and this could be a waste of valuable time.

Planning your career and next steps

When deciding what you want to do with your life, you need to keep these factors in mind:

- your strengths;
- the opportunities that are open to you;
- the limitations that you see yourself having.

For many young people about to enter post-16 education there are often difficult choices to be made. School offers students a wide-range of possibilities, and whilst this educates and helps to form the basis of a particular subject area, many young people are still left undecided on their future career path.

In the case of sport and active leisure, an A-level in physical education can often lead to further or higher education related courses, however, there are other options available to young people interested in forming a career in the sector. Apprenticeships and the Diploma in Sport and Active Leisure provide alternative routes to further or higher education and a career by providing practical experience and developing the skills and knowledge required by employers.

The Apprenticeship programme which has been designed to help businesses train their future employees to reach a high level of competency and performance is more appropriate to students who already have an idea of their chosen profession and supports their development with skills relevant to that industry. Within active leisure, learning and well-being there are a number of different Apprenticeship pathways available at level 2 and 3 including activity leadership, coaching, instructing exercise and fitness, playwork, leisure management, the outdoors, operational services and spectator safety.

The Diploma in Sport and Active Leisure is more appropriate for young people that have a specific interest in the industry, but are yet to discover their chosen pathway by providing an overview of the sector. It combines both class work and hands-on experience that gives students the opportunity to gain a fully rounded education through a number of learning methods within the environments of both the classroom and the workplace. The broad nature of the diploma means that studying at higher and advanced level offers a wide range of progression routes into the industry, whether it is a focused pathway in an advanced apprenticeship or employment or into a further or higher education course.

With the London Olympic Games and Paralympic Games on the horizon, sport and active leisure is one of the fastest growing sectors in the UK and it is an exciting time to be involvement within an industry. There are lots of potential opportunities for young people to achieve a career within a chosen industry but gaining the experience required by employers is essential to starting that journey. To find out more on the different types of career available within sport and active leisure, visit: **www.skillsactive.com/careers**

Your strengths

Throughout your decision-making process you should always remember what your strengths are. You will probably have done some work on identifying these at school. If you have not, you might like to draw up a list to remind yourself about them.

Action

Use a large sheet of paper and just blast out your thoughts and your strengths, scattering them on the page. Don't aim to sort them out into logical categories at first; you can do that later on. The following ideas may help you:

- Think about what you are good at. Don't just limit yourself to what you do at school; that is just a part of who you are!
- What were your best subjects at school? Are these your favourites? (Sometimes what we are best at is not necessarily what we enjoy the most.)
- Think about your hobbies. What do you do in your spare time? What are your real passions? Is there anything that you can't imagine life without (for example, were you born to play football, paint, run and so on)?
- What do you read, watch on TV, listen to? This will give you an idea about what your interests are.
- Think about your preferences. Are you an indoor type or an outdoor type? Are you fashion-conscious or not? Are you easygoing or serious?
- How do you spend your school holidays? Are there any activities that you nearly always do when you have a break from school? Is there anything you would like to do more of?
- What skills do you have in addition to any qualifications you have from school? Can you swim? Drive a car? Ride a bike? Juggle? Paint? The list is endless. It doesn't matter how frivolous you think the skill may be, add it to your list.
- Talk to your teachers, parents, siblings, other adults in your life. What do they say your strengths are? How do they see you?
- What dreams, goals and desires do you have?

Once you have written your ideas out on to a sheet of paper (be bold, don't limit yourself), aim to organise them into groups. You are free to make up your own category headings. Ideas that may help you are listed here, but don't let these headings limit you. Add your own or leave some of these out; whatever is most useful to you and the list of strengths that you have devised:

- indoor strengths and outdoor strengths;
- literacy strengths;
- numeracy strengths;
- science strengths;
- key skills (such as communication, information technology and so on);
- specialist knowledge (for example, are you an ace beekeeper or hotshot software designer?);
- personality traits (such as being helpful, considerate, having a sense of humour, being focused and so on).

These headings need to be devised to fit in best with your particular strengths. Have as many category headings as you need. Now you have an excellent resource to use whenever you need to identify your main strengths.

Opportunities open to you

There will be certain opportunities facing you that you can take advantage of right now. It would be foolish to say that anyone can do anything, but there will be opportunities that you can go for, or at least consider going for. This book will tell you what those opportunities are, but you should also talk to your careers adviser at school and your local Connexions service. Even if you are sure about what your next move will be, always look around to see if there is an opportunity you did not know existed or had not even thought of.

Remember, when you are looking at the opportunities that may be open to you, be realistic. You have to take your limitations into consideration. If you are terrified of water, training to be a lifeguard on the beach is not a realistic possibility!

Realistic opportunities... View from Naila

I always had this vague idea that I wanted to be a dentist. I was always fascinated whenever I went to the dentist and thought it would be a great job to do. But actually when I sat down to write out some thoughts about my career possibilities, there were lots of things that came out that didn't fit with being a dentist. If I'm honest, I sometimes dread going to the dentist myself, especially if I have to have treatment. That wouldn't make me a good dentist! I also realised that I think I'd rather work outside if I can, at least for part of each day. The final thing that did it was that I hadn't realised just how much science I'd have to study to be a dentist. That's not a strong point for me.

Realistically, it might have seemed like a good idea in the past but I can think of loads of other things that would be much more suitable for me. Being a dentist is not really an opportunity that's open to me if I'm totally honest with myself.

Limitations

If we are honest, we may feel that we do have certain limitations facing us. Someone who has a tendency to put on weight is not likely to make a prima ballerina or dancer, but need not abandon his or her dreams of a career in dance altogether. What other dance styles would be more suitable for this person? How about an ancillary role? It takes far more than just dancers to put on a performance! The team needs specialist make-up artists, lighting technicians, choreographers, costume designers… The list is long – and all these people work in the world of dance.

However, there are sometimes real limitations that we have to take into consideration. For example, some medical conditions rule out certain careers, and some learning needs can limit our choices. Sometimes people can limit us if they have strong opinions about what we should or should not be doing. One famous example of this involves Robbie Williams, who was apparently told that he would never make it as a singer!

Are there any limitations facing you? But remember, you never know what you cannot do until you have given it your best shot!

As you read further into this book, just keep in the back of your mind all your strengths, opportunities and perceived limitations. Be open to the suggestions that you read, and follow the pointers to further information about anything that sounds interesting. The most important thing you can do for yourself right now is to believe that you can achieve!

Tracking progress

You may well have been given information on ways that you can track your progress through education and work experience, especially as you work towards your qualifications and start thinking about moving into more study, travel or work. Most schools will have a method of helping you to gather information on what you have achieved to date and what you want to work towards next. This will usually involve some goal-setting exercises.

Often it is up to you to decide whether or not to track your progress in this way, and, unless you are already doing this in your own manner, it is definitely going to be worth following your school's suggestions. Organising your thoughts and plans, not to mention all your achievements such as exam results, and non-academic successes such as swimming certificates or other hobbies pursued, is a great way of keeping important information in one place and of helping to track where you have been and where you want to go.

One way of starting this process, if you are not given guidance on it at school, is to think about the following:

- What likes and dislikes do you have? How do you learn?
- What are you good at? What skills do you have?
- What are your successes? What have been your most important learning experiences and achievements?
- What do you want to achieve? What changes and improvements do you want to make and what goals do you want to reach?
- How will you achieve? What action plans do you have? Do you have SMART (specific, measurable, achievable, realistic and time-related) targets?
- Who has helped you to achieve? Who can help you in the future?

You might like to start recording your thoughts on those questions in a notebook or folder. Some kind of box or pocket file is useful for gathering certificates and other evidence of achievements together in one place. Adopting this approach helps you to get and stay organised, and to be in charge of your plans for the future.

As you progress through your later years at school or college you may want to start thinking about:

With the ACA the whole world's calling.

THE ACA. QUALIFIED TO SUCCEED.

At home or abroad, the ACA opens up a world of career opportunities.

The ACA is a business and finance qualification from the ICAEW, a world leader of the accountancy and finance profession and is highly respected in all industry sectors around the world.

If you're looking for variety, opportunity, and the best preparation for a career as a business leader, choose the ACA.

You'll be guaranteed a great reception anywhere in the world.

To find out more:
T +44 (0)1908 248 040
icaew.com/careers

With the ACA the whole world's calling!

Would you like a career where you could travel the world? Whether you're working for a large firm in a big city, or assisting a small company with their finances, you have the opportunity to succeed with the ACA qualification behind you.

The ACA from ICAEW is a professional business and finance qualification that attracts talented people from a variety of backgrounds. Our training produces chartered accountants and business advisers who are valued in all sectors, from practice to commerce, industry and the public sector. You will gain a solid foundation in finance, business, marketing, economics and management, ideal for opening doors to a wide range of career paths once ACA qualified.

The ACA puts you at the heart of business. It gives you the adaptable skills, expertise and experience needed to become a future business leader.

Earn while you learn

ACA training is a mixture of classroom tuition and work experience. When studying for the ACA you will work for an ICAEW authorised training employer on a training agreement. There are over 2,200 ICAEW authorised training employers of all sizes throughout the world who offer the ACA, in practice (chartered accountancy firms) commerce and the public sector. Your employer will generally fund all of your training and pay you a competitive salary at the same time, so you really do earn while you learn.

Routes to training

Organisations employ school leavers as well as graduates to study the ACA. There are a variety of opportunities available after your A-levels. You can train for the ACA straight from school or go on to study the AAT (Association of Accounting Technicians) qualification. After the AAT you can Fast Track to the ACA . Even better is if you choose the right modules we may be able to give you credit for prior learning (CPL) because you will have covered some of the ACA modules during your AAT. This means you could complete the AAT and ACA and become a chartered accountant in just four years!

If you decide university is for you, great, go for it! You can train for the ACA in just three years after you graduate, regardless of your chosen degree subject.

The only difference if you choose not to go to university is that you will take the first step on an exciting career ladder sooner than people who have chosen the university route.

Want a taster without the commitment?

If you like the idea of chartered accountancy but are not 100% sure if it's for you, why not try the Certificate in Finance, Accounting and Business (CFAB). CFAB gives you knowledge in finance, accounting and business fundamentals. It will enhance your employability by giving you the knowledge that employers have told us they are looking for. These computer based assessments are made up of the first six modules of the ACA, which means on completion you can obtain credits when starting your ACA study.

Entry Requirements

Entry requirements differ across employers, but as a guideline our suggested minimum entry requirements for the ACA qualification are;

- three GCSEs (most employers expect A or B grades in maths and English)
- two A-levels, or their equivalents, in any subjects. Many employers will be looking for a minimum of a 240-280 UCAS tariff score,
- a first or 2:1 in any degree discipline (or equivalent), if you decide to go to university.

Focus on........Forensic Accounting

Interested in investigating commercial fraud, money laundering and personal injury cases? Then with the ACA you can be in prime position in front of a jury giving a testimony of your expert findings of a legal case.

The work of a forensic accountant is to enable lawyers, insurance companies and other clients to resolve disputes. It's an interesting and dynamic side of accounting, perfect if you have an analytical mind!

Find out more:

E: careers@icaew.com
W: icaew.com/careers
T: +44 (0)1908 248 040

- Your personal development – what personal qualities, attitudes and interests do you have?
- Your experiences of work – what work skills, enterprise activities and work placements have you experienced?
- Career planning – what are your career management skills like? How do you apply your plans?

Once you get started, make sure you get in the habit of updating what you write in your file. This should be a living, breathing project, not a once in a lifetime effort! It is particularly important to do this to reflect your changing interests, skills and achievements. Obviously, what you were really keen on in Year 7 might not do it for you in Year 11, and having some way of tracking your progress is an excellent way of making sure that you acknowledge these developments. Think of it as a 'working file'; in a way, it is a work in progress, and always will be as you go through your life.

One word of caution: don't use this as a way of recording what goes on at school. The idea is that it should represent the whole you. In other words, what you do and achieve outside school should be recorded too.

As you get older, you can use this progress tracker to:

- build up your confidence to make the most of yourself – understand yourself better, set goals and targets, develop your study and other skills, keep a record of all your achievements and so on;
- make the most of opportunities – manage your learning, make successful applications to further education (FE) or higher education (HE) or employment with training;
- make your experience count – give others the best possible description of yourself, your achievements and your potential.

Why track your progress?

It isn't compulsory to keep a record of your progress and future plans but there are many reasons why it is a good idea to get into the habit. Tracking your progress can help you:

- to become more organised;
- to achieve higher grades or the qualifications you want;

- to make more informed decisions on the options facing you;
- to see how what you have done in the past and what you are doing right now fits in with what you hope to do in the future – to understand how aspects and dimensions of your life interlock;
- to work through a personal crisis or simply to change some aspect of yourself for the better;
- to focus on improving your skills;
- to ensure that you can make the most use of the feedback you receive all the way through your education and into work, where you are likely to be appraised on how well you are doing.

Summary

The key points from this chapter include the following:

- Career plans should not be set in stone; allow yourself to change your mind as your skills and goals alter over time.
- Writing down your strengths will help to focus your mind on what you might like to do with your life, or for your next steps at least.
- You should explore the opportunities open to you even if you think you know what to do next.
- Not everyone can do everything, but we all have opportunities and options facing us.
- Even if we think we have limitations, we do not have to abandon our dreams altogether.
- Keeping a file to track your progress can be an excellent way of planning your development and recording your achievements.
- It is not compulsory to track your progress in this way, but it is useful for many reasons.

Part Two
Education

4
Looking at education

This chapter looks at:

- how education is changing for 14- to 19-year-olds;
- thinking about further education (FE).

Reforms affecting 14- to 19-year-olds

The very first thing to say about education choices facing 16-year-olds is that a lot has changed over recent years.

Transformations in learning

The Government's overall plan for young people is to ensure that they are equipped to thrive in a globalised economy in the 21st century. This has meant making some changes to education which you will probably have experienced to some extent in recent years.

Since September 2008, schools have been teaching a new secondary curriculum. This curriculum has been designed to help you to become a successful learner, to gain in confidence and to become a responsible citizen. It covers attitudes and attributes, skills, knowledge and understanding.

Info

You can find out much more about the secondary curriculum from the Department for Eduction website: www.education.gov.uk.

At the time of writing, there are four learning routes for young people which will lead to qualifications:

- Apprenticeships – with an entitlement to a place by 2013 for all 16-year-olds who are suitably qualified;
- Foundation Learning Tier – with an entitlement by 2010 to study one of the progression pathways;
- General Qualifications eg GCSEs and A levels;
- Diplomas – with an entitlement by 2013 for all 14–16-year-olds to the first 14 Diplomas and for 16–18 years to all 17 Diplomas.

If there is a clear rationale for it, young people will be able to study qualifications that do not fall under these four routes.

Throughout the curriculum and qualifications routes there will be:

- functional skills in English, mathematics and ICT;
- personal, learning and thinking skills;
- personal, learning and thinking skills (team working, independent enquiry, self-management, reflective learning, effective participation, creative thinking).

Diplomas

A key dimension of the reforms to education for 14- to 19-year-olds is the introduction of the Diploma. This is a real alternative to the traditional qualifications young people used to be offered. Diplomas are a combination of theoretical and applied learning, and in that way they are a 'package' of learning, which helps to make sure that those who take them are as prepared for the world of work as possible, as well as being well educated.

Diplomas will develop your functional skills in English, maths and ICT, and these skills will be applicable in the work situations you find yourself in when you leave education.

The Diplomas will be available for students at three levels:

- Level 1 (foundation, or the equivalent of around five GCSEs);
- Level 2 (higher, or the equivalent of around seven GCSEs);
- Level 3 (advanced, or the equivalent of three and a half GCE A levels);
- Level 3 (progression, a subset of the Advanced broadly equivalent to two and a half GCE A levels).

There are currently 14 Diploma subjects to choose from:

- Business, Administration and Finance;
- Construction and the Built Environment;
- Creative and Media;
- Engineering;
- Environmental and Land-based Studies;
- Hair and Beauty Studies;
- Hospitality;
- Information Technology;
- Manufacturing and Product Design;
- Public Services;
- Retail Business;
- Society and Active Leisure;
- Travel and Tourism.

There has been talk that GCSEs and A levels might be abolished, but that isn't the plan at the time of writing. The Government says that it will make improvements to them where necessary, but these changes don't mean the end of exams! In June 2010 the Government announced that state maintained schools will be able to offer the International GCSE from September 2010.

Info

If you would like to find out more about the changes to education for 14- to 19-year-olds, you can visit the 14–19 website, http://yp.direct. gov.uk/diplomas/.

For information about countries of the United Kingdom other than England, visit the following websites:

Scotland: www.scotland.gov.uk/Topics/Education
Wales: www.wales.gov.uk
Northern Ireland: www.deni.gov.uk.

Thinking about further education

The education choices that you make at the age of 16 are important ones; they can affect your entire future. That is why it is really important to know exactly what is on offer to you, whether in the form of so-called academic qualifications or vocational ones, so that you can make an informed decision.

Staying on in FE is one of the best things that most young people can do for themselves. It offers the opportunity to gain valuable qualifications and skills that help directly with future career goals. Besides, there is real evidence to show that the longer you stay in education, the more money you will earn when you enter the workplace (see page 74 for more details).

For many, the choice is made easily and is a natural progression from their time at school, but for others it can be a difficult decision to make. Which category do you fall into?

Action

If you are really undecided about what to do when you finish school at 16, think about your answers to the following questions. It can help to write your responses down so that you have something to read over. This also helps to make sure that you don't forget any of your thoughts. The aim here is not to reach any mind-blowing conclusions but rather just to get you thinking about your attitude to going into FE. There is no need to show your answers to anyone unless they bring up further questions that you would like to discuss with someone.

- Did you enjoy school?
- Did you enjoy the process of learning?
- Do you want to learn new subjects and skills?
- Was there anything that you didn't enjoy about being at school?
- Is there anything that you don't enjoy about learning?
- Do you think you would be best doing academic subjects in FE or vocational subjects? Or perhaps a mixture of these?
- Do you feel that you really can't study any more and need to get out and go to work?
- How do you feel about the prospect of staying on to study? Generally positive or generally reluctant?

Reaching your conclusions

There is one very important thing to remember when you are thinking about the possibility of staying on for FE, and that is that studying at the post-16 level is nothing like being at secondary school. Even if you will literally be in the same school or on the same campus as you have been so far in your school career, you will find that the attitude of your teachers will be quite different from how it was when you were doing your GCSEs. You will have passed an important turning point in your life and will be seen more as a young adult than as a child. You will have new freedoms and different treatment but there will be certain expectations of you. In return for all this, your teachers will expect you to take more responsibility for your learning. This means excellent attendance, commitment to your studies and, it goes without saying, being cooperative and switched on in class!

Even if you would say that you do not exactly love studying, you will see that there are many new and exciting opportunities for you in FE that are unlike anything you have done so far. Keep an open mind as you make your decisions, and you will not miss out.

Did you know there are over 500,000 courses on offer around the United Kingdom? There is bound to be something that grabs your interest from all of those! It is obviously not practical to list all of these courses here – there are far too many – but if you want to browse a courses database, log on to the Connexions website, www.connexions.gov.uk.

Info

> *Other sources of information are:*
>
> *www.direct.gov.uk for details on all the different kinds of vocational and academic courses*
> *www.bbc.co.uk/schools/16guide for the BBC's pages on post-16 education and training*
>
> *Don't forget that you can always contact Connexions if you would like to talk to someone about your education choices at age 16 or 18: 080 800 13 2 19.*

If you still conclude that going to work really would be the best thing for you, do read through the following chapter on education first just in case there is something there that can change your mind. The following chapters in this book will also be of great help in organising your next steps to find a job or some work-based training.

Making decisions... View from Mack

I always thought that I wanted to leave school as soon as I could, but everyone around me told me I was mad. I was fed up with being in classes and having to be indoors most of the day. It's just not me.

But I hadn't looked into exactly what I could do at college, and to be honest hadn't taken that much notice of all those careers talks at school. I just knew I wanted to get out. My Mum went to the local colleges and picked up prospectuses for me to read through and I found out that I could do agricultural courses really close to where I live. This seemed to be a great solution as I wouldn't be stuck indoors all day and could learn real skills that I could use as soon as I left college. I knew that realistically it would open up more opportunities for me and that I'd be crazy not to go.

Luckily I wasn't too late to apply and I did get on the courses I wanted to do. Looking back now, it was the best thing I could have done. I was pretty determined not to listen to anyone's advice but I'm really glad I did in the end. I wouldn't be in anything like such a good position if I'd just left school and tried to get a job that suited me. I think I'd probably be unemployed and getting depressed about never having any money!

Summary

The key points from this chapter include the following:

- Education for 14- to 19-year-olds has changed, and the changes may affect you.
- Going into FE is one of the best things that young people can do for themselves.
- It is very useful to think about your attitude to going into FE to see if this can help you to make your decisions.
- Studying in FE is very different from what you have known at school so far.

5
Choices in further education (FE)

This chapter looks at:

- what to study in FE;
- the main qualification groups;
- where to study in FE;
- choosing a college.

If you have been reading this book from its first few pages, you will know by now that it emphasises that there are many decisions to be made. But the more information you have available to you, the easier these decisions will be. Just take it one step at a time and don't rush at anything; it is essential that you are happy with, and committed to, the decisions that you make.

Info

Education or training?

There is information on work experience and apprenticeships in Chapter 8. While these do still involve learning and education, this is done alongside your work in a particular company or organisation (although you usually would spend some time on day release at a local college). For this reason, work-based training schemes are covered in the sections on work in this book.

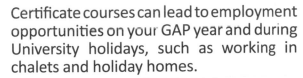

LEITHS

SCHOOL OF FOOD AND WINE

Leiths' reputation as a first-class training school for chefs attracts students of all ages from all over the world. With its dedicated teaching and friendly atmosphere, Leiths' guiding principle is to impart enthusiasm for the trade and instil a lasting love of good food and wine.

Whether you are going straight to university or taking a gap year, learning to cook will prepare you for the future. Leiths School of Food and Wine offers a range of courses that are ideal both for students leaving home who will have to fend for themselves and for those wishing to earn money and travel.

The 4-Week Essential Certificate in practical cookery takes place in late summer every year, making it especially suitable for those starting their gap year or going to university. The course enables you to cook simple, delicious food with an emphasis on essential practical skills. You will then be able to go on and earn money cooking to a family level in the UK and abroad, or practice your skills entertaining friends at university.

"Being at university means that you have to fend for yourself. The Leiths qualification has ensured that I can cook meals for not just myself but my whole house."

The 10-Week Foundation Certificate in Food and Wine is a thorough introduction to cooking. It is designed for the interested amateur and the potential professional, and includes an introduction to tasting and appreciating wine. The course teaches you to plan your time efficiently, cook with confidence, follow and understand recipes and to adapt them to suit your own cooking style. Graduates typically go on to work for ski chalets, villas, and yachts, or to cook privately in the UK.

"Leiths is a fabulous qualification, one which will stay with you forever."

The Intermediate and Advanced Certificates follow on from the Beginners Certificate. You can return at a later date to complete them or you can take them in succession. If you are tempted by a career in food, completing all three of these certificates results in the Leiths Diploma in Food and Wine. The Diploma course may be the right choice for you if you are keen to pursue a career and start training immediately in preference to University. The Diploma is a well recognized professional qualification in the food and wine world and a springboard to an interesting and varied career.

"During the holidays there are always jobs available, (via Leiths List) which is useful when cash-flow as a student is difficult!"

The School works in conjunction with Leiths List, an employment agency for chefs and Leiths Food Solutions, an enterprise that offers management advice for anyone setting up or wanting to improve a food business. There are numerous employment opportunities including private catering, restaurant positions, food writing, magazine work and food styling.

- Run by Managing Director Camilla Schneideman, Leiths excels on both the theoretical and the practical sides, benefiting from over 30 years' experience, whilst remaining fully abreast of contemporary techniques, styles and methods.
- The premises has a purpose-built demonstration theatre, seating 42, 4 fully-equipped teaching kitchens and a restaurant kitchen to create a realistic work environment.
- Leiths teaching staff are trained professionals with first-hand experience of restaurants and commercial catering. Renowned chefs, cookery writers and Masters of Wine regularly demonstrate or lecture at the School.

**Leiths School of Food and Wine, 16-20 Wendell Road,
London W12 9RT
Tel: 020 8749 6400   www.leiths.com**

What to study in FE

Before you can make a decision on what to study, you need to know the full range of courses out there. You can find this information out by talking to your careers teacher at school and also by browsing the careers library at your local Connexions office. Most schools and colleges of FE have prospectuses of post-16 learning opportunities too, so it is worth gathering these to work your way through.

You will need to ask your careers teacher and other teachers at your school for advice on what type of qualification you would be best suited to. They will be able to help you by talking to you about your current levels of attainment in school and what you both feel would be a good level to go for in FE.

Remember, it is up to you whether you want to apply for academic and/ or vocational courses. Both will give you valuable skills for the workplace, and with the ever-increasing emphasis on skills they are likely to ensure that you have the edge in the job market when you are ready for work.

Don't forget that it is possible to mix and match your studies at post-16 so that you can develop a programme that is just right for you. For example, you could combine A levels with NVQ units to build a programme of study that best suits your plans for the future.

Info

Your school may use an online or a paper method of tracking your progress through school and beyond. You can use this to focus on organising your skills, achievements and goals. Find out from your tutor or careers adviser whether your school has such a thing for you to work with. Tracking your progress in this way can help you to:

- *organise your time so that you don't miss any opportunities;*
- *record your achievements and track your progress against your goals;*
- *practise putting together a CV and applications for jobs and courses.*

The main qualification groups

Basically, if you want to study in FE, you can choose from the following main qualification types for 14- to 19-year-olds. This is not a list of courses, just a list of the groups of qualifications you may be able to choose from:

- A levels;
- Key Skills;
- Skills for Life;
- GCSEs and International GCSEs;
- Entry level;
- NVQs;
- BTECs, OCR Nationals and other vocational qualifications;
- Functional Skills;
- Diplomas;
- International Baccalaureate Diploma.

AS and A levels

The GCE A level is split into two parts: the AS and the A2. The AS (or Advanced subsidiary) is a qualification that can stand alone in its own right. It is the equivalent of half a full A level qualification and units are assessed as though the student is halfway through an A level course.

The A2 is the second, more demanding part of a full A level. Students are assessed as though they are at the end of a full A level. Again it is worth half of the full A level qualification but the A2 is not a stand-alone qualification in its own right.

The units of an A level are usually assessed by examination, but some are assessed by coursework, which can account for between 20 and 30 per cent of the marks.

> *Even if you know that you do not want to go on into higher education (HE), gaining A levels is still a wise move as they are so widely known and understood by employers and recruiters.*

Info

Key Skills

There are certain skills that are needed for success in study, work and life in general. These are known as Key Skills, and it is possible to take Key Skills qualifications that explore the way that you apply the skills in different contexts. The Key Skills areas are:

Main Key Skills
- communication;
- application of number;
- ICT (information and communications technology).

Wider Key Skills
- working with others;
- improving own learning and performance;
- problem solving.

Each Key Skill is assessed separately and assessment is based on a portfolio of evidence. For the three main Key Skills, you would also take a test.

Skills for Life

Skills for Life qualifications are designed for those who need to develop skills used in everyday life, for example, reading, writing and mathematics.
   You can take a Skills for Life qualification if you:

- are over 16 years of age;
- have left compulsory full-time education;
- do not have an up-to-date English or mathematics qualification at level 2 on the National Qualifications Framework (such as a GCSE).

Skills for Life are sometimes referred to as Basic Skills.

GCSEs

Although GCSEs are what you do at the end of your school career at the age of 16, you can still study them post-16 (particularly if you want to go on to do A levels or other qualifications that require you to have achieved a certain number of GCSEs and you need to resit any that you did not get the required grade in). GCSEs can be taken in over 45 subjects.

Entry level

Entry level is the first level of the National Qualifications Framework (NQF) – see below – and entry level qualifications are pitched below GCSE grade G, NVQ level 1 or vocational qualifications at level 1.

Entry level is subdivided into three levels: entry 1, entry 2 and entry 3 (the highest). From entry level 3 it is hoped that students will go on to level 1 qualifications (such as GCSEs) that appeal to them. If you opt for entry-level qualifications, it is probably because you have a learning need in a particular area, such as numeracy or literacy.

The National Qualifications Framework (NQF) for England, Wales and Northern Ireland sets out the levels at which qualifications are recognised. There are nine levels: entry level and levels 1 to 8. GCSE grades A*–C are level 2 qualifications and A levels are level 3 qualifications.

There is also a Framework for Higher Education Qualification levels, which run from C (certificate), I (intermediate), H (Honours), M (Masters) to D (doctoral).

NVQs

NVQs are work-related qualifications. They focus on the skills, knowledge and competences that you need in order to do a particular job really well. There are national occupational standards that NVQs are based on. These standards tell us what people in certain jobs or professions do and the standards that they do them to.

There is no specified time in which NVQs have to be completed, although they do have to be completed within a 'reasonable' amount of time. This is so that you could combine part-time work with study for NVQs. There are no entry requirements and no age limits. You get NVQs through a combination of assessment and training.

NVQs are at levels 1 to 5 on the NQF. Most 14–19 learners achieve levels 1–3. Getting to level 4 in that age group would be extremely rare, but it is certainly something to aim for!

At the time of writing there are currently new qualifications in the process of development which will be placed on the Qualifications and Credit Framework (QCF). The QCF is a framework which makes it easy to compare qualifications. There are three sizes of qualifications in the QCF:

Awards: 1–12 credits
Certificates: 13–36 credits
Diplomas: 37 credits or more

In this framework it is possible to have an Award at level 1 of the NQF or at level 8.

The new qualifications will eventually take the place of current vocational qualifications (but some NVQs will still be around!).

You can find out more about the QCF from the QCDA website: www. qcda.gov.uk/19674.aspx.

BTECs, OCR Nationals and other vocational qualifications

Mainly for learners aged 16 or over, BTEC qualifications and OCR Nationals are work-related qualifications. They are available in a wide range of subjects and have mostly been designed in collaboration with industry, so they help to make sure that you have the skills and knowledge that employers want. There is a real mix of theory and practice in these qualifications and you may also do an element of work experience too.

BTECs and OCR Nationals are available in a wide range of subjects, including:

- art and design;
- business;
- health and social care;
- information technology;
- media;
- public services;
- science;
- sport.

> *BTECS and OCR Nationals are currently being updated. They will be available as new qualifications on the Qualifications and Credit Framework by the end of 2010. To find out more about this visit: www.direct.gov.uk.*
>
> **Info**

You would usually study for these qualifications full-time at college, or possibly at school if it is collaborating with a college. It's also possible to take them part-time at college.

There are almost countless vocational qualifications that are linked in to the NQF at every level. You can really let your imagination run wild when thinking about what vocational qualifications you might like to have, because there is one to cover just about every industry sector you could imagine, from beauty to catering, secretarial skills to journalism.

There is a real push right now to get more young people to go for vocational qualifications, so if you are at all tempted, ask for details at your local Connexions office or from your careers teacher. As there are so many vocational qualifications being provided by so many different organisations, they vary in length, level and assessment arrangements.

> *There are also other qualifications that you might like to look into and your careers teacher or local Connexions office can help you to do this. One such example is the Free-standing Mathematics Qualification. It is part of the NQF and is for post-16 students. There are three levels – foundation, intermediate and advanced – and they are not attached to any other qualifications.*
>
> **Info**

Functional Skills

Functional Skills are practical skills in English, mathematics and information and communications technology (ICT). They will be fully launched in 2010. The key feature of Functional Skills is that they are not just about knowledge, but how and when to apply that knowledge in real life too.

Diplomas

The Diploma is a qualification for 14–19-year-olds. It is designed to be a more practical way of gaining essential skills for moving on to university or employment. Diplomas are available in 14 subject areas (see page 48–49).

The International Baccalaureate

The International Baccalaureate (IB) Diploma Programme is a Level 3 qualification for students aged 16–19 that is internationally recognised. It leads to a single qualification, and it takes the form of academic study of a wide range of subjects, including languages, the arts, science, mathematics, history and geography.

The IB is designed to encourage you to:

● learn how to learn;
● ask challenging questions;
● develop a strong sense of your own identity and culture;
● develop the ability to communicate with and understand people from other countries and cultures.

> **Info** *You can find out more about the International Baccalaureate Diploma Programme here: www.ibo.org/diploma/.*

Scotland

Scotland has a different education system from that in the rest of the United Kingdom, and if you want to find out about FE there, you should talk to your careers teacher at school or college as well as having a good look through the following website: www.skillsdevelopmentscotland.co.uk.

In short, Scotland's SVQs are equivalent to NVQs elsewhere in the United Kingdom, Standard Grades are equivalent to GCSEs and Highers are equivalent to A levels.

Where to study in FE

You may know that you definitely want to stay on for FE, but you still have decisions to make if you are not just staying on at school. Some of your options are:

- to stay on at school if yours has a sixth form attached;
- to go to the sixth form in another school;
- to go to a local college of FE;
- to go to a sixth form college;
- to attend a specialist college (for example one devoted to agriculture or aviation);
- to go to a private fee-charging college;
- to attend an HE college that offers some FE courses.

Sixth forms and sixth form colleges

Sixth forms are attached to, or part of, a school, whereas sixth form colleges are separate establishments. You can take a range of courses at sixth forms but they do tend, still, to specialise in A levels and GCSE resits (although not exclusively, by any means). Sixth forms in schools can offer you the potential benefit of being taught by teachers whom you already know – but for some students this is a distinct disadvantage and they prefer the opportunity to go somewhere new and start afresh!

Regardless of whether you entered a sixth form or a sixth form college, you would be expected to manage your own studies, time and deadlines.

Other colleges

Other colleges of FE vary tremendously, usually depending on the quality of the alternatives on offer or the size of the town that you live in. If there are very good sixth forms around, it is likely that other colleges will specialise in more vocational courses. Here you would have the option of studying full- or part-time, which may help to sway your decision.

Choosing a college... View from Andy

I knew that I wanted to do A levels, but when I went round the colleges on their open days I just didn't like the local sixth form college. Most of my friends were going there but I still felt that it wasn't right for me. The local college of FE had a really strong art department, and as that was one of my best subjects, I really wanted to go there. They do higher education courses at the FE college so it meant that I had the benefit of using the resources and equipment that the degree students were using while studying for my A levels. In the end there was no competition; I couldn't throw away that opportunity, so chose the college of FE over the sixth form college.

Choosing a college

For many students it is usually obvious which college they should attend, especially if they want to take a particular course which is only taught at one local college. However, if you have a choice to make, these ideas will help you. Ask these questions about any college you are considering attending:

- Can you do the combinations of courses and subjects that you are interested in?
- Does it have a good reputation for the kind of subjects you want to study?
- What are the results like there? Are they good? Do people achieve well there?
- Can you imagine being happy there?
- Do you know others who are going there? Does it matter to you if you don't?
- What is the atmosphere like? Do you think you could study there?

- What are the facilities like? Does it have strengths that you would be able to take advantage of?
- Are there any sporting opportunities? Does it matter to you if there aren't?
- What are the student welfare facilities like? Is there plenty of advice on offer?
- What's your gut instinct? Could you be happy and do well there?

The only really effective way of choosing where you are going to continue your studies in FE is to visit all the options that are open to you. All the colleges will have open days where you can look around, meet staff and students, try out taster sessions and chat to others who are thinking of going there. Your local paper will publish details of open days at the relevant times and your local Connexions office will have the details too.

Even if you think you know where you want to go, take the time to look at the other options in your town, or within commutable distance.

> It's a good idea to keep notes on the various colleges that you visit. This way, if you are stuck between a choice of two, you can use your notes to help you reach a decision.
>
> **Action**

Once you know where you would like to study, obviously you will need to apply for a place. The best advice here is to follow the guidance of your school or the Connexions service. You will need to fill in application forms and you may also be asked to attend for an interview.

Colleges want to be as sure as they can about two main things before offering places: that potential students will stay on their courses and not drop out; and that the students will get the best results they possibly can. No college wants dropouts and flunkers as students, so convince them that you will stay and will achieve the best you can!

You can get all the forms you need direct from the college itself if not from your school. Make sure that you meet all the deadlines you need to and ask for help if you are struggling with the application form. Most careers teachers and Connexions staff will be able to guide you through this process.

Info

The section on work will have some useful advice for you on making applications generally, which you will be able to apply to any applications you make (see page 127). There is also advice on interviews there too (see page 140), which will be useful if you have to have one to get into the college of your choice.

Summary

The key points from this chapter include the following:

- It is up to you whether you study academic or vocational subjects in FE. Some people choose to study a combination of the two.
- There is a range of types of qualification.
- There are several ways of studying in FE. You may be able to stay on at school, go to a separate sixth form college or go to your local college of FE; these are just some of the options you may have.
- It is important to choose the college that is right for you, and there are many factors to take into consideration.

6
Choices in higher education (HE)

This chapter will look at:

- what to study in HE;
- the main qualification groups in HE;
- choosing a university;
- applying through UCAS;
- starting your course.

Higher education is what you progress to after completing further education (post-16) courses, should you so decide (assuming you have the necessary entry requirements). HE courses can last anything from one to four or five years or more, and there is a variety of qualifications you can gain.

Going into HE is not just a matter of doing a degree or nothing. There are several options open to you, so you will need to do a little research to make sure that you take the path most suited to you.

THE COURTAULD
Institute of Art

"

STUDY AT ONE OF THE WORLD'S LEADING CENTRES OF ART HISTORY AND CONSERVATION

"

For more information
t: 020 7848 2635/2645
www.courtauld.ac.uk

THE COURTAULD
Institute of Art

The Courtauld Institute of Art is a dynamic international centre for the study of art history, curating and conservation, and is also home to one of the finest small art museums in the world. Based at Somerset House in the heart of London, The Courtauld and its Gallery are close to all the major cultural institutions of London and provide unsurpassed research resources and learning opportunities.

What is Art History?

Art history is a part of the wider field of history. It investigates all forms of visual arts and design. Art history explores the making and viewing of art, the social and political uses of works of art within their respective historical contexts - economic, social, philosophical, and cultural -rather than focusing solely on their outward appearance.

Why study Art History?

Studying art history will provide you with the sophisticated skills and vocabulary of visual response and critical expertise. It will also equip you with a range of other useful skills attractive to employers in the art, heritage and creative industries and beyond, for example: analytical ability; communication skills; presentation skills; writing ability; research skills; time management and team working skills.

A substantial number of Courtauld graduates progress to art-related careers both nationally and internationally as museum directors, curators, academics, conservators, critics, journalists, teachers and in the commercial art world. The most common openings are in teaching, curatorial, administration work in galleries and museums and other aspects of the heritage industry, and in commercial galleries and auction houses as well as in art publishing and journalism.

Recent Courtauld graduates have gained positions at the National Gallery, Tate and the Victoria & Albert Museum, the Barbican, Historic Royal Palaces, Christie's, New Statesman magazine, Frieze magazine and art fair, White Cube, and many other prestigious and exciting organisations. Many of our graduates also go on to further academic study either at The Courtauld or other universities in Britain and abroad in art history, conservation or museum curating.

Which A-levels should I study in order to take a BA in Art History?

Students who wish to apply for art history at undergraduate degree level should study three A levels, or equivalent (such as the International Baccalaureate) in relevant subjects. History, Art History, English and modern European Languages are the most relevant, but applications will also be considered from those studying other subjects. A levels that involve independent study and essay writing will provide the best preparation for degree level study.

Student Comment

Christopher Griffin
BA History of Art - 2004 to 2007 MA History of Art - 2007/8

"Looking back on my time as an undergraduate, and comparing my experiences with friends at larger universities, I realise how lucky I was to learn amongst such an intimate and enthusiastic intergenerational scholarly community. Despite being a specialist institute, students at every stage of their education are encouraged to develop their own approaches to art history and to share ideas and perspectives, cultivating a collaborative research environment which served me well in preparation for my postgraduate degree.

As well as fostering an environment for me to excel academically, the Courtauld offers all the social experiences anyone could want from university. With the support of a lively students' union there are regular social events, an ever-expanding selection of clubs and societies, and networks to other London colleges. The past four years really have been the best of my life and I owe them entirely to the Courtauld."

The Courtauld Institute of Art
Somerset House
The Strand
London WC2R 0RN
0207 848 2635/2645   www.courtauld.ac.uk

Are you trying to find a pathway into Graduate Entry Medicine?

BSc Medical Sciences and Humanities (MeSH) BV95 at Swansea University

Exploring the scientific and human sides of Medicine & Healthcare

This innovative, interdisciplinary degree explores the complex bio-psycho-social nature of health, illness, and the role of medical intervention. You will study biomedical sciences, but also human sciences and humanities in relation to medicine. Our degree was developed in 1999 with Swansea University's Medical School as an ideal platform for graduate entry into medicine, or to the para-medical professions (e.g. physiotherapy, health promotion, speech therapy). **Medical Sciences and Humanities'** students have a consistent, year-on-year track record of successful applications to study medicine at Swansea Medical School and other UK, European and Australian Medical Schools. The **MeSH** degree is also a proven pathway into professions allied to medicine, and managerial careers in healthcare, social services, local government, and the public/private sector in general.

Entry Requirements

- A minimum of 280 UCAS tariff points at A level
- There is no requirement for an A level in Mathematics or Science subjects

Graduates' Comments

Toria Harding, of Staffordshire, has progressed onto Graduate Entry Medicine at Swansea University:

'I lost confidence in my abilities when I didn't do as well as expected in my A-levels. I think this course has really helped me understand the career of a Doctor better. We do everything from medical science to medical law, from medical history to health economics. I feel more prepared for medicine now; looking back I wasn't ready to dive into such an intense course as medicine straight off the back of my A-levels. It's taken three years, but I finally feel like I've gained some of that self-belief back, looking back it's the best decision I ever made.'

Rusha Ashour, of London, has progressed onto Medicine at Dundee University:

'This is the only degree of its kind in UK; it is very special because it covers all areas of medicine from different perspectives. This is just the beginning of my career ambition. I feel all the hard work has been paid off massively, I am so happy and excited to graduate and to continue towards my ultimate goal since I was young: to one day be a genuinely good doctor.'

Contact Us
Dr Andrew Hull
+44 (0) 1792 518599
a.j.hull@swansea.ac.uk

Admissions
+44 (0) 1792 518531
shsadmissions@swansea.ac.uk

- *Eurydice (Scotland): http://eacea.ec.europa.eu/portal/page/portal/ Eurydice/ByCountryResults?countryCode=SC.*
- *National Database of Accredited Qualifications: www.accreditedqualifications.org.uk.*
- *Directgov: www.direct.gov.uk/en/EducationAndLearning/ QualificationsExplained/index.htm.*

Before you research HE courses, just take a moment to think about why you are even considering going into HE. Is it to put off getting a job or to study something you are genuinely interested in and/or to further your career? Make sure that you know what your motivations are and then read the following points:

- Around 22 per cent of students fail to complete their courses. Approximately 100,000 leave within a year.
- Estimates of student debt suggest that you could expect to graduate with around £20,000 of debt and possibly even more than that.

Are you still interested?

There are definite advantages to think about:

- The chances of you being unemployed are thought to be cut by half when you have a degree.
- You can expect your salary to rise faster if you have a degree. Estimates suggest that graduates can expect to be earning as much as 30 per cent more than non-graduates in the case of men and 46 per cent more in the case of women 10 years after graduating.
- University-goers develop marketable transferable skills.
- The opportunity for an 'all-round' education is open for all at university; the social and cultural life that's to be had helps to develop all-rounders who are not just fixated on their subjects!
- You get letters after your name!

Has that recaptured your interest?

For information about student life in the United Kingdom, log on to www.studentuk.com. Also check out www.uni360.com, providing virtual tours of universities and much more, and the National Union of Students website, www.nus.org.uk.

Info

What to study in HE

Not only do you need to know the full range of courses out there before you can make a decision on what you want to study in HE, but you also need to think about the following considerations:

- What courses are open to you with your current qualifications?
- What courses are you most interested in?
- Do you need a vocational degree to achieve your goals (for example, to be a vet or a doctor)?
- Are you studying anything at the moment that you want to continue with?
- Does it look as though you will get the results you need to do the course that you are interested in? Do you have a plan B in case you don't get enough points or the right grades?
- Do you have the relevant work experience you need (if this is a requirement)?
- Do you actually need to go to university for the career you want to pursue?

Even if you get on your perfect course, there will be times when the work seems too much (or you have put it off for too long and are now facing all-nighters to get your essays done!). Just imagine how this will feel if you have allowed yourself to be persuaded to do a course that other people want you to do or that you thought sounded fun at the time but did not really have a burning passion for!

Not all courses run to the same pattern. Some are modular (meaning that you can choose certain self-contained modules to study), others are sandwich (meaning that you will spend a year out either abroad or in industry), combined (two or more subjects making up a single course of study) and so on. Make sure that you find out exactly what kind of course it is that you are interested in. If you are unsure of any of the terms used your local Connexions office can help you. There is a huge amount of advice on the Direct.gov website, too: www.direct.gov.uk. This website aims to give you all the information you need to get started on the road to HE.

If you do not have a career path in mind, it is particularly important, essential even, to choose a course that will grab you and hold your attention until you take the final exam. University life will hold much to tempt you away from your studies, so if your heart is not completely in it, you are more likely to fall behind. Do something you get a kick out of and the chances are you will stick with it to the end.

UCAS is the central organisation that processes applications for full-time undergraduate courses at UK universities and colleges. You can do a full course search on the UCAS website, www.ucas.com.

The UCAS website also carries invaluable advice on how to apply for HE courses. Applications must be made online. If you don't have access to the internet at home and you have to compete to use it at school, you may want to use one of the online centres that have teamed up with UCAS to give students access to work on their applications. To find out more, visit www.ukonlinecentres.com.

Other websites that can help in the search for a course are www.ukcoursefinder.co.uk and www.hotcourses.com.

The main qualification groups

Basically, if you want to study in HE, you can choose from the following main qualification types. This is not a list of courses, just a list of the groups of qualifications you may be able to choose from:

- H (Honours) – Bachelor's degrees, graduate certificates and diplomas;
- I (intermediate) – Diplomas of Higher Education and Further Education, foundation degrees, Higher National Diplomas (HNDs);
- C (certificate) – Certificates of Higher Education.

Honours degrees

Honours degrees are the most common HE qualifications. They are called Bachelor's degrees and are either arts based (the Bachelor of Arts (BA)) or science based (the Bachelor of Science (BSc)). They take between three and five years of full-time study to complete. Honours degrees tend to be subject based rather than linked to specific careers or professions.

Foundation degrees

Foundation degrees are employment-related qualifications. They have been designed with employers and aim to put an end to skills shortages. They combine vocational and general learning, using flexible methods of study. Full-time foundation degrees take two years to study and part-time ones usually three or four years pro rata. There are no set entry requirements, so you can apply even if you do not have other qualifications; it is up to the university or college to decide whether you are a suitable candidate or not. If you successfully complete a foundation degree, you may be able to add a further 12–15 months' study to what you have done so far and convert it to an Honours degree. It is possible to study a foundation degree course while working.

> You can find out more about foundation degrees from the website www.findfoundationdegree.co.uk.
>
> Info

HNCs and HNDs

Higher National Certificates or Diplomas can be done in a wide range of subjects, usually linked to specific careers. Often, HNCs and HNDs are studied part time by people who are also working. They take two or more years to complete. Having an HNC can mean you can enter the second year of a suitable Honours degree, while having an HND can mean you can enter the second or third year.

Certificates and Diplomas of Higher Education

The Certificate of Higher Education is a one-year course that can be done if you feel you need to gain some confidence before starting further HE studies. The diploma is a two-year (three-year part-time) course often linked to specific careers. It is like a degree but has less content. It is sometimes possible to add a year of study to the diploma to convert it into a degree.

Info

You can find a list of universities and colleges on the UCAS website: www.ucas.com.

Choosing a university

There are many factors to consider when choosing a university – not least, does it offer exactly the kind of course you want to do? University is about much more than the studying you will do there. It is about meeting new people, having new experiences and widening your horizons, as much as anything else. So, with this in mind, when it comes to choosing where you want to apply to, think about these considerations:

- Does it offer the course that interests and motivates you most?
- Can you meet the entry requirements for the course you want to do there?
- Will it give you the opportunity to build on your past achievements and strengths?
- Is it close enough to home (if you will be living at home through HE) or within a distance you are happy to travel (if you will be moving away)?
- What reputation does the university have?
- What reputation does the course have?
- Does the university excel in any particular area? Would your course be sidelined in favour of its 'pet' courses or are all treated equally?

- Would you be able to study in a way that suits you? How many lectures would you have to attend and how much private study would be expected? Is there any practical work to do? Would you get a year out in industry or abroad?
- Would you get much one-to-one tutoring?
- What weighting do exams have on the course? Is any coursework taken into consideration?
- If you have any particular special needs, can the university cater for you?
- Would you get a chance to learn skills that would make you more employable than other graduates?
- Would you get a chance to do some work experience?
- Does the university have an active student union? What entertainments would there be on offer? Does it offer a good social life?
- How good are the sports facilities?
- Is it a campus university (where most of the university buildings, including halls of residence, are in one area, often with green space in between) or are the buildings spread out across a town or city?
- What kind of student accommodation is there? Would you be guaranteed a place in a hall of residence for your first year at least?
- What is your instinctive feeling about the place?

In a tough economic climate, some people question whether it's a good idea to go to university. This has to be your decision ultimately, but you might want to consider these points:

Info

- *While you're at university you'll be gaining skills, knowledge and expertise at a time when the economy may be moving towards recovery. Just when you're ready to leave with your qualification complete, things may have picked up a little.*
- *It is likely that the more qualifications you have, the better your chances are on the job market when you are ready to start looking.*
- *Even though things may be tough in the economy, as a student you're still entitled to the same funding (in terms of grants and/or loans) as before the recession kicked in.*
- *It is always most positive to follow your goals if at all possible, regardless of what is happening in the wider economy. If you have always wanted to go to university, there's no reason to put that dream on hold just because the country may be in recession.*

BISHOP GROSSETESTE
UNIVERSITY
COLLEGE
LINCOLN

www.bishopg.ac.u

Here at Bishop Grosseteste University College Lincoln, we offer undergraduate BA (Hons) and BSc (Hons) courses in:

Drama in the Community
Early Childhood Studies
English Literature
Heritage Studies
Primary Education (QTS)
Education Studies and Art and Design
Education Studies and Drama
Education Studies and English
Education Studies and Geography
Education Studies and History
Education Studies and Mathematics
Education Studies and Music
Education Studies and Sport
Education Studies and Theology

Just over 2,000 students currently study with us, creating a unique academic community where support is always on hand and every student is treated as an individual. Our attractive, single-site campus is situated within historic uphill Lincoln, within easy walking distance of the city's main attractions.

Why not come along to one of our Open Days to see for yourself and find out more. Our next Open Days are:

Sunday 10 October 2010
Sunday 13 March 2011
Sunday 5 June 2011

For more information on any of our courses, call us now on **(01522) 583658**, email **info@bishopg.ac.uk** or visit **www.bishopg.ac.uk**.

Bishop Grosseteste University College Lincoln (BG) offers undergraduate, postgraduate and work-based foundation degree courses, with an emphasis on enriching the lives of its students, staff and the community it serves. BG is located in the heart of historic Lincoln, a city with over 2,000 years of history behind it. Originally a Roman settlement, Lincoln was a thriving Medieval centre and now finds itself as one of the fastest growing cities in the UK, a captivating mixture of the old and the new.

BG began life in 1862 as an Anglican teacher training college for women. To mark the centenary in 1962, it was renamed Bishop Grosseteste College in honour of Robert Grosseteste, the thirteenth century scientist, philosopher, educator, and Bishop of Lincoln. In the summer of 2006 the name was changed to Bishop Grosseteste University College Lincoln after a successful application for taught degree awarding powers.

The University College has changed considerably over its 148 years of existence. The past few years have seen a considerable growth in student numbers, and in September 2009 the University College was bigger than it had ever been, with just over 2,000 students.

The University College still occupies its original site in uphill Lincoln and the buildings of the original 1840s college are still in daily use, though these have been extensively extended and refurbished. Today the attractive 18-acre site also houses many modern developments, including purpose-built learning and teaching accommodation in the Robert Hardy Building, as well as dedicated facilities for music, science and technology, a theatre and library.

Recently, a brand new Sport and Fitness Centre was opened on campus, providing students with a well appointed gym, specialist fitness equipment and indoor sports hall. In 2008, the University College unveiled the state-of-the-art Human Performance Laboratory (HPL), primarily to be used by the students on the new BA (Hons) Education Studies and Sport programme.

Along with the recent improvements at BG, there are plenty more developments in the pipeline for the next few years (including plans for an enlarged library) all of which are designed to improve the lives and experiences of BG students in the years to come.

BG remains a small and cohesive academic community where staff and students alike are valued as individuals and encouraged to think of others. The biggest change in recent years has been the beginning of life as a University College (a university college is like a university in every way except size, having less than 4,000 students).

Steve, BA (Hons) English Literature graduate of BG – "The great thing about BG is that it is whatever the students make it. The students and staff all know the importance of constantly developing and working to improve things in order to make sure we have the best experience possible. What else could you ask of a university college?"

You can find out more about BG by visiting
www.bishopg.ac.uk.

Open days

The only way to know if you will be happy at a particular university is to visit it and have a look round. All universities have open days, and you should definitely attend any at universities you are thinking of applying to. Even if the journey seems like a hassle, do it!

> **Info**
>
> *For information on open days, visit www.opendays.com. This website even allows you to book an open day online.*

> **Info**
>
> *The online 'Push' guide to university is an independent guide to finding the right university for you. It can be found at www.push.co.uk.*
>
> *You might find www.unofficial-guides.com of interest too.*

Applying – UCAS

UCAS, pronounced 'you-cass', is the Universities and Colleges Admissions Service. It is responsible for handling nearly all the applications for HE courses.

> **Info**
>
> *To get a clear idea of the application process you need to log on to the UCAS website, www.ucas.com, where you will find detailed guidance. It's a good idea to note key dates in your diary so that you don't miss any important deadlines.*

Applications to UCAS are made online via the UCAS website. You can apply for up to five courses in five different institutions (but you can just apply to one if there is only one course in the whole country that you want to do; alternatively, you can apply to five courses at one university if you are sure that you want to go there and are not too bothered about what you study).

The UCAS application asks for details about your qualifications so far and grades achieved. You will also need to complete a personal statement to sell yourself! Your school or college can help with this, as can Connexions, and there is even a website, www.personalstatement.info, although writing from your own ideas and own 'voice' will always be best.

Your school or college will help you through the UCAS application process. There are some important deadlines so make sure that you don't miss them. At the time of writing, if you are applying to Oxford, Cambridge or for medicine, dentistry or veterinary science/medicine, you will need to submit your application by 15 October of your final year of FE. Other applications need to be submitted by 15 January of the year of expected entry to HE except if you are applying for some art and design courses, in which case your application needs to be in by 24 March. You can find out more from the UCAS website: www.ucas.com.

> *UCAS has a tariff that compares all the different qualifications that can get you into HE. Points are assigned to each type of qualification and grade. It can seem quite daunting to go through at first, but it is not that bad if you get the help of your tutor at school or college. The Connexions service can help with this, too.*
>
> *To find out more about the UCAS tariff, visit www.ucas.com.*

Info

- There is a fee to pay. As an example, the fee for students starting university in 2011 is £21 (£11 for those who apply to one course at one university).
- Once your application has been submitted, UCAS will send an acknowledgement back as well as sending your application to the admissions tutors in the institutions you have chosen.
- UCAS will inform you whether you have been successful in your application.
- You may be called for an interview (see the section on page 140 for general advice on interviews).
- If you are offered a place, this will probably be conditional on your achieving certain results in your exams. If you already know your results (for example, if you have taken a year out), any offers of places are likely to be unconditional.
- If, when your results come out in August, you do not have exactly the grades you needed, the institution may agree to take you anyway.

- If you do not get offered a place when your results are known, you can enter the 'clearing' system. This is basically when all the courses that are not yet filled and all the students who do not yet have a place try to match up with each other! It's a busy time as courses have to be filled between the end of August and the start of term. If you need to go through clearing, your school or college will be able to help you through the process. Basically, you will have to keep a close eye on the broadsheet newspapers and the internet to find out what courses still have places. Do not be tempted to leap at the first thing that looks vaguely interesting. Not surprisingly, of all the students who do not make it through to the end of their HE courses, a relatively high proportion have entered through clearing rather than having got on to the course of their choice. This is worth keeping in mind.

Info

'yougo' is a student community site brought to you by UCAS for year 12, S5 or equivalent students among others designed to help you to get ready for life in higher education. UCAS says that by joining yougo you'll get a range of benefits including:

- Access to the yougo community.
- A discount card to cut the cost of shopping at many high street outlets.
- Regular web chats with experts, including UCAS, universities and colleges; as well as friends of yougo, such as Lonely Planet, TARGET Jobs and the Rugby Football Union (RFU).
- All the essential information about higher education courses and places of study.
- Online UCAS advisers to help you with the UCAS application process.
- Regular newsletters with news and advice at key stages of the application process.
- Access to institution profile pages: 'talk' to the colleges and universities online.
- Three copies of The Independent's 'You Can' magazine, the essential guide to higher education, delivered to your UK address.

yougo is free to join. You can find out more by emailing support@ yougofurther.co.uk or calling 01242 544804. Register online at: www. yougofurther.co.uk.

If terms such as 'clearing', 'deferral', 'firm offer', 'conditional offer' and 'entry profiles' leave you a little baffled, take a look at the UCAS jargon buster. Commonly used words and phrases that you're bound to come across during the application process are all explained here: www.ucas.com/students/ucasterms.

Extra enables students who find themselves without an offer of a course to have an additional choice through UCAS. If you take the Extra route, you don't have to wait until clearing to carry on with the search for a place.

You can apply via Extra from the end of February to the end of June in the year of intended entry to HE. So, for example, if you were aiming to start a course in the autumn of 2011, you would go through Extra from the end of February of that year. You are eligible to apply if:

- *all five of your choices have been used up;*
- *you have not had any success with any of your choices;*
- *you have declined all offers made to you.*

You can find further information about Extra at www.ucas.com/students/offers/extra.

Starting your course

Congratulations! You are off to university! Whether you are actually leaving home or staying put, this is a good opportunity to get yourself sorted before launching into your next phase of studying. These ideas may help:

- How prepared are you emotionally? Is there anything you want to talk about before you take the plunge? Have you got any concerns or anxieties?
- Make sure that you read Part Six of this book, especially the sections on finding somewhere to live and money.
- Is there a chance you could take a holiday before your course starts? This will give you a chance to gather your thoughts about what is ahead.

- Do you need anything new to take with you? Do you have enough clothes and shoes?
- Have you got plenty of paper (for note-taking) and any other resources you need for your course?
- Is there a book list you need to be looking at? It might be worth scouring some second-hand bookshops to see if you can get some bargains. Some online bookshops sell second-hand copies of books too, but check that you get the right editions.
- Do you know how you are going to get you and all your stuff to university?
- Spare a thought for your parents and close relatives as you are getting ready to leave. It might be incredibly exciting for you, but the chances are they will really miss you. Make a promise to keep in touch and stick to it!
- Set off with a really positive attitude about what is ahead of you. Aim to really enjoy it. After all, you deserve to after all your hard work so far!

Leaving home... View from Ashley

It wasn't until I had graduated that my Mum told me how upset she'd been the day she and Dad drove me to university for the first time. Apparently she had cried most of the way home that day! I really appreciated the fact that she didn't tell me at the time as I would have thought it was a really big deal. I'm glad I made the effort to stay in touch with my family and friends when I went away, and I made sure that I didn't go more than six weeks without going home for the weekend so that we could all catch up with each other. It was quite a learning curve for me; we don't always realise what an impact we have on other people and I think we have to be sensitive to what others close to us might be feeling at such turning points in our lives.

Summary

The key points from this chapter are:

- There are distinct advantages to studying in HE, not least that graduates typically earn considerably more than those who have not studied in HE.
- It is essential to make the right choice over what to study in HE to give yourself the best chance of success, especially if you do not have a career choice in mind.
- Choosing a university is easier said than done. There are many factors to take into consideration.
- It is a good idea to go to the open days for the universities that you are interested in.
- Applications for most places on HE courses are handled by UCAS.

Make Aberdeen your next choice

Choosing a degree course has always been one of the most important decisions that an individual will make – it sets them on a career path and determines which doors will be open in future and which will be closed. In the wake of the financial crisis the decision takes on renewed importance, as questions arise as to what the economy – and by extension the job market – will look like in the future.

In this context a degree that is highly-regarded both for its intellectual rigour and for its transferable skills offers obvious attractions to students and to prospective employers. A law degree has in recent years increasingly come to be seen as the most desirable general degree in addition to being the first step on the road to employment in the legal profession.

As many as a third of law graduates now pursue careers outside of the profession, with employers recognising that the degree's focus on problem solving, argument construction and clarity of communication produces individuals with highly-developed skills that are valuable in a range of business settings.

This trend certainly favours long-established institutions such as the University of Aberdeen with a proven track record of providing high-quality legal education to meet the needs of today's students and their future employers, both in law and in business more generally.

Build Your Future in the Sixth Century of Law at Aberdeen

Law has been taught at Aberdeen since its foundation in 1495. Today, the school consistently ranks highly in UK University League tables. With a tradition of excellence in research and international scholarship, the Law School offers a range of modern, flexible programmes.

We welcome applicants to all programmes at both Undergraduate and Postgraduate levels.

For further information about:

- Our extensive range of programmes
- Current and future activities
- Funding opportunities

1495

UNIVERSITY
OF ABERDEEN

www.abdn.ac.uk/law

Thinking about the future?

We understand that coming to University is about more than receiving your qualification. It's about giving you the knowledge, skills and experience to ensure you get a great job after you graduate. But while you're working hard, we also want you to be able to enjoy your student life and get the most out of going to University.

The Faculty of Health & Social Care offers a wide range of health care programmes so you can choose a subject that interests you. The majority of our programmes have a work placement element to them, which ensures you have the skills and hands on experience to maximise your employability on graduating.

But don't take our word for it, here's an insight into Matt Evans' day, a third year student, studying BSc (Hons) Podiatry.

advertisement feature

A day in the life of Matt Evans

7.30am I get up, have breakfast and check my social networking sites. I put on some music and get ready for Uni. I normally set off at about 8.30am as it's fairly close to home.

9.00am I arrive at Uni and grab a quick coffee in the Neo Café. I'll then go over to the podiatry clinic on campus, put my uniform on and set up ready to see patients.

9.30am – 12.00 noon I see about four patients in the morning clinic which is good as I prefer to be busy. This means I learn more about the different types of conditions which can affect people's health. The morning clinic is based on musculoskeletal conditions.

12.00 noon – 1.00pm I head over to the Neo Café to eat my sandwiches. My mates are usually in there so we have a catch up about recent media events or what was on telly the night before.

1.00pm – 4.00pm I go back to the clinic in the afternoons to treat a range of sport injuries in children and adults. Sometimes I'll be in the gait lab custom making insoles for patients or attending the lectures depending on which day it is.

4.00pm – 7.00pm If I'm not coaching swimming after Uni I'll head home and do a bit of studying or I'll go to the Trafford Centre.

7.00pm – 11.00pm I'll put some music on, prepare dinner for me and my girlfriend and we talk about our day. I'll put a film on or go on Facebook and chat to my friends. I have friends who live abroad so I use Skype to keep in contact with them. I usually go to bed around 11.00pm so I can be fresh and alert for the next day in Uni.

If you'd like to learn more about our programmes, student life and studying at Salford please contact us on:

T: 0845 234 0184
E: fhsc@salford.ac.uk
W: www.fhsc.salford.ac.uk

Part Three
Work

7
Types of work

This chapter looks at:

- getting work at 16;
- getting work at 18;
- types of work that you can do.

Getting a job is not just about going for a cosy nine to five with one of the major employers (if there is such a thing as a 'cosy' job!). There are many types of job out there, not to mention the on-the-job training and apprenticeships, and work experience, that you can undertake.

At the time of writing, a recent change to the law means that all young people will stay in education and training until age 17 from 2013 and until age 18 from 2015. That means that those who started in Year 7 in September 2009 will stay on in education or training until they are 18.

According to the former Department for Education, this doesn't necessarily mean that young people will stay in school. They may choose between:

- *full-time education in school or college;*
- *work-based learning such as apprenticeships;*
- *part-time education or training for those who are employed, self-employed or volunteering for more than 20 hours a week.*

Info

850 different people. Same sense of pride and achievement.

APPRENTICESHIP PROGRAMME

It doesn't matter who you are or what you do at Tesco – you can achieve great things on our Apprenticeship Programme.

The Apprenticeship Programme is an opportunity to achieve a recognised qualification while you work. Over 850 people from the ages of 17 to 67 took part in this years programme and we are proud that our success rates are among the best in the industry.

The qualification, which includes a Retail Certificate (NVQ), Technical Certificate and Key Skills Maths and English, is equivalent to five GCSEs.

The programme is available to Tesco employees of all ages who are not in full-time education, and is delivered in your store. It's also a superb opportunity to carry on earning your normal wage and working your usual hours, while gaining a City & Guilds qualification that will improve your future job prospects.

To find out more and enrol, please speak to your Personnel Manager.

YMCA TRAINING
inspire - develop - transform

www.tesco-careers.com

Tesco is an equal opportunities employer.

TESCO | *Every little helps*

You can find out more about the raising of the participation age from the Department for Education website: www.education.gov.uk/14-19/.

Getting work at 16

As you read through the next few chapters, you'll find out about some of the options that are open to you if you want to find work at the age of 16 (after you have left school). For example, you may start work on an apprenticeship scheme, which means that you will be working and training at the same time.

Initially, the places to go for advice if you are thinking of getting a job straight after leaving school are your school's careers teacher and your local Connexions office. Visit www.connexions-direct.com for further information, or telephone 080 800 13 2 19.

Info

While the decisions you make in your life are ultimately for your benefit, it is a really good idea to get on to an apprenticeship or training scheme. You will be able to gain vocational qualifications as you are working and earning money, and keep up with the competition in the workplace. If you leave school and go straight into a job that offers you no further training, education or development, you could find yourself falling behind the others in your age group whom you will be competing with for jobs throughout your life.

What to do next

If you know that you are going to try to get a job at 16 rather than stay on in FE, these steps might help you:

- Ask your form tutor and careers teacher about work experience. They may be able to arrange something for you to do after school or in one of the school holidays in your final year to give you that little extra advantage on the job market.
- Attend every session that your school runs on careers. The school may have a careers fair where local employers come to talk to students

WHO SAYS YOU LOOK BETTER WITH A DEGREE?

Trainee Management Options Programme We think you look great just as you are – with your 180 UCAS points (three A-levels grade A-D (or equivalent)) and GCSE Maths and English grade A-C. After all, these qualifications can put you on the fast-track to the very top at Britain's number one retailer. Our 12-month Trainee Management Options Programme is perfect for people who want to get on with their careers; people who aim high and want independence, responsibility and a salary – instead of university debts. For more information, visit our website **www.tesco-careers.com/trainee-management-programme**

Tesco is an equal opportunities employer. **TESCO** | *Every little helps*

about the world of work from their perspective. If your school runs a careers fair, make sure that you go; you could make really useful contacts and find out about options that you had never thought of.

- Ask your careers teacher about work-based training schemes and apprenticeships. He or she will be able to give you all the latest details and tell you about any local schemes that may exist.

- Get a notebook and write down all the information you gather. Even if it is not useful now, you never know when it might come in handy! Make sure that you read through these notes frequently to remind yourself of what tips and information you have picked up.

- Do not be tempted to take just any job, particularly if it doesn't offer you any future prospects. Always think about what you can progress to. It is important to think about your working life as a series of steps or stages, and to get stuck in a dead-end job at such a young age will not be good for you.

- Do not take a job that you know is too easy for you. You will get bored very quickly and that will destroy your chances of getting any job satisfaction at all.

- Make sure that you know exactly why you want to get a job and not stay on in FE. You might consider rereading the first few chapters of this book to see what choices you have, particularly in FE.

- If your final decision is to go for work, make sure that you read this chapter thoroughly. Your CV and letter-writing skills will need to be excellent and the chapter on going to an interview will be very useful too.

Getting work at 18

If you want to get a job at the age of 18, you can still use the Connexions service for advice, as well as your local Jobcentre Plus. You may also want to consider doing a training scheme so that you learn additional skills alongside your job. This would be the best idea for most 18-year-olds who decide not to go into HE.

What to do next

If you know that you are going to try to get a job at 18 rather than stay on in HE, these steps might help you:

- Talk to as many teachers and tutors at your school or college as you can. Use their expertise and advice. In particular, make use of the careers library and any specialist careers help that might be on offer.
- Get into the habit of visiting your local Connexions office as often as you can. Ask about the vacancies that they know about and any training schemes that you might be suitable for. You are not too old for a training scheme such as an apprenticeship and there just might be the perfect opportunity for you!
- Aim to get your next move sorted out before you leave school or college so that you do not have any periods when you have nothing to do.
- Use the careers library at your local Connexions office. Ask for support and guidance; there may be someone there who can spend some time going over possibilities with you.
- Ask at your local Jobcentre Plus if they have an adviser who specialises in your age group. Ask if you can make an appointment to see him or her.
- Do not reject any ideas without fully considering them. You may not have thought of them as possibilities before, but could they be for you?
- Read all the information in this book about how to find vacancies, apply for jobs and attend interviews.

Types of work

It would be impossible to list here all the possibilities that exist in the world of work today. The Information Age is helping to ensure that the pace of change is rapid and we all need to make sure that we can remain employable by:

- getting the qualifications we need to be able to thrive and compete in the working world;
- developing our skills and looking out for new opportunities and experiences;
- having high standards in certain key skills such as ICT, communication, numeracy and literacy;
- being willing and able to cope with change;
- being willing to look at the possibility of pursuing several careers through our lifetime.

With the right attitude and a commitment to show employers that you have what it takes and that you have the qualities that are needed in the workplace, there's every chance that you can succeed in getting a job if that is what you want.

The different sectors

The world of work can be split into three main sectors: the private and public sectors, and a new non-governmental 'Third Sector'. They all have quite different approaches and philosophies, and they feel very different to work in. You may feel that you are naturally more suited to one than another, depending on your personality and nature.

The public sector

There are certain organisations that belong to the state (which means that we all 'own' them). These include:

- the National Health Service;
- the maintained education system;
- the Civil Service;
- the police;
- fire and rescue services;
- central government;
- local government;
- a wide range of other organisations.

The public sector exists to provide a service rather than to make money (although there is a drive for the public services to save money by being more cost-effective). The wages of people working in the public sector are paid out of money that the Government has collected in tax.

The private sector

The private sector includes all companies that are not owned by the state and that provide goods and services – for example, manufacturing companies, retailers (such as high street shops), the hotel industry, banks, insurance companies and so on. This sector exists to make a profit, and the wages of people working in this sector are paid out of this profit and not by the Government out of taxes.

The 'Third Sector'

The 'Third Sector' is the name given to the group of organisations that can be described as being non-governmental and that typically use their profits to reinvest in social, cultural and environmental projects. These organisations might be charities, voluntary and community organisations, social enterprises, not-for-profit organisations, cooperatives or mutuals. The 'Third Sector' is growing in the United Kingdom and makes a huge contribution to society as well as to the economy and the environment.

> **Info**
>
> *You can find out much more about the 'Third Sector' and the job opportunities that it might hold for you from the following websites:*
>
> - *www.cabinetoffice.gov.uk/voluntary-sector.aspx – This is the website of the government departments which leads work across government to support voluntary and community groups, social enterprises, charities, cooperatives and mutuals.*
> - *www.thirdsector.co.uk – This is the website of a UK publication for the voluntary and not-for-profit sector. You will find information about the sector, latest news and job opportunities here.*

Other ways of viewing the world of work

As well as splitting the world of work into the public, private and Third sectors, we can also split it into the following:

- the leisure industry (including hotels, sports centres, leisure centres, holiday companies and so on);
- the financial sector (including banks, building societies, accountants, insurance companies and so on);
- the health sector (including the NHS, private hospitals, private health-care practitioners, the world of complementary and alternative medicine, and so on);
- the so-called 'invisible' sector (including tourism, imports and exports, and foreign students);
- the farming industry (including farms, dairies and so on);
- the manufacturing industry (including companies that produce goods such as cars to sell in the United Kingdom and abroad);

- the construction industry (including building contractors, engineers, architects and so on).

There are, of course, other sectors that could be added to this list, but this is just to give you an idea of the range that exists.

Job categories

Table 7.1 shows some of the jobs that you might consider going into. It is not a definitive list by any means but will offer you some ideas.

> To find out more about work categories and the kinds of jobs they include, take a look at www.jobs.ac.uk. If you are interested in eco-friendly employment, visit www.environmentjob.co.uk, which lists jobs and volunteering opportunities in the environmental sector. There is also a 'definitive guide to careers with a conscience' called 'The Ethical Careers Guide', which can be found at www.ethicalcareers.org.
>
> **Info**

The armed forces

One option open to school leavers at both 16 and 18 is to enter one of the armed forces. The armed forces in the United Kingdom are the British Army, the Royal Navy and the Royal Air Force. There is an incredible array of jobs on offer in the forces and in the Ministry of Defence civilian careers (take a look at the websites below for more information).

Being in the armed forces is also an opportunity to undertake FE. Welbeck – The Defence Sixth Form College – admits students 'with a career ambition' to join the Royal Navy, the British Army or the Royal Air Force or to become Ministry of Defence Civil Service engineers (see the website listed below for further information).

Working in the armed forces is not all about active service by any means. There are amazing opportunities to be had if you like the idea of seeing the world, or pushing your body to its ultimate in fitness. It is not for everyone, though, and if you think a career as a Royal Marine commando is up your street, remember what the advertisements say: 99.99 per cent need not apply! But the armed forces are not all like the Royal Marines, and if you think you might be tempted, do spend some time browsing the relevant websites to see exactly what opportunities are out there for you.

Table 7.1

Sector	A few examples of types of work or jobs in each sector
Agriculture and food	Farming, food preparation, food science
Construction	Bricklaying and plastering, surveying, civil engineering
Health and medical	Doctor, dentist, pharmacist, homeopath, osteopath, nurse
Scientific	Zoology, botany, horticulture
Computing	Software engineer, database manager, hardware technician
Architecture and planning	Town planning, environmental technologies
Environment	Sustainability, conservation, ecology, pollution
Sport and leisure	Sports coaching, leisure management
Civil Service, politics and government	Social worker, tax inspector, administrator, clerical officer
Business administration	Marketing, human resources, land and property management
Education	Teacher, nursery nurse, classroom assistant
Financial services	Bank and building society work, insurance, sales and so on
Forces	The armed forces, police work
Librarianship	Librarian, information service work
Creative arts	Design, music, drama, beauty and hairdressing
Media	Journalism, PR, publishing and so on
Entertainment	TV work, actor, writer
Retail	Sales assistant, manager, personnel
Self-employment	Anything at all!

If you thought that being in the armed forces was all about combat, think again! There are 140 different trades available across seven main job groups: engineering; logistics and support; medical; human resources and finance; intelligence; IT and communications; combat; and music and ceremonial. For just about any career path you can think of, there's an opportunity in the forces.

Joining the army... View from Andrew

I joined the Army after doing my GCSEs and I'm now an equipment mechanic in the Royal Engineers. I chose the Army as a vocation as well as an experience. My Dad was in the Army and I always wanted to do the same. I was looking to get a vocation as well as gain some life experience, so I chose the Royal Engineers because of the range of trades available, plus you get to do extra tasks such as demolition and bridge building. My duties include fixing any vehicles that come in with a problem, and when preparing for an overseas tour we make sure all the vehicles and kit are ready to go.

For more info about a career in the armed forces, take a look at the following websites:

www.welbeck.mod.uk
www.mod.uk
www.raf.mod.uk/careers
www.armyjobs.mod.uk
www.royalnavy.mod.uk.

Info

Take a few moments to think about the kind of work environment that you would like to work in. Here are some examples of the kinds of possibilities there are; you could work:

- alone;
- with others in a team;
- in a building;
- outside;
- in a factory;
- in a shop;
- in an office;
- on a ship;
- in the air;
- above ground;
- underground;
- with others of your age;
- with others of various ages;
- with people of the same level of education as you;
- with people of various degrees of education;
- at night;
- in the daytime;
- in uniform;
- in your own clothes;
- in smart clothes;
- in casual clothes.

These are just some ideas, but they should help to trigger your own thoughts on the kind of environment that you would like to work in.

Aim to draw up a shortlist of possibilities. Do also pay attention to anything that you really would not like to do. For example, if you hate being on an aeroplane, a career as a flight attendant is probably not for you. Use your conclusions to help you in your job hunt.

Summary

The key points from this chapter include the following:

- You need to spend time researching your job prospects if you want to leave school at age 16.
- Work-based training schemes are a very good idea for many 16- and 18-year-old school and college leavers.
- The world of work can be subdivided into many different sectors. One way is to split it into the public sector, the private sector and the 'Third Sector'.
- There is an enormous range of jobs that school leavers can do.
- You need to think about what kind of job would suit you best of all.
- The armed forces are another possibility for 16- and 18-year-old school and college leavers.

8
Work experience, job shadowing and work-based training

This chapter looks at:

- doing work experience and job shadowing;
- apprenticeships;
- Entry to Employment;
- the Connexions Card.

Work experience

Rather than offer help to organisations as you do when volunteering, work experience and job shadowing are purely for your own benefit. That said, many companies are keen to take on young people for work experience. You never know, if they like you and you like them there may be a job for you at the end of it!

Taking someone on for work experience or job shadowing does entail a fair amount of work on the part of the organisation, so they do want to see quite a high level of commitment in return. Effective work experience programmes usually involve planned and supervised activities so that you can really get a taste of what it might be like to work in that company or industry.

Work experience... View from Neil

Doing work experience was one of the best things I have ever done. I always thought that I wanted to be an accountant and when I was at college I got the chance to spend one afternoon a week in a local accountant's office. It was so amazingly boring! I'm not saying that accountants are boring, but for me the time went so slowly and I hadn't really understood how much fine detail the job involves. I got really impatient and it really taught me that the job's not for me.

I love maths and want to make sure that I can use the maths I've learned when I'm working, and I thought that accountancy was the obvious option. But I was glad to have had the opportunity to find out that it wasn't before I started the training process.

I was talking to one of the accountants in the office about what other options I might have and she had some really good ideas for me to follow up. So, it was definitely a worthwhile thing for me to do.

You will almost certainly have done some work experience while at school. If this is the case, think back over your experiences. What did you learn? How did you learn? If you are yet to do work experience, think carefully about what you would like to do and where. Is this something you can arrange by yourself in your own spare time?

Arranging your own work experience

If you want to try out what it might be like to work in a particular place, you can arrange your own work experience to carry out in your spare time. Even if you cannot offer full days because of study commitments, you could perhaps do some hours after school or college, or spend a week or more somewhere in your holidays. You can use your initiative over this and arrange whatever would fit in with your schedule.

There follows a sample letter that you might like to use when approaching companies direct to ask for work experience.

Your address here:

2 Orchard Street
Worksworth
West Shire
WW2 4HY

Date here

Address of the person you are writing to here:
  [Make sure you find out the name of the person you need to write to]

Mrs B Short
Human Resources Manager
Worksworth Electronics
Worksworth
West Shire WW3 7RT

Dear Mrs Short

I am writing to request a period of work experience at Worksworth Electronics. I have just completed my GCSEs and I am very interested in working in the electronics industry.

Ideally I would like to spend two weeks with your company and I would be particularly interested in experiencing the manufacturing side of your business, but I would be very grateful for any time and experience you are able to offer me. I am very willing to learn and to undertake whatever tasks you think it appropriate for me to do.

I have enclosed my CV, which contains my full contact details, and I look forward to hearing from you.

Yours sincerely

Your name here

If you do not hear anything within about 10 days of sending your letter, you can always ring up to check that it arrived and to see if it is possible to make arrangements over the phone. Try to be as accommodating as you can. If the organisation offers you a day's work experience when you really want a week, take it; one day is better than nothing.

Once you are doing work experience try to identify the transferable skills (more on this on page 198) that you are learning. At the end of each day it is a good idea to jot down what you have done and what you have learned. You will be really grateful for this when you come to write job applications or apply for a place at college or university.

Work experience... View from Caz

I didn't get the work experience I wanted when I was at school so I decided to arrange my own in the summer holiday after I finished my GCSEs. I've always wanted to be a hairdresser but thought I should really get some experience first before making a commitment to a course.

I wrote to the manager of my local branch of a hairdressing chain. I wanted to go for one of the bigger salons in my town so that I could see a whole range of cuts, colours and treatments. I'm also really interested in hair fashion and styling, so I thought the bigger the salon the better.

The manager invited me in for a week and asked one of the senior stylists to look after me. I was dreading it being cliquey but it wasn't at all. They were all really friendly and even got me washing hair by the end of the week. I learned how to mix colours (although they didn't let me loose on the customers!) and how to answer the phone and make bookings on the computer. I absolutely loved it and definitely want to go into the profession.

To anyone thinking of arranging their own work experience, go for it. You've nothing to lose and you might have as much fun as I had. At the end of the week I really didn't want to leave and I still go in there if I have a spare afternoon. You have to be willing to get stuck in; I swept up so much hair that week it's untrue! But overall I found it a great experience.

Just as Caz found, there may well be certain tasks that are too difficult or technical for you to do on your work experience. If this is the case, the chances are that you will 'job-shadow'. This simply means watching closely while someone else does the job. This is not as tedious as it might sound, especially if you give yourself mini tests on how things are done and what techniques are used. Remember, when you are job-shadowing, to ask if there is anything you do not understand. And if it looks as though there is something you can do (like Caz when she learned to wash clients' hair), ask if you can do it. They can only say 'no' and just might say 'yes'.

Info

The National Council for Work Experience (NCWE) is an organisation that aims to provide young people and employers with everything they need to know about work experience and work-related learning. They can help students to:

- *put theory learning into practice;*
- *consider career options;*
- *find out what they like or do not like doing;*
- *get some practical experience and start to develop 'employability' skills.*

You can find NCWE's website at www.work-experience.org. The site has a great resource centre too, which is well worth checking out. As NCWE is not a placement agency, it does not accept CVs.

The website carries a really useful list of links for young people wanting to do work experience. Click on the '15–18-year-olds' button for more information.

Internships

You may have heard of work experience being described as an 'internship'. This is just another way of describing the kind of experience you can get in a workplace while you are at school, college or university. It is sometimes possible to get an internship when you have completed your studying and before getting a contracted job.

All kinds of internships and work experience can be an invaluable step on the career ladder. They are a superb way of gaining experience that will be meaningful in your future career. The chances are you will develop your skills and you may even be more employable as a result too.

Great People, Real Opportunities – Compass Group UK & Ireland

As the UK and Ireland's largest catering and support services organisation, Compass employs over 52,000 people across 7000 client sites. Our people are at the heart of Compass Group UK & Ireland and central to our ethos is employing Great People and providing them with Real Opportunities. Training and development is a key part of this culture and ensuring that our people have the necessary training to deliver the high levels of service and quality expected by clients is essential.

At Compass we fully believe in the benefits of vocational qualifications and on-the-job training. We appreciate that A-Levels and university aren't necessarily the best or most appropriate route for every school leaver and that there should be a wide range of options available so people can choose a career suited to them.

A large proportion of Compass employees have no formal qualifications so in 2009 we launched our Qualifications for All programme, offering all employees without formal qualifications the opportunity to undertake a NVQ Level 2 in subjects relevant to the business and enabling these employees to learn while they earn. Since 2009, when the programme was launched, 2000 of our employees have undertaken an NVQ.

The Qualifications for All programme is managed by employees' line managers so that the employees undertaking the qualifications know where to go to for advice and assistance and the line managers, by being fully involved, also learn and benefit from the process. Our Qualifications for All programme is part of a broader learning framework which enables employees to progress throughout the organisation and which encompasses a number of different training programmes tailored to the needs of our varied employees.

As part of this learning framework, we run an extensive apprenticeship programme and currently employ approximately 450 apprentices throughout the company, a number set to double by September 2010. Apprenticeships are available to all employees who have worked with the company for at least three months on a permanent basis, for at least 16 hours a week. Embarking on an apprenticeship with Compass can open many doors and lead to career progression opportunities. Our apprenticeships cover a range of disciplines including: Professional Cookery; Food Preparation and Cooking; Food and Drink Service; Hospitality Supervision; Retail; Business Administration; Customer Service; and Cleaning.

In addition to this we have created the Compass Academy, our flagship two-year apprenticeship programme which was launched with 20 apprentices in October 2008 and now has 95 people on the scheme. The Compass Academy builds on the Government's Apprenticeship Framework and is designed to nurture and grow talented people of all ages, developing Compass Academy apprentices into fully rounded business managers and aims to show people that working in this industry can provide a career for life. Apprentices on the Compass Academy learn while they earn and are funded through the Academy programme. At the end of the programme, apprentices will have achieved two nationally recognised qualifications which are relevant to their role and are free to apply for roles within Compass.

The Academy adds many extra elements to traditional apprenticeship programmes, such as:

- A relationship with a dedicated mentor for the two year course
- The requirement to produce a frequently updated learning log and reflective statements
- In-house, on-the-job training
- An assessed business project in year two
- Compulsory work experience across the various sectors in which we operate including; business & industry; sports, leisure and hospitality; executive and fine dining; healthcare; education; defence, offshore and remote
- Practical days such as: visiting Compass suppliers; visiting Compass' food distributors; visiting support services and catering clients.

Linked to the Academy is Evolve, a programme launched in 2009 designed to develop existing ambitious general managers. Evolve is an 11-month programme that gives 100 of our most promising managers the opportunity to hone their management skills and position themselves for the next big move. The programme balances a combination of on-the-job and offsite learning, covering leadership and coaching skills, account management, change management, and mobilising new contracts.

Compass is committed to attracting, progressing and retaining great people and providing truly great opportunities. We constantly have a wide range of job opportunities available up and down the country and across the diverse sectors in which we work. We are always looking for enthusiastic, talented and passionate people with a can-do attitude and a willingness to learn and our training and development programmes enable employees to develop their skills and knowledge and progress up the career ladder.

We would encourage school leavers to research the catering, hospitality and support services industry and look at the opportunities that exist and the options open to them within this diverse, dynamic and hugely rewarding industry.

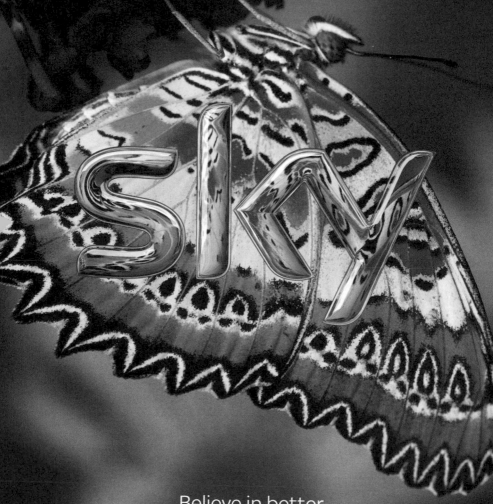

The potential to be amazing

Everything is possible at Sky. Wherever you join us on our wide range of school leaver and graduate programmes, we'll make sure you develop to be the very best that you can be. Discover how at **www.workforsky.com**

Believe in better
www.workforsky.com

Sky delivers some of the most diverse content and services on the planet, and we value the same diversity within our business. We provide a culture of entrepreneurialism and opportunity for one and all.

Believe in better for everyone

At Sky we believe everyone deserves the best. That's why we're always finding new ways to bring people the entertainment they love, and the services they enjoy. It's a passion for us. A passion that drives us to provide great service to over 9.7 million Sky customers around the UK.

We're a true people business driven by our 16,000 employees and their shared desire to delight customers through incredible products and services. There's great TV and high-speed broadband for a start. And, where Sky+HD has taken picture quality to a whole new level, our new 3DTV in the home promises to take the viewing experience into a new dimension. We've also recently been named Britain's Most Admired Company by Management Today.

What could be more exciting than kick-starting your career with us? Whether it's as an Engineer or Advisor the Sky Apprenticeship Scheme is all about doing things for real. Developing transferable life and professional skills.

As well as a salary and a permanent role, you'll also have the opportunity to gain two nationally recognised NVQ/SVQ qualifications. From your side you'll need to be 16-17 years old, a great communicator and passionate about customers.

Join us and you'll enjoy lots of benefits – like free Sky+HD and Sky broadband plus paid time to study at college so you can earn while you learn.

We want our people to be the best they can be. That's why all our development programmes closely mirror our values – being tuned in, irrepressible, inviting and fun.

If you want to be part of our team visit
www.workforsky.com

It is a good idea to make sure that you get answers to the following questions before starting work experience or an internship:

- What is the purpose of the experience? Are there clear benefits for you and the 'employer'?
- How much of an insight will you gain into that particular world of work? Will what you do be linked to what you would like to do as a career?
- Might there be any possibilities of future work at the company? Even if this is just holiday work, it's always worth asking.

If any internships or work experience start to feel exploitative, carefully discuss this with your key contact at the placement. There will usually be a win/win element to these kinds of arrangements but it shouldn't feel like you are working for very little and not gaining the kind of experience you need.

You can find out more about internships, including information about the circumstances under which you should expect to be paid, from the National Council for Work Experience website: www.work-experience. org (see the previous info box).

Apprenticeships

If you intend to leave school at 16, you may be able to get a place on an apprenticeship scheme. These schemes offer the opportunity to learn on the job and to build up the knowledge and skills that you need while also gaining qualifications and earning money at the same time. Can't be bad!

At the time of writing there are no set entry requirements for apprenticeships apart from the following conditions:

- You need to be living in England (see the Information point below for details for people living in Scotland, Wales and Northern Ireland).
- You must be aged 16 or above.
- You must not be in full-time education.

There are different kinds of apprenticeship available in a wide range of industry sectors and it depends on your experience and the opportunities in your area as to which one you should go for. Most Apprenticeships fall into one of three categories:

- Those that are equivalent to GCSE level ('Apprenticeships').
- Those that are equivalent to A level ('Advanced Apprenticeships').
- Those that are equivalent to a degree ('Higher Apprenticeships').

Apprenticeships usually take between one and four years although they have no set time limit. On an apprenticeship you would be paid a wage by your employer (one that reflected your age, skills and abilities) and receive targeted on-the-job training. You would also spend time at a local college or other learning provider gaining all the valuable skills you would need really to understand the job and succeed in that field.

The National Apprenticeship Service has responsibility for the delivery of apprenticeships. To find out more, visit www.apprenticeships.org.uk.   **Info**

Employment rights and responsibilities

Employment rights and responsibilities are an important part of apprenticeships. The reason for this is to help apprentices to learn all about:

- the rights and responsibilities of workers/employees;
- how workers/employees are affected by public law and policies;
- issues such as discipline, representation and the organisation of the relevant industry.

To find out more about apprenticeships in England, visit www. apprenticeships.org.uk or telephone 08000 150 600 or Connexions on 080 800 13 2 19.   **Info**

If you live in Wales, visit www.careerswales.com. If you live in Scotland, the website to look at is www.careers-scotland.org.uk. Those living in Northern Ireland should visit www.delni.gov.uk.

Entry to Employment (E2E)

E2E is a scheme for people who are not yet ready or able to start an apprenticeship, further learning or a job. It is a work-based programme that will have been devised to match individuals' particular needs, but the schemes do have a focus on improving motivation, personal effectiveness and employability. At the end of E2E you would go through a transition programme that would help you to progress into either employment (with training), apprenticeship, FE or training.

Info

To find out more about E2E, e-mail E2Einfo@lsc.gov.uk or telephone 0870 900 6800.

Action

New projects designed to help young people get into work seem to be quite common, so it is always a good idea to call into your local Connexions office to see if there is anything, whether it be a local or a national initiative, that you can take advantage of. If you are not 'in the know', you may be missing out on some great opportunities.

Summary

The key points of this chapter include the following:

- Work experience is an excellent way of finding out whether a particular job is for you.
- You can arrange your own work experience to do in your spare time.
- Apprenticeships offer school and college leavers a chance to learn and work at the same time.
- E2E is a scheme that people who are not yet ready to do an apprenticeship can do.

HOW OFTEN DO YOU HAVE A GOOD DAY*?

You can have a GOOD DAY every day. A GOOD DAY comes from being part of a skilled workforce, playing an important part in peoples' lives. A GOOD DAY depends on good people, and a GOOD DAY comes from a job well done.

Kieran Lacey
Technician, Hotchkiss

Mary-Ann Wright
Senior Engineer, FaberMaunsell

Christopher Jenkins
Electrical Apprentice, RDM Electrical Services

Want a career you'll really enjoy? See for yourself in the case studies opposite

Visit **www.goodday.org.uk** or call **01908 303960**

Summit SKILLS

The Sector Skills Council for building services engineering

When was the last time you had a really Good Day?

All the systems we take for granted, such as plumbing, heating, electrical power, air conditioning, ventilation and refrigeration, all provide the comfortable environment that we live and work in. To work in building services engineering is to play an important part in people's lives.

Read on and find out how you can have a career that you'll actually enjoy...

Kieran Lacey, a computer-aided design draftsman, completed a four-year apprenticeship. He said, "I've spent time in a whole range of different departments and got real experience out on-site from very early on. I completed a BTEC in Building Services Engineering and then a two-year HNC."

Mary-Ann Wright, a senior engineer, graduated in Mechanical Engineering, and completed an MSc in Building Services and Management. She said, "My ideas crystallised in the Sixth Form when I went to a lecture about women in engineering. I love the fact there's a new challenge every day and the opportunity to help the environment by implementing new energy-efficient technologies."

Chris Jenkins left his job as a deputy manager in retail to become an apprentice electrician. He said "I felt that my career prospects in retail were limited. Building services engineering caught my imagination because there's scope to work in all sorts of different areas. One of the things I love about the job is there's no such thing as a typical day. Even if I'm doing the same sort of work, the challenges are always different. I've worked in bus stations, hotels, restaurants, offices and factories – even a holiday village!"

Choosing a career is a big decision to make. Discover how you can have a Good Day, every day, in your new career - visit **www.goodday.org.uk** to read more about the sector, find out what training you'll need and the options that are available to you.

The Sector Skills Council for Building Services Engineering

9
Finding and applying for jobs

This chapter looks at:

- finding out what you want to do;
- where to look for vacancies;
- researching jobs;
- applying for jobs;
- filling in application forms;
- writing a CV;
- writing a covering letter;
- writing a letter of application;
- making speculative applications.

Knowing that you really should get a job is one thing; knowing exactly where to look for what you want is another. This chapter should help to make sure that you do not miss out on the perfect vacancy for you.

What do you want to do?

The level of success we have in our working lives does seem to be linked to the attitude we have to our work. We are unlikely to have a positive attitude to it if what we do for a living is far removed from our hobbies and interests. Before you can even start looking for jobs, you have to have some idea of what it is that you would be happy doing. As well as the information in this chapter, the following activity may help to give you some ideas.

This activity will help you to work out what it is that grabs you and what you might like to do for a job.

Answer the following questions by writing your responses down on a sheet of paper. Your answers can be as detailed as you like. They are for your eyes only, so make them as useful as they can be for you.

- What interests you?
- What are your hobbies?
- Do you have a career plan? What is it?
- Would you describe yourself as an indoor or an outdoor person?
- What are your skills? (Remember: skills are not the same as interests.)
- What are your abilities? (For example, can you drive? Do you have any vocational qualifications?)

Some careers experts split job activities into four categories: working with objects, information, concepts and people.

- Are you an 'objects' person? Do you want to work with goods, building them perhaps, or designing or selling them?
- Are you an 'information' person? Do you want to analyse, gather, manipulate, record or publish information?
- Are you a 'concepts' person? Do you want to communicate, create, debate, market or teach concepts?
- Are you a 'people' person? Do you want to represent, manage, direct, guide, share with or motivate people?

These are just a few ideas. There is information in Parts Four and Five that will also help you to find out what motivates you.

Your local careers or Connexions office will be able to offer more information and ideas on what you might like to do next. You can find the contact details for your local office in the Yellow Pages *or at your library.*

Where to look for vacancies

You have to be good at research if you are to find the right job for you. Knowing where to look for job vacancies is critical, and that does not just mean flicking through the jobs pages of your local paper. To give yourself the best chance possible, your job hunt will need to be far-reaching, covering newspapers and the internet, your personal contacts and your local Jobcentre, to name but a few. Get your vacancy radar tuned so you do not miss out! Table 9.1 will help you to focus your search.

Stay positive as you look for vacancies. Even if the job market seems dead, you have to be creative and use your initiative. Is there something that you can apply for that will take you one step closer to what you really want to do? Might it open up opportunities for you once you are in post?

When to look

Vacancies occur all through the year, but some may be seasonal. You will need to do some research into the kind of job that you are interested in to see whether vacancies are more likely at certain times of the year than others. Even if you find that this is the case, it is still worth looking all the time anyway. You never know when the perfect job might turn up, and if you are not looking in the right place, you will miss out on it.

Researching the job

For every job advertisement you see that you would like to apply for, you need to ask yourself a few key questions:

- Does it look like the kind of job you could do? This is not as obvious as it sounds; some job advertisements give very little away about what is involved. Do you need to find out further information before you would be in a position to apply?
- Do you have the appropriate skills and qualifications needed?
- Do you need to be knowledgeable about any current affairs or industry inside information in order to get through the application stage? Should you look at any trade publications?

Table 9.1

Where to look	What to look for
Your local library	Local and national newspapers, specialist magazines, local jobs bulletins, careers books, local business directories
Your local Jobcentre Plus	Vacancy cards, leaflets, one-to-one advice, website, books
Your local career/ Connexions service	Careers library, one-to-one advice
Your school or college	Careers section of library, careers adviser, one-to-one advice
The internet	There are literally hundreds of jobs advertised online. It is best to do a search for what you are looking for, but these are good for starters: www.direct.gov.uk www.jobsite.co.uk www.fish4jobs.co.uk.
Job agencies	There is almost certainly at least one job agency on your local high street. Call in or make an appointment for some one-to-one advice about whether they can help you. Most will have job vacancies displayed in the office, too.
Your local radio station	Most local radio stations have a jobs slot. Ring up to find out when it is.
Your local community	Shop windows, post offices, information points and so on often have posters, leaflets and postcards about job opportunities.
Friends, family and acquaintances	Make use of all your contacts.

- Is the job with the kind of company you would like to work for? Can you find anything out about the company before applying for the job? Does it have a website? Do you know anyone who works there who can give you some inside information?
- Would you be able to get to work if you got the job? Could you drive there or travel by public transport? Would you have to move or could you stay living where you are now?
- Does the job offer any training opportunities?
- Is the pay good enough? Would it allow you to pay your living expenses as well as have some left over for spending money or savings?
- Do the prospects of the job look interesting?

Applying for jobs

Everything you have read, thought about and acted on so far should help you to understand that it is best not to just go for any vacancy you see advertised. It helps tremendously if, first, you know a little about what you want to do and where you want to do it. Do not bother even applying if you cannot do it with enthusiasm and intent. You need to intend to get any job you go for. If you don't, your lack of drive and enthusiasm will shine through far more brightly than any of your great selling points. You need to show that you are hungry for that job, not any job.

Once you have found an appropriate vacancy to go for, you need to start the process of actually applying. There are usually two stages to this process: the written application stage and the interview stage. This means that you will have to be good at presenting yourself on paper as well as in person. It is not enough to be good at one and not the other.

Every application you make (whether for a job or a college place) will require you to follow certain instructions. It goes without saying that you need to follow these exactly. If you are required to fill in an application form, do not send in your CV instead, however wonderful it may be! Always do exactly what is asked, otherwise you risk your application going straight in the bin without even being considered.

It is well worth stocking up on some good-quality A4 writing paper and matching envelopes and blue or black ink pens that will not splodge or smudge. If you are asked to complete an application form, you will find A4 envelopes useful too so that you do not have to fold the form to send it.

Before even making the first mark on your paper, think carefully about exactly what you have to offer. All job applications require a fair amount of 'selling', so do not go any further without establishing what it is that you have to sell.

Action

Your unique selling points
While many of the activities in this book are optional (you only need to do them if you think they will help you), this one really is important. Write your answers down and use them to refer to when you are making applications.

● What have you got to offer a company?
● Why should they employ you?
● What are your unique selling points? (Think of skills, achievements, accomplishments and so on.)

These questions are deliberately open-ended so that you are not restricted in your thinking or limited by any suggestions that could have been listed here. Think as widely as you can; you will be trying to sell yourself on the job market, so make yourself as attractive as possible.

Selling skills... View from Jas

I hate doing this kind of stuff. It seems a bit phoney to me. But then my Mum told me that it's just a process you have to go through. Once you've got your job, you don't have to keep selling yourself unless you want to go for promotions really quickly. In a way, it's like a game but it's one that everyone's playing, so if you don't want to be left out, you have to join in. My advice would be to always be honest, though. Putting a positive spin on stuff is one thing, but lying is completely different! If you lie about your skills you'll quickly be found out.

Mistakes to avoid

Always bear in mind that most employers won't even look at any applications that are:

- not exactly what they asked for (for example, a CV instead of their application form);
- not appropriate for the job (for example, it is a job that requires catering qualifications and you do not have any);
- messy, untidy or illegible;
- lacking in vital information such as your contact details;
- not unique to that job; no prospective employer wants to read an application that has obviously gone off to loads of different companies.

Filling in application forms

Many jobs require candidates to complete application forms. This is usually so that they can be sure they get the information they need and can judge candidates equally. Although the whole form-filling process can be time-consuming, the advice here may help it to go without hitch:

- Find out when the closing date is and do not miss this deadline.
- Before doing anything, take several photocopies of the form so that you can have practice runs, but remember that you can only send in the original.
- If you have to download the form from the internet, make sure that you have the right one before starting.
- Gather together all the information you might need – for example, your schools and the years you attended them, qualifications and exam results, the names of your referees, your full contact details, your National Insurance number and so on.
- Always follow the instructions you are given exactly. Some ask you to use blue ink and some black. If this is not specified, use blue or black, but no other colour. Even in the so-called creative industries, pink or green ink would probably be frowned upon!
- If you make a mistake, start again. If you are using the original form, simply cross out the error with one neat line. Do not use liquid paper or multiple scribbles over the mistake.
- Answer every question. If a question does not apply to you, put 'n/a' (not applicable) in the box rather than leaving it blank.
- Be scrupulously honest. That said, do not be shy about your achievements.

- Aim to show what each experience has taught you. If you have spent time volunteering on a play scheme, state what transferable skills that has given you (see page 198).
- Look carefully at the person specification for the job. You will almost always be given an outline of the kind of person they are looking for. For example, job details might say, 'must be motivated, honest and reasonably fit', in which case you would need to show specifically in your application that you are all of those things, preferably with examples for each.
- Always get someone to check over your rough version first, before taking the plunge and doing it neatly. Ask the person to look out for spelling mistakes, grammatical errors, inconsistencies, potentially negative points and areas that simply do not come over well. If he or she helps you to do any rewrites, make sure that the language is what you would use yourself.
- Make sure that you have practised fitting your writing into the space available.
- Write a covering letter to go with the application form. This need not be lengthy, but should be on good-quality A4 paper, and laid out as you would lay out any formal letter. Make sure you have the name of the person you should send it to, and underneath where you write, 'Dear X', write the title of the post that you are applying for. Underline this if you are writing the letter by hand or type it in bold if you are using a word processor. Include any reference numbers the job may have, too. Do not repeat any of the information you have included on the application form but simply say, 'Please find enclosed my application for the post of XYZ.' You may also like to add, 'I look forward to hearing from you.' You then need to add something that will encourage the reader to look at your application (see the section below on writing covering letters). End your letter formally with 'Yours sincerely' (assuming that you know the name of the person you are writing to). Do not attach the letter to the form in any way. As long as your name is on both (which it should be), the recipient will be able to tie them up together. (See more tips on covering letters in the section below: Writing a covering letter).
- Take a photocopy of all the forms and letters that you send.
- How does the form need to be returned? Can it be e-mailed (in which case you will have completed an electronic version of it)? Or should it be posted? Or can you deliver it by hand?

- Make sure that you get the form in on time. Most companies will not consider any applications that arrive after the closing date.
- If you want acknowledgement that they have received your application, include a stamped addressed plain postcard that can be posted back to you. You may like to write on the postcard something like 'confirmation of receipt of application to XYZ company'.
- Be sure to make a note of when you send in your application.

Referees

Many application forms ask you to give the names of one or two people who would be willing to act as referees for you. This means that these people will be contacted by the company (should the company want to interview or employ you) and asked to provide a character reference about you.

Most employers will look carefully at the status of the people you appoint as referees, so it is best not to list your best mate! Choose referees who will be in a position to sell your skills to the prospective employer by matching your qualities to the job's requirements. You want them to be as supportive as possible, too, so always ask their permission first before putting their name down on the form. Good choices for referees might be a family friend who has known you for some time (especially if he or she is in business or a member of a profession) and your school or college tutor. If you have had a job already then your current or previous employer might be willing to act as a referee.

What if you do not hear anything?

You may need to follow up your application if you do not hear anything within a few weeks of sending it in. Usually, all you need to do is make a quick telephone call. Look up the name of the person you need to speak to and call from somewhere quiet and private. Have with you the date when you sent the application and the exact title of the job you applied for.

You should be told what stage your application is at, but if you are not, ask if it is possible to know when you might be told. Do not telephone again unless you do not hear anything by the time the person has said you will.

What if you get turned down?

It is not a disaster if you do not get invited for an interview. It may be very disappointing, but it is best to cultivate the attitude that the job obviously was not meant for you and that something better will come along in the future. That is not to say that you can sit back and wait! As soon as possible get back out there, make another application and get some more possibilities in the pipeline.

One positive thing to remember is that each time you apply for a job you are gaining valuable experience. If you do not get called for an interview, look back over what you sent in and see if you would do anything differently with hindsight. Some employers will offer feedback on unsuccessful applications. If this is offered to you, take it. If it is not, ask for it. Information like this can be invaluable when it comes to applying for jobs in the future.

Writing a CV

CVs (curricula vitae; in the singular, curriculum vitae) are essential in the world of job hunting. Even if you are not looking for a job, it is important to have one prepared and up to date so that when you do come to apply for jobs you have a CV ready to go.

It is easy to procrastinate about preparing a CV. It can take time to get together and can be difficult to get looking just right. It helps a lot if you have access to a computer so that you can manipulate the information on-screen. In the end, though, you just have to take the plunge and get stuck into it!

Why have a CV?

Your CV is your summary of your life and achievements. It is an important part of job hunting but it will not get you a job on its own. You should see it more as a useful tool.

Once you have written your CV, you can either send it to prospective employers in response to a job advertisement or you can use it to make speculative applications. Even if you are asked to apply by completing an application form, the fact that most of the information that you need is gathered together in one document will be really helpful when it comes to filling in the form.

How to write a CV

There is no single format for writing a CV, but the way in which you present the information is critical. Research has shown that it can take the average reader less than 10 seconds to glance over a CV and make a judgement. It is critical that your CV captures the interest of its reader immediately so that he or she reads it for long enough to be captivated!

Your CV may have a difficult job to do in seducing readers into employing you, but that does not mean that you can misrepresent yourself in it. Honesty is always the best policy. Besides, you never know when those little white lies are going to get you!

Some people choose to head their CV with 'Curriculum Vitae'; this isn't strictly necessary, as it should be obvious what the document is, but you won't lose points if you decide to do this. Then you will need to divide your CV into sections under the following headings:

- Personal details (in which your name, address and contact details go; whether you include your date of birth is up to you).
- Education and training (in order, starting with your secondary school(s) and including the qualifications and grades gained).
- Employment (starting with your most recent experience first). Make sure that you add a little detail about your roles and responsibilities. You may also like to add work experience here, but be sure to make it clear that it is your paid work you are describing.
- Voluntary work.
- Hobbies and interests. (Aim to show all aspects of your personality but do be honest! Remember that this section should support your job application.)
- Additional information (sometimes called a 'skills summary' – this is basically your best bits!).
- Referees (usually two – make sure that you have already asked their permission).

There are some 'dos and don'ts' when it comes to preparing a CV. These ideas may help:

- Do type your CV and print it out from a computer. Always make sure that you have a few copies handy. Use good-quality paper and stick to one typeface.
- Don't bind or staple your CV in any way. It does not need clipart or borders and should be on plain paper. Selectors want to see your skills and achievements, not your artistic talents.
- Do take care over the layout. Make sure that the type is well spaced yet does not cover more pages than it needs to. No more than two sides of A4 is adequate for most people.
- Do not include any salary information. That can all be discussed at interview.
- Do not include personal details such as height, weight, marital status, parenthood status and so on. Age is optional but strictly not necessary. If age restrictions apply to a job, the application form will give details. Photos should not be included either.
- Don't include testimonials from other people.
- Do remember that skills are more important than experience, and accomplishments are more important than responsibilities.
- Do use short bulleted statements rather than long, flowery sentences.
- Do remember that your CV will develop over time. Keep it up to date and vibrant.

There are many books and websites that can help you to create a winning CV. One of the books is *Preparing the Perfect CV* by Rebecca Corfield (see the Appendix for details).

Writing a covering letter

Covering letters are essential in the job application process. Whether you are sending in a CV or an application form, you will need to send a covering letter with it. Your covering letter does need to state that there is a CV or application form enclosed, but it also needs to grab the reader enough to make sure that he or she looks at what you have sent.

Use these tips when writing a covering letter:

- Always find out the name of the person you need to write to. Do not use 'sir' or 'madam'.
- Include a sentence or short paragraph that explains why you are enthusiastic about the job.
- Include a sentence that shows how appropriate you are for the job.
- End with an expectation of a reply ('I look forward to hearing from you').
- Always write a fresh covering letter for each job you apply for. Never be tempted to send generic letters, as the employer will not feel that you have made an effort.
- Remember that your covering letter is likely to be the first representation of you that a prospective employer will see. Make sure that it is concise, structured and faultless.
- Always keep a copy of the covering letters you send out.

Writing a letter of application

Sometimes you may be asked to send a CV with a letter of application rather than fill in an application form. This can be a daunting task as you really have to sell yourself, but not having the restrictions of an application form does have its benefits.

Your main goal when writing such a letter is to make sure that you can fit the profile of yourself with the profile of the person the company wants to employ. Whatever they are looking for, show that that person is you!

Selling your skills

Think about this for a moment: you have unique selling points that no other person in the world has. What you can offer an employer will not be repeated in anyone else.

Follow these ideas when writing a letter of application:

- Write a list of key points that you know about the job. What sort of person are they looking for?
- Make a list of the unique selling points that you would like to include (use your responses from the activity on page 36 to help you here).
- Make sure that your first sentence really grabs the attention of the reader. Try to end with something memorable, too.

- Aim to convey a sense of your personality – let you shine through from the page. For example, what motivates you?
- Write about your qualities. These ideas may inspire you:
  - friendly;
  - approachable;
  - thoughtful;
  - supportive;
  - energetic;
  - enthusiastic;
  - open to learning new things;
  - fit and healthy;
  - non-smoker;
  - punctual;
  - neat;
  - hard-working;
  - keen for challenges.
- Make sure the main body of the letter is filled with your skills and achievements.
- Do not include anything negative, or use potentially negative language. Always emphasise positive things about yourself.
- Lay the letter out as you would any formal letter, with your address and the address of the person you are writing to at the top, the date and a reference to the job you are applying for. End with 'Yours sincerely' if you know the name of the person you are writing to.
- Write in concise sentences rather than lengthy scrawls. Avoid over-using 'I did' and go for 'action' words instead. These examples may help you:

accomplished	formulated	proposed
achieved	generated	provided
arranged	implemented	recommended
assessed	improved	redesigned
compiled	improvised	reduced
composed	incorporated	regulated
concluded	initiated	renegotiated
conducted	inspired	reorganised
consolidated	instigated	resolved
created	instructed	reviewed

cultivated	introduced	revised
defined	invented	revitalised
delivered	launched	shaped
demonstrated	led	simplified
designed	maintained	streamlined
developed	managed	strengthened
devised	modernised	structured
documented	monitored	supported
effected	observed	tightened
eliminated	organised	uncovered
enacted	originated	unravelled
engaged	performed	utilised
established	prevented	visualised
evaluated	produced	vitalised
expanded	promoted	volunteered

- Write about what your experiences have taught you so far.
- If you have travelled, done voluntary work or have any hobbies that may be relevant then mention this too. Always link back to why this makes you great for the job.
- Never be tempted to reuse the same letter of application for different jobs. Always tweak it or rewrite it completely so that it fits the requirements of each application.
- End your letter of application with the expectation of a reply.

Making speculative applications

You may not have seen a job vacancy but know that you want to work for a particular company. If this is the case, then make a speculative application. This means sending in your CV with a covering letter explaining why you want to work for that company and a little about yourself and your main selling points. End your letter by asking whether you can visit the company to look around or even attend for an interview. There may not be a vacancy for you to fill immediately, but most companies will keep letters and CVs sent in speculatively and look through them when a vacancy arises. Look at it this way: it is pretty flattering for most companies!

Here are some points to remember when making speculative applications:

- Always telephone the company first to get the name of the person your letter should be addressed to.
- Include a stamped addressed envelope for a response.
- Plan your covering letter carefully. You need to include your achievements and outstanding skills, so refer to your responses to the activity on page 36 to help you out.
- In your first paragraph, state what you want – for example, 'I am particularly interested in working for your company. I understand that there are no vacancies at present but I would like to be considered for any that arise in the near future.'
- Then add a paragraph detailing your main achievements and skills. This need not be very long; it is best to make every word count and refer readers to your CV for further information.
- End by asking for an interview. You can even give broad suggestions of when this might be (for example, 'I am available to attend for an interview on most days and can be available at short notice').
- Say something that indicates that you expect a reply – for example, 'I look forward to hearing from you and enclose a stamped addressed envelope.'
- Keep your letter concise and punchy. If they want to know more, they will invite you for an interview.
- Use good-quality paper. Always check for errors. (Getting someone else to as well is a good idea; two brains are better than one, and it is easy to miss your own mistakes.)
- If you do not hear back within about 10 days, it is perfectly reasonable to make a follow-up call asking to speak to the person you wrote to in order to find out whether your letter has been received.

Speculative applications... View from Nick

I really wanted a job in my local bookshop. It's a really good one and one of the few independent ones left. There wasn't anywhere else that I wanted to work at the time and I was so frustrated that they never seemed to advertise job vacancies.

Then I decided to send in a letter to the manager just to see if they had anything going. I explained in my letter that I was really keen to work there and why, and actually asked if I could have an interview in case anything came up in the future. I included my CV too. It felt a bit pushy but I knew I didn't have anything to lose.

About a week later I had a phone call from the manager offering me a job! I couldn't believe it! I asked him if he wanted to interview me and he said no, he liked my handwriting and was happy to offer me the job! He told me when to turn up for my first day and that was that.

When I started work there, I found out that every person employed there had written in speculatively. It's obviously how the manager found his staff. I really loved my time there and only left when I moved away. Since then I've got two more jobs by writing speculative applications, so I know that it works. Sometimes your letter hits the right desk at the right time and you're in luck. I'd definitely recommend trying to get a job in this way.

Summary

The key points from this chapter include the following:

- Success in life can be linked to the attitude we have to life.
- Job vacancies are advertised in a wide range of places. You have to make sure that you look at as many sources as possible so that you do not risk missing out on your ideal opportunity.
- Don't just go for any job vacancy. Make sure that you research each possible vacancy to see if it is suitable for you to go ahead and apply.
- You have to sell your skills in every job application you make.
- A CV is a summary of your life and achievements. It is a vital part of the job application process.
- Even if you don't see a vacancy advertised for a particular company, you can still make a speculative application asking if they have any jobs going and whether they would consider you for an interview.

10
Interviews

This chapter looks at:

- what interviews are;
- how to prepare for an interview;
- what to do on the day of an interview;
- psychometric testing;
- starting work.

What are interviews?

Interviews are simply an opportunity for an employer to decide whom they want to employ for a job. They are also an opportunity for candidates to decide whether they want to work for that company or organisation. It is most definitely a two-way thing!

It is a good idea to think of interviews as fun. OK, that may not sound very realistic when you are nervous about being interviewed, but the more you can think about interviews as opportunities to meet people and find out about a new workplace, the better.

Regardless of the outcome, an interview is always a positive experience. Even if it goes so badly that you do not have a hope of getting the job, or you realise that the place is a dump that you could never work in, you will have learned valuable things about the whole process. For this reason, it is a good idea to jot down a few of your thoughts after an interview. For example, how did it go? Would you do or say the same things again? What would you change? And so on.

Preparing for the big day

If, after sending in your application for a job, you are invited for an interview, you will usually be given some notice. This can be valuable time to prepare for the big day. A word of warning, though: try not to get too wound up about your preparation or you will get too stressed out to perform to the best of your ability.

When preparing for an interview, make sure that you:

- Confirm as soon as possible that you will be attending for the interview. You can do this by letter or telephone (or e-mail if the company has given you an e-mail address for correspondence).
- Find out all you can about the company.
- Work out how you will get to the interview. If possible, do a dry run so you know exactly how long it will take you to get there. Always leave extra time for traffic jams or train or bus cancellations.
- Some organisations will pay travel expenses but others will not, so it is worth checking in advance. If you need to stay overnight the night before in order to be there on time then make the necessary arrangements in good time. Again, check whether these expenses will be paid and what sort of budget you have to keep to. Remember to get receipts for everything that you will be claiming for.
- Sort out your outfit as early as possible. Make sure that it is comfortable, clean and appropriate for the job. If in doubt, wear a suit and tie, or smart jacket and trousers/skirt. Nothing too baggy, skimpy, flesh-revealing or bright! Remove piercings. Whether it is right or wrong, instant judgements will be made about you based on your appearance, so give yourself the best chance possible. Clean your shoes, too. If you are not sure about your outfit, ask the opinion of someone you trust.
- Do not smoke or drink alcohol anywhere near your interview clothes; the interviewers will be able to smell it a mile off!

- Write the name and telephone number of the contact person on a piece of paper to take with you just in case you get held up and need to ring them.
- Gather together any exam certificates you may be asked for.
- Read through your application form and CV to remind yourself what you wrote.
- Get an early night before the interview. The last thing the interviewers want to see is bags under your eyes.
- Be positive about the interview. If you go into it thinking, 'I'll never get this', you probably won't! A positive mental attitude is one of the most effective ways of standing out from the crowd.

The day of the interview

Even though you may be nervous, make sure that you have a good breakfast so that you have the energy you need to get you through the day. Drink plenty of water, too, as this will help you to keep a clear mind.

There is no real way of knowing exactly what the day will bring unless the company gives you a detailed breakdown of events in advance. However, most interviews follow this pattern:

- They take place in a meeting room or private office. There may be a desk between you and the interviewer(s) or you may be seated on comfortable chairs around a coffee table, or any number of scenarios.
- There may be one or more people interviewing you.
- These people should be introduced to you.
- They may start by asking you simple questions to break the ice: something like 'Did you find the place OK'? or 'How was your journey?'
- There will be a period of questioning about a variety of things to do with you, the job and possibly other issues too.
- You will be asked if you have any questions. (Make sure that you have thought of some. If you really cannot think of anything, say, 'No, I think all of my questions have already been answered, thank you.')
- You may find that you are interviewed at the same time as other candidates in a group interview.
- You may be asked to do some psychometric tests (see page 146).

- You may be shown around the workplace either before or after the formal interview (although remember, even when you are being shown around you are being interviewed).
- You may be offered the job there and then or they may say that they will contact you when they have made up their minds.

What interviewers are looking for

The person or people who interview you are looking for key things. They want to make sure that the person they eventually employ will be:

- able to match the job specification;
- able to fit in with the existing staff;
- willing to make a positive contribution to the organisation;
- respectful of the management;
- motivated and conscientious;
- able to do the job;
- willing to learn;
- very likely to stay in the job if employed.

All of this will be far easier for them to find out if you answer all the questions as fully as possible. If a question could have more than a yes or no answer, give it. They want to see that you are comfortable talking and engaging in conversation. If there is anything you do not understand, ask them to repeat the question. If you still don't get it, say so; don't guess at an answer!

Possible questions

It is impossible to know what you will be asked at an interview, but the following could come up:

- What can you offer this organisation?
- Why should we employ you?
- Why do you want to work here?
- What are your strengths?
- What are your weaknesses?

- How have your past experiences prepared you for this job?
- What did you enjoy most about school/college?
- What are your goals and aspirations?
- Where do you see yourself in two years' time?

Sometimes you may be asked about your likes and dislikes, hobbies, what films you enjoy and what books you read. All of this can help an interviewer to build up a picture of what you are really like. It can also help him or her to make a decision over whether you would fit in well and make a positive contribution to the organisation.

Touring the premises

A tour of the premises, whether that be an office, factory, shop or whatever, will usually be a feature of any interview. If it is not, it is well worth asking whether you can be shown around. You will probably find that certain questions come to mind as the tour progresses and it is fine to ask these as they arise. You may be shown around by yourself or with the other candidates.

There are certain things to look out for and think about when looking round a potential place of work:

- Does it feel like a place you could happily go to every day to work?
- How are people working? Is the place in silence? Can you hear chatting? Are people working hard? Does it seem like a relaxed atmosphere?
- Are people talking to you as you go around? Does it seem friendly?
- Does it look safe? Does it feel as though there is fresh air and enough light? Is it too warm or too cold?
- Are you shown round the whole workplace? Do you see where you would be working?
- Do you get to meet your potential work colleagues? The person you would be reporting to? The boss? Do you get to speak to them and ask any questions that you have?
- Can you visualise yourself working there?

As you take your tour, keep all of these questions in mind. There is no need to make written responses, but it is really important to take notice of any gut feelings that you have about a potential place of work.

Body language

It has been said that body language can shout louder than any words you may use. Body language is the non-verbal communication that we use. Without realising it, we reveal our thoughts through body language as well as reading the thoughts of others through theirs. These tips will help you in interviews:

- Smile. It shows that you are not hostile.
- Give a firm handshake. It shows that you are not timid.
- Make eye contact. It shows that you are sincere.
- Nod. It shows that you are listening and 'with' the speaker.
- Sit up straight. It shows that you mean business.

Whatever you do, don't:

- turn your body away from the speaker;
- cross your arms and legs;
- slouch;
- jig about or swing your leg;
- touch your face, hair or any other part of your body.

What if things go wrong?

Once you are at an interview, don't worry if things seem to go wrong; it really doesn't matter. Just do the best you can. If you forget your train of thought when you are halfway through an answer, just stop, smile and say something like 'I think I'll start again.' You are only human, and so is the interviewer. The chances are that he or she will know exactly how you are feeling. Remember that it is not so much the 'mess' you get yourself into (if you do, that is!) as the way you get yourself out of it that counts!

Whatever happens at the end of an interview, don't forget to thank your interviewer(s) as you leave.

If you find that you are attending interview after interview and not getting anywhere, ask someone you trust to give you a mock interview. You may be able to get advice on this at your local Connexions office. You might also like to read a specialist book on interviews (see the Appendix for further information).

Psychometric testing

Some employers do what is known as psychometric testing on candidates for jobs. Psychometric testing falls into three main categories:

- ability testing (testing people's potential);
- aptitude testing (similar to ability testing, although aptitude testing looks at a person's job-related abilities);
- personality questionnaires (testing a person's characteristics, in particular those that may be relevant to the job).

Probably the most common of these are aptitude tests, so for the purposes of this book we will focus on these.

Aptitude tests

Aptitude tests are a way of testing a person's general intelligence as well as specific abilities such as reasoning skills and thinking skills. The tests are objective, meaning that the results should not be influenced by the personal feelings and interpretations of the employer using them. The most often used tests aim to assess verbal and numerical logical reasoning skills – in other words, how well you understand and manipulate language and numbers.

Many organisations, both large and small, use aptitude tests to help them recruit new staff. The tests give them a broader picture of each candidate than a simple application form can give them.

Although it might seem like a big hassle to have to go through these tests, they will almost certainly work in your favour. Many interviewers are pretty biased people. They can make snap decisions based on their first impressions of your appearance and the general feeling that you give off. Aptitude tests help them to make sure that the first impressions they had of you were not wrong.

If you are going for an interview as either a potential student or an employee, you should be told in advance if you will have to sit a test as part of the interview process. It should not be sprung on you at the last minute.

It is possible to prepare for taking aptitude tests. You will not know exactly what you will be faced with when attending an interview, but you will at least be familiar with the style of question that is likely to be asked, and this can really put you at an advantage.

It is quite easy to obtain sample tests. There are several on the internet, and this book's Appendix contains some useful book titles to look out for. Practising aptitude tests is a really good idea. Research suggests that about 3 out of every 10 people invited to sit an aptitude test do not bother to turn up on the day. It is always worth turning up; you never know, you may pass with flying colours!

Aptitude test questions tend to follow particular patterns. They usually (but not always) ask you to:

- find a missing word;
- spell;
- check for mistakes in printed text;
- identify the odd word out;
- continue a number sequence;
- perform mathematical calculations;
- fit shapes together;
- match symbols;
- ask how strongly you agree with certain statements (such as 'I like helping people').

Each test is usually designed to cover a broad range of skills and aptitudes. Some of the questions will have right or wrong answers, others will be more open to interpretation. Usually, these tests are not marked in terms of passing or failing, but it could be that you turn out to be so different from the intelligence or personality profile that they are looking for that your application goes no further. For example, if your test scores show that you are quite shy and introverted, despite being really good at verbal reasoning, it is unlikely you will get into training as a flight attendant.

If English is not your first language, these tests can be more difficult, especially if they are testing quite high levels of language understanding. If this applies to you, make sure that you read through the section on discrimination on page 252.

Aptitude tests... View from Pete

The first aptitude test I had to take went really badly. I hadn't done any preparation and just wasn't into how to do them. I didn't finish in time and probably did hopelessly. I didn't get the job, anyway! After that I went to the library and got some books out and did practice tests. You can soon get to work out the kinds of questions they ask and it gets easier to see what each question is asking you to do. The more you practise, the easier it is when you are faced with one at an interview.

I'm on my third job now since leaving school and I've had to do an aptitude test at every interview. Not everywhere uses them but you have to do them for a lot of office-based jobs.

It really pays to focus on your weak areas. I was never that happy with the numeracy-type questions but the verbal reasoning ones were fine. I had to force myself to sit down and practise the number sequences and so on until I felt reasonably happy. I've done a few of the online tests too and they're really good.

My advice to anyone who hasn't yet done an aptitude test is: don't be afraid of them. They're not as bad as they sound!

Info

There is some very interesting research looking into the kind of mindset we might most usefully have for future success in the workplace and in life generally. Howard Gardner, Hobbs Professor of Cognition and Education at the Harvard Graduate School of Education, has written a book called Five Minds for the Future *(Harvard Business Press, 2008). In it he explains how we might thrive in a world of rapid change without being overwhelmed by information. It is well worth reading to find out more about ways of equipping yourself for a happy and successful future!*

Safety

When attending interviews, keep your safety in mind. Make sure that:

- the interview is being held on the organisation's premises, or at least in a public place such as a hotel (not in a car or car park, or some other location that could affect your safety);
- you tell someone where you are going and what time you expect to be finished;
- you never accept a lift from your interviewer, even if you think he or she can be trusted (better to be safe than sorry);
- you do not answer questions of a personal nature (politely say, 'I don't want to answer that', and leave if you are at all unsure).

Possible outcomes

You have found a job vacancy, applied for it, got through the first stage of selection, been invited for an interview and had the interview. So, what are the possible outcomes?

- You are offered the job. Congratulations! Accept it if you know that you want to work at that organisation and you want that job. Then make sure that you ask what the next arrangements will be. Will they send you a letter of confirmation? Will they send you a contract? Do they need to receive your acceptance in writing?
- You are invited back for another interview. This is a second chance for both sides to see whether having you do this job would be the right thing. Prepare for, and treat, a second interview in exactly the same way as you would a first interview but make sure that you have thought of some specific questions to ask. Be prepared for second interviews to be quite different from first interviews.
- You are not offered the job. Don't worry! This will have been an excellent experience and something that you will undoubtedly learn from. However disappointed you are, make sure that you look for another job to apply for as soon as possible. (See page 252 for information on discrimination.) Don't let failure hold you back.

Pay

It probably goes without saying that you'll be paid according to what you do and that different jobs offer different salaries. Generally (although this is not always the case), you will get paid more if you are:

- well qualified;
- experienced;
- able to prove you have a good track record with a particular company;
- good at what you do;
- reliable;
- flexible;
- successful in promoting the cause of the company or organisation;
- able to negotiate a rise!

Some jobs will pay you according to where you are on a pay scale that will be relatively fixed, whereas others will have less formal pay structures, with salaries being negotiated as and when appropriate.

Info

For further details on money, taxation and the National Minimum Wage, see the chapter on money on page 225.

Action

How important is money to you? Of course everyone needs to earn money in order to pay their way, but do you want to earn enough or far more than that? Take a moment or two to think about how important money is to you and what your financial goals are. Do you want to be as rich as possible, or is job satisfaction, regardless of how much you earn, the most important thing to you?

Location

Where do you want to work? Would you be happy moving away from your family and friends? Or do you want to stay in the area in which you grew up? Or perhaps you would be happy to work abroad? Depending on where you live, it may be that there are greater opportunities open to you if you move away. However, moving away is not necessarily the best thing to do if you end up homesick or feeling socially isolated and lonely. If you are thinking about moving away, do consider how this might make you feel. A bit of mental preparation will really help you to make a success of it.

Do also consider whether you want to take a job that would mean a journey into work. If you are losing an hour in the morning and an hour in the evening just in getting to and from work, will you be happy about this? Or would you prefer to live closer to your work (or for your work to be closer to where you live)?

> *The Trades Union Congress (TUC) has published a guide on employment rights for young people. The guide, called* Workwise, *can be downloaded free of charge from www.tuc.org.uk/extras/ YMNWorkWise.pdf.*
>
> **Info**

Starting work

When you are offered a job, it can feel as though that is the goal achieved! In a way it is, but you have still got to go through the following stages: signing a contract and starting work on your first day.

Before you actually start work, you should have been told all about the terms and conditions of your employment. These will usually be explained in a written contract that you will have to sign. Terms and conditions are what is expected from you and what you can expect from your employer. They cover things like the hours that you must be in attendance at work, what paid holidays you are entitled to, your job role and description, sick pay entitlements, the notice period required on both sides, your salary and so on. If you have not received a contract and the first day of the job is looming, get in touch with the person who interviewed you and ask whether a contract has been sent to you. Some companies cover this kind of thing on your first day at work as they 'induct' you into your new workplace.

Before you start work, make sure that you know:

- When to arrive.
- Where to arrive.
- What to wear (especially if there is a uniform).
- What to bring. (Is there a canteen there where you can buy lunch, or can you leave to go to local shops? Will you have to take your own lunch with you?)

On your first day:

- Look around to see how other people of your level dress. Do you fit in? If you are in any way unsure about how you look at work, ask the person you are working with whether your clothing is OK. It is better to be safe than sorry, and if you have asked someone's opinion, they will know that you are serious about wanting to make a good impression.
- It goes without saying that personal hygiene should be excellent and your clothing should be clean and tidy.
- It is a good idea to take a notebook and pen with you so that you can make a note of anything you need to remember but are likely to forget.
- Go in with a positive attitude. Show that you are keen to do well and committed to the job and the company or organisation.
- Talk to people and make an effort to introduce yourself. The people you meet early on are likely to be those that you befriend as time goes on.
- You can expect someone to spend time with you on the first day going over all the information that you need to know such as health and safety considerations and practical things like where the toilets are. This is often known as 'induction' and can last anything from a few minutes to several days.
- Expect to be pretty tired by the end of the day. It might be a longer working day than you are used to, and the tension of starting a new job can be pretty draining, too.

It is a good idea to keep a mini-diary of your first few weeks at work as it is likely that your boss will want to know how you are getting on after you have been there for a month or so. If there is anything that you are not enjoying, do not quit until you have really given it a good chance. You never know, there may be an opportunity to change some aspects of your work after you have been there for a while – and remember, there are aspects of any job that can be gritty and unenjoyable! It is just a question of making the most of things, and if after a few months you know that you will never be able to settle there, maybe that's the time to start looking around for something else.

For many people, starting work is an exciting time in their lives offering more advantages and opportunities than anything else. Let's hope that this will be your experience, too.

Your local Connexions office or Citizens' Advice Bureau can tell you all about your rights at work. If there is anything you are not sure about in your contract, you can ask someone there to read through it for you and explain the parts that you don't understand.

Info

Summary

The key points from this chapter include the following:

- Interviews are a two-way process for employers to see whether they want to employ you and for you to see whether you want to work for the organisation.
- It is essential to prepare for interviews to enhance your chances of success when interviewed.
- Interviews can take a variety of formats.
- To improve your chances during interviews, you will need to answer all the questions you are asked as fully as possible.
- Some interviews include psychometric tests. It is possible to prepare yourself for these.
- Body language can give away your inner thoughts. It is important to be aware of how you sit, stand and generally conduct yourself.
- Most jobs offer some form of induction for new employees.

Part Four
Travel

11
Studying and working abroad

This chapter looks at:

- whether travelling is right for you;
- studying abroad;
- funding studies abroad;
- working abroad.

Travel – is it right for you?

It can be easy to get swept along with the tide of opinion among your friends about travelling. In some groups it will be seen as the thing to do, and anyone not jetting off to slum it in some far-flung corner of the planet might be viewed as playing it just a little too safe for comfort. There is no doubt that travelling can be a valuable and worthwhile experience, but not everyone feels the need or the desire to do it. Don't even think about surfing the internet for great travel deals until you have sat down and thought about whether or not travelling is really for you.

eurodesk ★uk

Fancy doing something special?

Have a European adventure!

We are a free, unbiased information service providing you with the knowledge you need to **work, study, travel** and **volunteer** in Europe.

Eurodesk is an internet based youth platform with partners throughout Europe. We all work together to provide you with the information you need.

There are thousands of opportunities right on your doorstep; so why not see what's on offer for you, have a look around and get **back to us with your questions!**

www.eurodesk.org.uk

Let us point you in the right direction

 BRITISH COUNCIL Education and Culture

Fancy doing something special?
Have a European adventure!

"My European Voluntary Service was a life-changing experience! Looking back I'm quite surprised how much I got out of it", says Martin Schippan, a 22 year old German who took part in an EVS programme in Brighton in 2005/06. "It is amazing that I made so many new friends from all over Europe. And taking part in this programme looks great on my CV." Like Martin, each year, an increasing number of young Europeans spend time abroad to experience different cultures, backgrounds and languages and to meet new people. "Even if I didn't speak other people's languages there were no barriers and we all had a brilliant time together. In fact those were the situations where I learned most about other cultures."

There are many opportunities available for young people in Europe and there is no reason why you shouldn't benefit from them. If you are interested in going abroad but you don't know where to start, visit Eurodesk.org.uk.

Eurodesk is an information and advisory service for young people and those working with them. The website provides information on European study, work, travel and volunteering opportunities. It is a first point of call to gather information on both UK-wide and European youth projects. Whichever European opportunity you are looking for, Eurodesk UK can point you in the right direction and find something suitable for you.

Whether you are interested in a cookery course in Spain, or a European volunteering programme for six months or more, with all your costs covered, the Eurodesk website offers you a great overview of what's on offer for young people. You could learn a new language, or even get a summer job in the sun.

There is a Eurodesk in more than 30 European countries with 900 partners working together to provide you with the information you need. Here's an example: If you fancy working on a Greek Island over the summer, Eurodesk UK can contact their Eurodesk partner in Greece and ask them for details of local websites, tips for getting a job and what you will need to prepare. It's that simple!

There are thousands of opportunities right on your door step so, why not have a look around, see what's on offer for you and find out where to start your European adventure!

Check out the Eurodesk UK website: www.eurodesk.org.uk

Or contact Eurodesk UK at:

British Council
10 Spring Gardens
London
SW1A 2BN
United Kingdom
Tel: +44 (0)20 7389 4030
Fax: +44 (0)20 7389 4033
Email: eurodeskuk@britishcouncil.org

Education and Culture
Youth in action

Action

When thinking about whether travel might be the right thing for you to do, consider the following points. You may like to make a note of your responses to help you to clarify your thinking:

- Do you definitely want to do it; you have no doubts at all?
- Would you like to do it in an ideal world but at present have too many concerns?
- Do you envisage difficulties but nothing that will stand in your way?
- Can you not see the point of it?
- Would you do it if you had the money but not otherwise?
- Do you see travel as a way to contribute to the world or a way to see the world, or perhaps both?
- Do you associate travel with holidays or working opportunities?
- Do you associate these working opportunities with volunteering or with earning money?

Aim to get to the core of why you do, or do not, want to travel. Be totally honest with yourself. There are no right or wrong answers, but you do need to work out what lies at the heart of your personal motivations before taking any further steps.

If you have written your responses down, put them away for a few days and then reread them. Do you still feel the same way? Is there anything you would like to add to your responses?

Studying abroad

There are many opportunities out there for young people to study abroad. You can use the services of one of the many dedicated companies and organisations offering opportunities to study abroad, or you can organise your own studies. You may even find that if you do a course in HE you get to study abroad through an exchange system or a placement abroad.

The European Economic Area (EEA) agreement came into force on 1 January 1994. This agreement is concerned mainly with four freedoms:

- movement of goods;
- movement of persons;
- movement of services;
- movement of capital.

This has helped to create many opportunities for people belonging to European Union (EU) member states such as the United Kingdom. With the barriers to movement around the European Economic Area breaking down and the European Union ever-expanding, you might want to look into the opportunities for studying, as well as working, abroad that this may offer you.

> *At the time of writing, there are 27 member states of the European Union: Austria, Belgium, Bulgaria, Cyprus, the Czech Republic, Denmark, Estonia, Finland, France, Germany, Greece, Hungary, Ireland, Italy, Latvia, Lithuania, Luxembourg, Malta, the Netherlands, Poland, Portugal, Romania, Slovakia, Slovenia, Spain, Sweden and the United Kingdom. There are also three countries that are candidates to become members of the European Union: Croatia, the former Yugoslav Republic of Macedonia, and Turkey.*

Info

Studying abroad is not the 'be-all and end-all' – there are plenty of young people who choose to stay in the United Kingdom for their studies – but there are certain advantages in taking this step if you think that it is a good idea for you:

- It would help you to start to understand another country – which could be a distinct advantage if ever you wanted to apply to work there.
- It would undoubtedly show you new approaches and techniques in your chosen area of study
- You would learn another language as it is spoken by its people – invaluable in today's economic climate.
- You would certainly be attractive to any UK business that might want to expand further into mainland Europe.
- It would give you invaluable experience if you think you may want to be self-employed in the future, seeking to take advantage of the markets that Europe offers.

As an EU citizen you can apply for any HE course in any EU country. That said, it would only really be wise to do this if you were fluent in the language of your chosen country and, most likely, if you had pre-existing links with that country (for example, if you had lived there for some time in the past or had relatives there).

You can also apply to HE institutions around the world outside the European Union, but would need to satisfy visa requirements and have sufficient funds to pay for what could be comparatively expensive course fees. Do not forget, too, that many UK HE institutions offer the opportunity to go abroad for at least part of a course, allowing you to live and study in another country – usually for about a year, sometimes less.

Studying abroad... View from Mike

I was offered the chance to spend a term in Sweden on an exchange programme and leapt at the opportunity. I was in my second year of a nursing degree course and couldn't wait to see how things were done in a different country, especially one that's got such a great reputation for healthcare. A small group of us went over there and we lived in nurses' accommodation in Stockholm. We weren't that far from the city centre and took every opportunity to get out and about and see what life in Sweden is really like. As well as the actual practical experience in hospitals there, which I'd say was invaluable, I found the whole thing such good grounding in so many ways. It was the longest I'd been away from the UK and I learned a lot about myself during that term; probably more than in any other term at university. I'd say to anyone who's given the chance, do it! It doesn't matter what you may be missing at home and on your course, the chances are you'll be getting far more from the experience of going away than you would from staying put.

The EU Lifelong Learning Programme

The EU Lifelong Learning Programme is made up of four main sectoral programmes, meaning that there is one for each of the main sectors of education. The Comenius programme is for school education, Erasmus is for higher education, Leonardo da Vinci is for vocational training and Grundtvig is for adult education. These programmes have the aim of promoting lifelong learning as well as fostering 'interaction, cooperation and mobility between education and training systems within the EU'.

Info

If you think you might be interested in taking part in one of the opportunities offered by the EU Lifelong Learning Programme, you can contact the British Council on 0161 957 7755 or enquiries@britishcouncil.org. There is also a website you might find useful: www.lifelonglearningprogramme.org.uk.

The Youth in Action Programme

The Youth in Action Programme encourages the involvement of all young people, including those with fewer opportunities and those aged between 13 and 30. It has five key actions:

- Action 1 – Youth for Europe: supporting exchanges and youth initiatives and encouraging young people's participation in democratic life;
- Action 2 – European Voluntary Service: encouraging young people to take part in a voluntary activity abroad that benefits the general public;
- Action 3 – Youth in the World: encouraging cooperation with partner countries by building networks, promoting the exchange of information and assisting with cross-border activities;
- Action 4 – Youth Support Systems: promoting the development of exchange, training and information schemes;
- Action 5 – European cooperation in the youth field contributing to the development of policy cooperation in the youth field.

If you would like further information on the Youth in Action Programme and how it may benefit you, or if you want to become involved in the programme, you can e-mail eac-info@ec.europa.eu. You can also find out more at the programme's website: http://ec.europa.eu/youth/index_en.htm.

Info

IAESTE

IAESTE is the International Association for the Exchange of Students for Technical Experience. It allows science, technology and engineering students to do paid work placements abroad (as long as they are course related) lasting 8–12 weeks. These placements take place in the long summer break.

To find out more about IAESTE, log on to www.iaeste.org.uk or e-mail info@iaeste.org.

Info

Info

You can find out more about the opportunities that exist for you to study abroad from the following websites. (Don't forget that as well as doing your own searches on the internet, it's also worth talking to your careers teacher or adviser; there are lots of opportunities out there for you.)

www.britishcouncil.org/new – The British Council
www.acu.ac.uk – the Association of Commonwealth Universities
www.careerseurope.co.uk – for general advice
www.studylink.com – particularly for opportunities in Australia

Your local Connexions office will also be able to give you more information on studying overseas. Ask if they have the Exodus database for you to browse. This can also be accessed via the Careers Europe website (see above).

Funding studies abroad

If you do decide to pursue the idea of studying abroad, you will need to think carefully about how you will fund yourself. Studying in a foreign institute of HE or a university will almost certainly mean paying course and tuition fees as well as your living expenses while you are abroad, and this could be more expensive than staying in the United Kingdom.

There are organisations that can help with the financial aspects of your plans to study abroad. Grants and loans are available, so talk to your college's careers adviser and also to Connexions. Do also take a good look through the Appendix to this book, as well as your local library, for further ideas and information. Do be aware of the timescales involved in applying for study places abroad. Meet all the relevant deadlines and you will not find yourself having to kill time.

Working abroad

There are almost countless opportunities for young people who want to gain some experience working abroad. For example, you could:

- teach English as a Foreign Language almost anywhere in the non-English-speaking world (a TEFL qualification is nearly always needed);
- do childcare or domestic work, for example as an au pair (although there are age limitations, and requirements can vary from country to country);
- do catering work, particularly in the popular tourist areas of countries;
- go for seasonal work in a ski resort in the French, Swiss, Austrian, German and Italian Alps, Andorra, Spain, Scotland and elsewhere;
- work on a kibbutz or moshav in Israel;
- do farm labouring and fruit picking (particularly in hot countries);
- go for summer camp work as a counsellor (particularly in the United States and Canada);
- work as a representative for a package tour operator;
- work in a theme park, for example in Florida.

There are many organisations that can help you to find suitable work abroad. It is well worth talking to as many people as you can who have done it, spending some time browsing the shelves of your local library and settling in to a few hours online. Good starting points on the internet are www.ciee.org/representatives/ and www.gapwork.com.

If you want to work outside the European Union, you will probably need a work permit and visa. The relevant country's embassy in London will be able to tell you more. You can find the addresses and contact details of embassies at the Foreign and Commonwealth Office website, www.fco.gov.uk.

Your local Jobcentre Plus will have a Euro adviser who will be able to offer you advice on working within the European Union as well as information about the European Employment Service (EURES). To find your local Jobcentre Plus office, visit www.jobcentreplus.gov.uk, and to find out more information about the European Employment Service, visit http://ec.europa.eu/eures/.

Working abroad... View from Natasha

OK, I know it wasn't the most glamorous of jobs, but I loved the time I spent working in a ski resort in Switzerland. The pay wasn't exactly fantastic and it's incredibly labour-intensive work, especially if you're working in the chalets, preparing food for guests, cleaning and sometimes entertaining. But the whole experience was so good for me and I did get my accommodation and board thrown in. I met young people from all over, especially Europe and Australia, and I'm still in touch with many of them. I really improved my skiing too, which was an added bonus.

I wasn't tempted to stay there for ever, and by the end of the season I was ready to return home. I missed my own bed, my friends and family, but wouldn't have given up my time there for anything. One of the great things about working within Europe was that you don't have the hassle of having to get work permits or visas. It really is quite easy to organise, I think.

A friend of the family got me in touch with the company that I worked for, but I know that there is plenty of information on the internet about working abroad, especially in the skiing industry. Now I've done it in Europe, I might try somewhere further away in the future – who knows! But for now I'm going to get into my course and try to forget about the freedom of the slopes!

I'd recommend spending some time working abroad to anyone. You're never going to make your millions out of it but it's usually a pretty 'casual' way of seeing somewhere new, learning some new skills and earning enough money to get by. Although it was hard work, I found it relatively low-pressure, which meant I had plenty of time and energy to make the most of it.

Action

Is working abroad for you?

It's all very tempting when you hear about the experiences of others and their jaunts around the world, but working abroad is not all about holidaying (although it's usually possible to fit a fair amount of that in!). Think about your answers to these questions when deciding whether working abroad is for you:

- How do you feel about possibly knowing little about the country and culture that you would be working in?
- How happy are you to 'learn on the job'?
- Are you open to fairly menial or manual work?
- Do you like to make new friends and get to know strangers possibly from totally different cultures than yours?
- How happy are you to learn a different language?
- Are you likely to feel homesick? What strategies have you learned to deal with this?

- Are you happy in your own company? You may have to spend time alone.
- What about your religious beliefs? Would you be happy working in a country that has differing beliefs?
- Are you open to learning new customs?
- Are you open to new culinary experiences?
- What would you do if you really wanted to come home? What contingency plans would you make for this?

Aim to answer these questions in as much detail as possible. Note your answers down if that would help you. Add any other thoughts and reflections you have as you think about it all.

Summary

The key points from this chapter include the following:

- It is important to take time to think about whether you want to go travelling and, if so, what you hope to achieve by travelling.
- There are many opportunities for young people to study abroad. Some of the programmes are Erasmus, Leonardo da Vinci, Youth in Action and IAESTE.
- It is possible to get grants and financial help to study abroad.
- There is a wide range of jobs that young people can do abroad.

12
Taking a gap year and volunteering

This chapter looks at:

- what gap years are;
- what gap years can give you and why you might want to take a gap year;
- gap year guides;
- travel precautions;
- volunteering abroad and in the United Kingdom;
- vinvolved;
- coming home.

A gap year

Taking a gap year simply means taking time out from your life plans to do some other activity, either paid or voluntary, or to take an extended holiday. Although the majority of people taking a gap year do it after university, a significant number do it before university. Each year, it is estimated that around 50,000 18-year-olds take a gap year, each spending an average of £3,000–£4,000 on their trip. Most stay away from the United Kingdom for around four months.

If you decide to take a gap year, be really clear in your mind about what it is that you want to achieve. It is all too easy to let the time, which usually runs to a full academic year plus a few summer months, slip away if you are not focused and committed to making the most of it.

What can a gap year give you?

- The chance to save money for your time in HE. Even if you have managed to finish college without having any debts, the chances are that if you go into HE, you will need to take out student loans and an overdraft. Although you can start to repay these loans only when you are earning a certain amount (there is more on this subject in Part Six), obviously the more you borrow, the longer it will take you to repay, despite the fact that student loan interest rates are relatively low. The more money you have saved to begin with, the easier your financial situation will be. That said, the other side of this argument is that you should be able to earn more money when you have left HE than before you start your course, so some may say that this should be taken into consideration. However, many students do report that the more money they have in the bank before starting in HE, the more secure they feel. This depends entirely on the kind of person you are and how comfortable (or otherwise) you feel about being in debt.

- A break from formal education while you recharge your batteries; completing A levels can leave some students pretty exhausted and in need of a decent break from studying. This does not mean that you will not go back to studying the following year, but taking a gap year can allow you to indulge in some interests that you are not going to be tested on! If you're interested in doing this, the Universities and Colleges Admissions Service (UCAS – www.ucas.com) has further information for you on deferring entry to HE.

- The chance to 'see the world'. Think about it! You could travel by train, yacht, aeroplane, car, bike or foot! The opportunities are seemingly endless. And for someone of student age, there are amazingly good-value deals to be had. However, do not fall into the trap of thinking that this is the only chance you will get to travel. At present, the fastest-growing group of 'gappers' is people from the 25–35 age bracket seeking a break from their careers.

- A way of helping others through voluntary work. Doing something useful will nearly always lead to a sense of satisfaction. You do not need to jet off halfway round the world to achieve this, although of course if that is what you fancy, there are plenty of opportunities out there for you. Just remember that voluntary work can start at home, too. Employers will generally be impressed by time spent doing voluntary work, and there is no doubt that this can help you to gain invaluable life skills, too.

- An opportunity to gain work experience to kick-start your career. There is a developing trend, particularly in some professions, for employers to want prospective employees to have gained some practical experience in the field before they are taken on. In some professions, such as teaching, practical experience is pretty essential before even getting on a training course. Taking time out to gain this, either in a paid capacity or as a volunteer, is invaluable for those who know exactly what direction they want their career to head in.

- The chance to taste the world of work before continuing your plans. Whether you want to go into HE or straight into work, taking time out to try different kinds of workplace can help you to decide where you really want to be. There are some organisations that sponsor students through their degrees, and they often want them to spend some time working in the field before committing to a course. Getting stuck in is the only way really to know whether the job will be right for you. Leaping in one particular direction could see you feeling trapped and wanting to backtrack to take a different path; work experience can help you avoid that.

- Time to think about what direction you truly want to take in life. For some people, taking a year out can give them the time and space they need to make some long-term plans about their lives. The pace of life up to the age of 18 can be so fast that this is the only chance to think clearly about the future. If this is the case for you, it is really important that you take steps to make your decision rather than putting it off indefinitely. If you know you want to study but you are unsure about what course to go for, take some advice from your school or college. You could even start by making a list of what you do not want. That can sometimes help you to focus on exactly what it is that you do want.

Who is impressed by gap years?

Generally, employers and institutes of FE and HE are pretty impressed by those who have taken a gap year to do a structured and specific activity, even if that activity is travelling on an extended holiday. It helps if you can answer questions on why you did it, what you got out of it, the changes you think it brought about in you and the benefits you could bring to a university, say, or a company because of it.

If you have taken, or are considering taking, a gap year, make sure that you can answer the questions mentioned above. Ultimately, you need to be able to explain to an admissions tutor or employer precisely what your gap year gave you. Here are some ideas to get you started:

- knowledge of different communities;
- increased confidence;
- physical fitness;
- valuable work experience;
- specific skills such as keyboard skills;
- a greater understanding of yourself.

Make sure that you think as widely as you can about your gap year so that you can paint the picture of it in the best colours possible.

Action

Gap years... View from Alice

I definitely knew that I wanted to take a gap year but I just wasn't sure when. In the end, I decided to take one after my A levels and before going to university.

I knew that many universities run taster courses, but I decided that I wanted to have a break from academic study. My long-term plan is to be a teacher, so to me it was important to give myself the opportunity to see different parts of the world and have a bit of fun before getting back down to work and three years at university followed by another for my PGCE. I didn't want to go from school to college to university and then back to school as a teacher without ever taking a year out.

My cousin and I decided to go travelling for six months. This gave us time to work and save up some money. I worked in a day nursery during the day and at my local theatre in the front-of-house team in the evenings. I didn't have much spare time but I wanted to be focused on saving as much money as possible. Sometimes it was hard, but you have to keep your mind on what you're going to be doing later in the year! We didn't want to have to work while we were travelling, and this seemed to be the best way of achieving that.

There were key places that we wanted to see. Mostly these were in Europe, so we decided to plan a roughly circular train trip taking in all that we wanted to see. This took us six weeks, and then, after a brief visit home to get our stuff washed and to repack, we flew out to Australia. We have family out there so we were able to stay and sample real Australian life rather than just the backpackers' trails, which was an amazing experience. From there we went to New Zealand and then back home via Malaysia.

It cost more than we'd anticipated, but once you're out there, you may as well take advantage of the opportunities you've got. I think it was the best thing I could have done with that year.

Working in the nursery really confirmed to me that I definitely want to be a teacher, and seeing so many places abroad not only helped me feel a little more 'worldly' but also helped me to realise that I love living in this country!

Action

Before you even start planning a gap year, think carefully about your answers to the following questions. Jot down your responses if you think it will help you to make your decision.

● Will I be able to get the most out of a gap year?
● Can I afford to take a gap year?
● Am I motivated enough to plan it and save for it if necessary?
● Do I know what I want to do when I return from whatever gap year activity I choose to do?
● Can I create a gap year that will fit in with my plans for the future?
● Overall, will my life be enhanced by taking a gap year or will I just be killing time?
● Do I want to do this with all my heart?

Gap-year guides

Gap years need meticulous planning if you are to get the most out of them. There are many sources of information on this for young people now and most of the formerly broadsheet newspapers such as *The Times*, the *Independent* and the *Guardian* run stories about gap years in the summer months following exams. A list of gap-year guides can be found in the Appendix.

> *There are a number of excellent websites that can help you to learn about, plan and prepare for taking a gap year. While it is usually a good idea to do an internet search on the kinds of activities you are specifically interested in, the following websites will also be helpful:*
>
> *www.gapadvice.org*
> *www.statravel.co.uk*
> *www.gapyear.com*
> *www.gapyearjobs.co.uk*
> *www.gap-year.com*
> *www.lattitude.org.uk*
> *www.yearoutgroup.org.*
> *www.realgap.co.uk*
> *www.gapyeardirectory.co.uk*

Info

Travel precautions

Plan any travel that you do in your gap year very carefully. There are many books and websites available to help you to do this. Talk to the adults in your life about your plans, too. Those close to you are bound to have concerns about your jetting off, and if you talk through your plans and all the precautions you have in place, they will feel happier and more able to support you. Remember, this plan may be as new for them as it is for you!

Wherever you decide to travel to, make sure that you have a passport that will be valid right through until after you plan to return to the United Kingdom, and adequate insurance, including health insurance. There have been some reports recently of Britons abroad who were not given the medical treatment they needed until they could prove that they had insurance to cover the cost. Make sure that you carry all the relevant documents with you at all times and have photocopies of them in your luggage as well as leaving copies behind at home. It's an old cliché, but it's better to be safe than sorry!

A search on the internet will bring up companies to approach for insurance quotes. Always read the small print; cheapest is not necessarily best.

You may be feeling daring, but there is little point in putting yourself in undue danger. The Foreign and Commonwealth Office (FCO) website is packed with current information on where not to travel in the world because of political instability, and, although you may be able to get to these places, you'd be well advised to heed what the FCO says. Besides, if you did travel to one of the countries currently off limits, your travel insurance might well be invalidated.

Personal safety

Whatever you do in your life and whenever you do it, being aware of your personal safety is really important. Although attacks on travellers are relatively rare, some countries are deemed more dangerous than others, and it will always be worth knowing how to look after yourself and others in the event of trouble. Be realistic about it: in all likelihood you will be perfectly safe, but it can be all too easy to throw caution to the wind when you're away from home and having a great time. This isn't about not having fun; it's about going about it as safely as possible. As the Ultimate Gap Year website (www.ultimategapyear.co.uk) says, 'Travel is not without risk. The risk needs to be kept to a minimum acceptable level without eliminating the sense of fulfilment for individuals.'

There are several courses that would-be travellers can attend to learn all about staying safe while taking a gap year. You can find out about these from the website mentioned in the previous paragraph, and your school may also run sessions on how to stay safe while travelling. There is essential safety advice and knowledge that you should have before setting out, so be sure to find out as much as you can. Don't assume that you are streetwise and know all there is to know, and likewise don't let fears about safety put you off from travelling at all!

To find out more about travel safety, try these sites for starters:

www.ultimategapyear.co.uk
www.safetrek.co.uk
www.suzylamplugh.org.

Info

For further information on this, visit www.fco.gov.uk or telephone 020 7008 1500 for general enquiries.

Books and websites (particularly those listed in the Appendix) will be invaluable in planning your gap year. Taking the time to focus on exactly what it is you want to achieve from your year out will help to ensure that you reach your goals, even if they are simply to relax and have fun.

The Year in Industry scheme

If you think you may want to work for a full year before starting HE, consider taking part in The Year in Industry. This is a scheme, administered by the Engineering Development Trust, for gap-year students to gain experience of industry, before or during university, backed by comprehensive 'off-the-job' training. The main features of The Year in Industry are that it:

- is tried and tested;
- is available nationwide;
- targets the most able young people;
- matches students to companies' needs;
- arranges real work in industry;
- selects students pre-degree, at their most receptive and enthusiastic;
- fosters continuing links between companies and undergraduates.

Students taking part in The Year in Industry agree to:

- follow the company's terms and conditions of employment;
- show initiative and self-motivation;
- be present for all training sessions offered.

In return, the company agrees to:

- employ the student between around September and July;
- offer 'useful and challenging' work;
- free students up to attend The Year in Industry training courses;
- pay students a wage, typically from £9,000 to £14,000.

For further information on The Year in Industry, visit www.yini.org.uk.

Info

Looking for a year out?
Take a year in with JVC Britain!

- Aged between 18 & 35?
- Passionate about social justice?
- Want to live in community with volunteers from all over Europe?
- Keen to try living a simple lifestyle?
- Willing to explore and develop your spirituality?
- Looking for a fully-funded programme that will change your life?

We'll fill your gap year or summer break with experiences you'll never forget. You'll live in one of Britain's inner cities and work as a full-time volunteer, making a difference to the lives of homeless people, refugees, children, or people with physical or learning disabilities.

See our website at
www.jvcbritain.org
or call us on 0161 832 6888.

**Jesuit
Volunteer
Community**

In any one day JVC volunteers will be... *accompanying an **asylum seeker** to court... supporting someone with **learning difficulties** to speak out for their rights... baking bread with **homeless** people... helping someone learn to read... making a cup of tea... growing vegetables with **refugees**... playing football with **young people**... restoring a chair... meeting with **grassroots communities**... helping **children** learn about the environment... organising an action campaign... listening to someone... the list goes on...*

Adam, who works with refugees, says "Yet at the end of a frustrating working day, my overall thought was that I wouldn't have changed it for the world."

For 23 years, young people who are passionate about social justice have been changing people's lives, and their own, for good.

Contact us if you are looking for an opportunity to deepen your faith, meet people from other countries and experience a year that you will never forget.

Volunteering

If taking an extended holiday for your gap year does not quite do it for you, there are plenty of opportunities to take part in volunteer projects all around the world. Many agencies exist to help young people find suitable voluntary work, for example Camp America (recruiting people to work with children on summer camps in the United States), GAP Activity Projects or au pair agencies (looking for people to work in families looking after children and generally helping in the house). With these kinds of projects you may need to supply the money for your air fares.

> *www.worldwidevolunteering.org.uk is an enormous database of organisations and volunteer placements. Your local Connexions office may have access to it, so if volunteering is for you, it is well worth asking.* **Info**

There are also opportunities to volunteer closer to home. Volunteering England and Community Service Volunteers are just two of the organisations in the United Kingdom that help find placements for would-be volunteers. There are many conservation organisations, too, and these are often seeking volunteers. This is a great way of getting involved in helping to preserve nature or your local heritage, as well as making sure that you are not going to be stuck behind a desk from nine to five!

> *Community Service Volunteers (CSV) offer what they describe as high-quality volunteering and training opportunities. Through taking part in a CSV project, you would have the chance to help real people, significantly improving their lives. Check out www.csv.org.uk for more information.* **Info**

vinvolved

v is an independent charity which seeks to inspire volunteers aged 16–25 in England. The way it works is by funding voluntary organisations all over England to create inspiring, diverse opportunities. It also helps to overcome barriers that stop people from taking action to improve lives, communities and the planet. **v** aims to create a culture where volunteering comes naturally, so that the benefits of volunteering are understood and celebrated by all. **v**involved is the national youth volunteering programme which is split into two strands: **v**involved teams and **v**involved projects.

> **Info**
>
> *You can find out all about **v** and **v**involved from the website: www. vinspired.com.*

Coming home

If you are planning to spend any time away from home during your gap year, or as part of your studies, make sure that you do some mental preparation about returning home. The chances are you will have had some amazing experiences – possibly even life-changing experiences – and you may have a slightly altered perception of your home life as a result. Before you even start packing your rucksack for your outward journey, make sure that you have firm plans for what you are going to do when you return, even if those plans are simply to spend a fortnight fully researching your options and re-evaluating your life after the experiences that you will have had. Above all else, you need to avoid coming back to an apparently empty life as this could lead to huge feelings of anticlimax.

That said, you should be aware that what you thought you wanted to do before you ever set foot on the plane may be very different from what you now want to do having spent six months in the Australian outback! Be open to the changes and personal developments that take place and do not try to squeeze yourself into plans that no longer fit you. The pitfall you need to avoid is drifting on your return until something as exciting as what you have just been doing turns up. With that frame of mind, it probably never will!

Coming home... View from Jon

I was so excited about getting away from my village that I didn't put any thought into what it would be like when I got back. I got really depressed and demoralised because I'd been working on a kibbutz among other things; it'd been fantastically hot and a totally new experience for me. I got back to my quaintly English village in the middle of winter and everything felt wrong. I know I upset my family and I felt really bad about that. It wasn't their fault; they'd always supported me.

Looking back, I can see that I was just kicking out because I didn't want to face up to the fact that I needed to get on with the rest of my life. It really helps if you can get something organised before you leave so you don't end up in the state I was in. The lower I felt, the harder it was to get up off my backside and make future plans. I ended up wasting a year when I got back from travelling just trying to get my head around what course I wanted to do and where I wanted to be. I don't recommend that to anyone.

If you're not careful, all the benefits you gain from travelling and working abroad can be lost in a second if you just go home and coast. Get it sorted! Just make sure that even if you're not exactly sure about what you want to do next, you're at least thinking about it and not putting off the decision making until some point in the future. If you're not careful, that point will never arrive – and then what?

Summary

The key points from this chapter include the following:

- Each year, around 50,000 18-year-olds take a gap year.
- Gap years can give you a wide variety of experiences and opportunities.
- It is essential to plan your gap year as much as possible. Don't drift into it, or you may fritter the time away.
- Employers and university admissions tutors are generally impressed by people who take a gap year.
- There is a tremendous amount of advice out there for young people who are thinking of taking a gap year.

- Voluntary work can be an excellent way of spending all, or at least part, of a gap year.
- If you are planning to spend any time abroad, you must think first about what you plan to do on your return. Don't drift!

Part Five
Other options

13
Self-employment and beyond

This chapter looks at:

- all you need to know about self-employment;
- other options such as franchises and cooperatives;
- job sharing;
- portfolio working;
- work–life balance.

Leaving school at the age of 16 or 18 means that you face many choices. The obvious ones are either to go into FE or HE, or to get a job, but there are other options that you may not have thought of. Self-employment is something that many people consider at some point in their lives. It would be relatively unusual for someone to go into it straight from school, but if you think that it might be something you would like to explore later on in your life then you could bear this in mind when making choices now. Voluntary work or unpaid work such as job shadowing are two other choices. It is important to take time to make sure that you opt for what is best for you at the moment. Above all else, think about your options in the broadest way possible. So-called conventional employment is not all that is open to you.

Let's just get real for a moment, though. Doing anything other than getting a job can lead to periods of what some may describe as 'intense poverty'. Unless they have a private income from a loaded family, probably every student, entrepreneur, volunteer and self-employed person has been through it. Opting for one of the alternatives can mean risk taking and insecurity; it takes guts and commitment. That said, the benefits are potentially immense. Are you up for that?

Self-employment

Not many school leavers go straight into self-employment, and even at graduate level the figure stands at only about 2 per cent, although this is thought to be rising. But self-employment shows all the signs of being a growth area of the UK economy. You may have long-term plans for self-employment, so this chapter could offer you some useful ideas.

What is self-employment?

Self-employment literally means employing yourself – being your own boss. Whether this is a lifetime choice or a lifestyle choice – that is, either permanent or temporary – is down to you.

Most self-employed people get work (or contracts or customers/clients) from many sources, yet no single company or client is responsible for them. This has its advantages and disadvantages, but one thing to keep firmly in mind is that as a self-employed person you do not get sick pay, paid holidays, a regular salary, or any of the other benefits or bonuses associated with being employed, such as medical insurance and access to a company pension scheme.

As a self-employed person, your income would come from work completed that you then invoice your customer for. You would need a steady flow of contracts to ensure that you do not have any periods with nothing to do. This would also ensure that your cash flow remained healthy.

Being self-employed means having to be responsible for your tax and National Insurance. When you are employed by a company, these would be taken 'at source', meaning that tax and National Insurance are collected before your wages reach you. Consequently, all the money you earn is yours to spend (once all your bills are paid!). When you are self-employed, you have to make sure you save some money from each cheque received to pay for tax and National Insurance (in two lump sums through each year).

Any profits you have left when your bills are paid (including any savings and pension contributions you may be making) could be put back into your business. For example, you might need to buy a newer vehicle or rent larger premises.

Types of self-owned business

If you start up your own business (as opposed to simply working for yourself on a freelance basis), you will probably choose to run your business as either a sole trader, a partnership or a limited company.

Sole trader

A sole trader runs a business in which just that one person is the owner. As a sole trader, it is still possible to employ other people, but you do not need to go into the complexities of setting up a formal business. Another term for a sole trader is an 'unincorporated business'. Any profits made belong to the sole trader (although they will be subject to tax as appropriate).

Partnership

A partnership is a relationship between two or more (usually up to 20) people for the purposes of running a business and making a profit. Profits are split between all the partners and taxed as appropriate.

Limited company

Limited companies must have at least one shareholder, at least one director and a company secretary. If you run a limited company you will need to submit certain documents to the Registrar of Companies as well as produce accounts and file an annual report.

It is probably best, if you are thinking of self-employment as an option, to start out as a sole trader or partnership.

You may also want to consider a franchise (see page 189) or a social enterprise.

Why be self-employed?

There are many reasons for being self-employed. For many people, the example of their family has a large influence. If self-employment is a way of life for your parents or siblings, you are more likely to view it as a viable option for yourself – provided they run successful businesses, that is!

In addition, some people are just better suited to it than others. Whether you know this from early on or learn it as a result of work experience, you will know whether self-employment is a way of life that you could thrive in.

Certain types of work are typically more usual for the self-employed. For example, jobs in the media seem increasingly so, as are many artistic and design-based jobs.

Pros and cons of self-employment

Pros	Cons
You can be your own boss.	You are the only one in charge.
You can set your own hours.	You need strong motivation and drive.
You can promote your own ideas.	Your ideas and concept may be 'stolen'.
You may be able to work from home.	If working from home, you can never get away from your home office.
You can build up many sources of income.	You have to deal with job insecurity.
It may not matter where in the country you live.	You can end up feeling socially isolated.
You can decide when to take time off.	You do not get holiday and sick pay (nor the time to have a break!).
You have greater control of your life.	You have to stay on top of your business's direction.
You can dictate what your prices are.	Clients rarely pay on time.
You get to use a wide range of skills.	You do not have time to update your skills.
The profits you make are yours to keep.	You will have no retirement income if you do not make your own arrangements for a private pension.

Is self-employment for you?

To be self-employed, you need to offer a product or a service, preferably something that is not commonly being offered already (or that has a unique selling point). If nothing springs automatically to mind, think about your skills and aptitudes, hobbies and talents. Is there anything in that lot that you can market as being unique?

Remember, too, that if you take the plunge and go self-employed you will need to become expert at finance, sales and marketing, advertising, management, administration, human resources (if you employ others), ICT, the law as it relates to your business, and much, much more. Your levels of self-motivation will need to be so honed and so reliable that you will be able to ride out every storm as it strikes. You will need excellent support to draw on as and when necessary, and a very friendly bank manager!

Above all else, your vision must be realistic yet ambitious. There has to be a genuine need for what you want to offer and a willingness in you to reach the prize you desire through creativity, honesty and innovation. Does that sound like you?

Is self-employment for you?... View from Neil

I've always known that I want to run my own business. I don't want to spend my entire working life being someone else's employee. But I've watched my Dad run his own business and have seen how much work is involved. I knew I wasn't ready for that when I left school, so I got a job with him and I'm earning money and learning about running a business now. At the moment I have fairly fixed hours, so I can make the most of my time off, too. But I will be starting my own business within the next five years. I don't want to leave it any later than that. I know what I want to offer and am in the process of doing some research into how viable my idea is. It's looking good at the moment, so I won't reveal anything about it!

Help starting up

A quick search on the internet will confirm just how much support there is out there for young people wanting to start up their own businesses. In particular, contact:

- Livewire – www.shell-livewire.org;
- The Prince's Trust – Business – www.princes-trust.org.uk;
- the New Deal – www.jobcentreplus.gov.uk;
- Business Link – www.businesslink.gov.uk.

Info

You will find a lot of information on starting up as a self-employed person on the HM Revenue & Customs website, www.hmrc.gov.uk/ startingup. In particular, take a look at the booklet Are You Thinking of Working for Yourself?, which you can download free of charge from http://www.hmrc.gov.uk/leaflets/se1.pdf. There is also a helpline for the newly self-employed: 08459 15 45 15. For help with self-assessment tax you can call 0845 9000 444, and advice on National Insurance can be found at www.hmrc.gov.uk/nic. The self-employment contact centre can be reached on 08459 15 46 55.

What if your business fails?

Many small businesses do not make it through their first two years, so it is important to be prepared for possible failure. This in itself is not a reason to back out of your dream if you really want to be self-employed, but it is certainly something to be aware of. Success for the self-employed person is not a foregone conclusion.

There are sometimes wider factors that have an influence on how successful your business can be – factors such as the state of the national and global economies, interest rates, house prices, domestic politics, international politics (such as wars and conflicts), trends and fads for and against the product or service you are providing and so on, all of which have an impact on the profits that businesses can make. Even if you are doing the best you can, working as hard as is humanly possible, these other factors could conspire to make your business fail.

As a self-employed person you need to be as forward-thinking as possible. Taking out relevant insurances and expanding at a sensible pace will help, as will seeking advice and support as soon as you detect problems, but there are still no guarantees that you will succeed. That said, the belief that self-employment is the riskiest way to earn money no longer holds true. Your income may be irregular and working hours long, but this can also apply when you are employed by another person or organisation.

Alternatives

As well as being employed, or going for self-employment, there are still other options that you might want to consider.

Buying a franchise

Franchises are other people's business ideas, sold on. Rather than growing their business in the conventional way, some business owners (franchisers) choose to sell a licence for other people to use their idea, allowing the franchisee to trade under that company's name. Business outlets are owned by the individual franchisees, while the franchiser retains control over key aspects such as marketing, quality and standards.

Franchises can be shops, restaurants, clubs – almost anything! Examples of franchises that you might have heard of (and may have used) include the following:

- Clarks Shoes;
- Coffee Republic;
- Haagen-Dazs Café;
- Hobgoblin Music;
- Jo Jingles;
- Millie's Cookies;
- Neal's Yard Remedies;
- Specsavers.

There are many advantages to buying a franchise, not least that it is a tried and tested business idea that is known to work. As you can see from the list above, many franchises are household names, and it is an opportunity to have a relatively independent role in a nationally recognised business. However, one potential disadvantage is the amount of money that would-be franchisees have to put up front. Franchises are not altogether risk-free, either, so, as with any business proposition, careful thought and planning would be required before proceeding.

> **Info**
>
> *For further information and all you need to know about taking out a franchise, make sure that you visit the British Franchise Association website: www.thebfa.org.*

Job sharing

There are many jobs that can be split and shared between two (or sometimes more) people. Even some headteacher posts in schools are shared between two people. Although job sharing is still pretty rare, it is on the increase, and employers do generally seem to be quite supportive of the idea.

Job sharing is different from basic part-time work. When job sharing, although you would be working part time, you would be contributing, with your job-share partner, to a full-time post. This means that you are more likely to be able to do fairly 'high-level' work, whereas if you were to take a part-time post it would be less likely to be particularly high-flying. Getting promotions as a part-timer (as opposed to job sharer) does seem to be potentially difficult, too.

There are pros and cons to job sharing; really, whether it appeals comes down to personal preference. Ultimately, people choose to job-share if it means they can pursue other goals such as further study, building up their own business in their spare time or looking after a family or a sick relative.

Job sharers usually split the tasks of the role, pay, holiday and any other benefits that the job may have according to the hours each person works. Needless to say, job shares are as successful as the relationship between the job sharers. If that is based on trust, cooperation, support and respect, among other things, the job share has a far better chance of working.

There are several options open to job sharers when dividing out the work. The job could be shared by:

- working alternate weeks;
- splitting the week into two full days and one half-day each;
- splitting the day into a morning and afternoon session;
- working two days one week and three days the next;
- working to an uneven split, with salary and tasks reflecting this pro rata.

Can you job-share?

If you think you might like the opportunities that job sharing can offer you, take a moment to think about the questions below as to whether you fit the profile of an effective job sharer. In order to job-share successfully, you need to be a particular type of person. Job sharing is no good for 'control freaks' who like everything to be just so! Could you job-share in the future? To help job-sharing arrangements work effectively, job sharers need, at the very least, the following:

- excellent communication skills;
- skills of cooperation rather than competition;
- flexibility;
- compatible, but not necessarily identical, methods of working;
- commitment to the arrangement;
- complementary knowledge and skills.

The question is: how well do you fit this profile?

Action

Portfolio working

It is probably true to say that there is no longer any such thing as a 'job for life', if there ever was. Many people are now wanting to work to a different pattern rather than the traditional Monday to Friday, nine to five, and employers are responding to this by offering a range of possible contracts. This means that one person may have a portfolio of several jobs. For example, you might be employed on a part-time contract for one company for 15 hours a week, do some freelance work for another 15 hours and teach an evening class for 5 hours a week.

'Outsourcing' has increased over recent years, meaning that freelance employees and contractors have to be relied upon. This has helped to change many people's views about work. We all need to make sure that we remain employable, whether on a short-term or a permanent basis, by keeping our skills up to date and our minds tuned to the idea of lifelong learning. This can greatly help the portfolio worker.

Portfolio working may not suit everyone; some prefer the thought of being employed full time by one company. But for others, it is the ideal way of working, as it best suits their personality.

Portfolio working... View from Dave

I think I'm pretty unusual among my friends because they've all got full-time jobs but I knew that wouldn't be right for me. My main interest is music. I love everything about it. I know that ultimately I'd love to record my own; not necessarily to be famous, but for the pure pleasure of creating something that I can keep for ever. If I make anything out of it, that would be great!

I wanted to get a job in a record shop, and not just for the discount! I work three days a week in a small independent shop and I get given a budget to order some of the stock. That's brilliant, seeing what deals I can get, trying to research stuff that I think will sell well, getting to know customers and their tastes and so on. It's fascinating being that bridge between musicians and record producers and listeners. You find out so much about the whole industry from that central point.

On my other two days I work (for peanuts!) in a recording studio. Again, I see it as a way of gaining valuable knowledge and insight into the way the music industry works. Sometimes I'm little more than the tea boy, but I have worked on some interesting projects and learned so much.

I also play the guitar and keyboard myself and am gaining in confidence as a singer. I play in a band and we often get gigs at the weekends, so that also brings in extra money. I see everything that I'm doing now as a route to my ultimate goal. I've got a portfolio of jobs but they are all connected and are teaching me different skills from various angles of the same business. I've got no regrets at all about choosing to do things this way. And if I'm honest, many of my friends are quite jealous, even though I'm sure they're probably earning a bit more than me right now!

Short-term contracts

Short-term contracts can have various names, for example specific task contracts (where you would be employed to cover, for example, a maternity leave) or fixed-term (for example, to cover the busy Christmas season in a shop). The contracts have a fixed finishing date and help to allow employers to increase or decrease their workforce as and when they need to. Some people thrive on short-term contracts, liking the variety and flexibility that they offer. They can also mean the opportunity to gain experience in a wide variety of work settings, which can be particularly useful if you are not completely sure of what you want to do and where you want to do it.

Cooperatives

Cooperatives are democratic organisations owned and run jointly by their members, who share their profits among themselves. These profits shares usually depend on an employee's level within the company (often linked to salary). People choose to work in cooperatives as a way of starting a new business while having the security of working with others.

There are many different types of cooperatives, from those offering transport services to a community to babysitting circles, building services to wholesale food supplies. Some even operate their own forms of currency as a way of trading skills within a group.

> *The Co-operative Group is an example of a large and successful coop-erative in the United Kingdom. Infinity Foods is another example. Visit their respective websites for further information:*
>
> *www.co-operative.coop*
> *www.infinityfoods.co.uk.*

Info

Communes and communities

OK, it is just a relatively tiny percentage of people who live and work in communes, but rising numbers have passed through one at some stage of their lives. Communes appeal to those people who do not feel completely comfortable with the realities of the world of work, seeking to do things in an alternative way. Different communes have different reasons for being, but, in general, members share accommodation and resources (to a certain extent) and work together on a common project such as making things or growing crops, to be self-sustaining or offering educational programmes.

Info

Two examples of successful communities are the Findhorn Community in Scotland, www.findhorn.org, and the Pilsdon Community in Dorset, www.pilsdon.org.uk.

Work–life balance

Rather shockingly, employees in the United Kingdom work the longest hours in Europe. In fact, only employees in the United States work longer hours out of the whole of the developed world! This, combined with the way that new technologies have impacted on our lives, means that personal time is being squeezed. There is no doubt about it, you will need to work hard at creating a division between work and leisure and ensuring that your life has a healthy work–life balance. Whether you live to work or work to live is up to you, but you will need to leave time to relax and pursue hobbies and leisure if you are to avoid the strains of negative stress.

Working hours

Full-time, permanent jobs used to mean, in the main, being in your place of work from nine to five, Monday to Friday. Now, flexible hours (flexi-time), shift work, opportunities for part-time and term-time work, working from home and so-called hot-desking (shared desks for employees such as sales representatives who are not in the office long enough to have a desk each) mean that there is far more variety in working hours to be had out there. Overall, it is estimated that over 2 million people work from home, and the number of those who do at least some work at home is likely to be far higher. In fact, some people estimate that as many as 60 per cent of workers spend at least some time working from home, whether employed by a company or self-employed. Do not get locked into thinking that you will be doing the same thing in the same place at the same time each day; working life does not need to be like that any more.

Summary

The key points in this chapter include the following:

- Self-employment means employing yourself, or being your own boss.
- Although not many school leavers go straight into self-employment, it is something that many people consider at some stage of their lives.
- There are several types of business that you can set up, including being a sole trader, or running a partnership or a limited company.
- There are pros and cons of self-employment that need to be fully considered before taking the plunge.
- There is plenty of help available to you if you want to start up your own business.
- If you have difficulties running your own business, there are several sources of support.
- Buying a franchise can be one way of running your own business in a relatively safe way, although there are still risks attached.
- Job sharing is another possibility for young people who want some time spare to pursue their own interests or to continue studying.
- Portfolio working is when you have several jobs from different sources or employers.
- Cooperatives are democratic organisations that are owned and run jointly by their members.
- Whatever you decide to do, it is important to pay attention to your work–life balance.

14
Voluntary work

This chapter looks at:

- voluntary work as an alternative to paid work;
- reasons to be a volunteer;
- transferable skills.

The voluntary sector

Rather than getting a job or starting your own business, you may want to spend some time doing voluntary work. (For information on doing work experience and job shadowing, see Chapter 8; for information on volunteering in a gap year, see Chapter 12.) Although doing voluntary work will not provide you with an income (although expenses may be paid), it does offer the chance to gain useful experience, to develop skills and to find out exactly what it is like to do a certain job. Many feel that it is worth going without an income for a period in return for these benefits.

The voluntary sector in the United Kingdom is huge and covers just about every area of society. The turnover of the voluntary sector is around £16 billion and there is every indication that this will only go one way – up. Around 5,000 new charities are registered each year and add to the approximately 150,000 charities already in existence. Some can afford to have paid staff (such as Oxfam), whereas others are run almost entirely by unpaid volunteers.

International agencies make up by far the largest part of the voluntary sector. After them come the cancer charities and a little further down the list come animal protection charities (interestingly, above children's charities).

Working in the voluntary sector as an unpaid member of staff can be a great way of eventually getting a paid post there. Charities nearly always need administrators, fundraisers, project managers, press and PR staff and many more. If you have got your eye on any of those roles, starting out as a volunteer could be a wise career move.

Do you want to work for no pay?

Working unpaid is not such a weird concept, really. In fact, some people go so far as to pay their own travel and living costs in order to work for free! It all depends on what the perceived benefits are. If you think about it, there will be jobs and activities in your life that you will be happy to do for no immediate financial gain (although it is important to remember that you may well end up earning slightly more because of your experience than you would have done had you not volunteered). Doing voluntary work is simply about expanding that outwards into your community to see whether you can spend some time helping others and achieving an end goal.

Why be a volunteer?

There are many motivating reasons to choose to do a period of voluntary work. Have a think about these ideas. You could do voluntary work in order to:

● gain knowledge and skills that will be useful in the future;
● benefit society and your local community;
● try out new ways of working;
● be part of a team of people working together to achieve a common goal;
● gain a way into an organisation;
● gain experience of a career you might like to enter;
● travel.

Why be a volunteer?... View from Geraint

I've been working part-time in my local Oxfam shop for the past two years. It's not staffed entirely by old ladies! Most of the volunteers are about my age and we've all got our own areas of interest. Because the shop's in quite a wealthy area we get a lot of decent clothes to sort through. Some are vintage originals, which we have to get advice on; others aren't up to much but still sell. Any clothing we can't sell to customers can be sold to a recycling company. Nothing gets wasted.

My favourite part of the job is sorting through the books as they come in. We've had quite a few first editions and some really valuable titles. I'm getting far better at spotting the potentially valuable stuff, but again, we can get advice on this.

Obviously I can't do this for ever; I've got to earn enough money to live. But I've never wanted to be rich. I just want enough to get by. I hope I never have to give up doing some voluntary work as it really keeps me grounded. It's a great way of knowing that you're giving something back to your local community as well as learning first-hand about other people's experiences of life. It's easy to shut yourself off from the needs of others if you never give your time to a charitable cause. I don't want to preach about it, but for me, I need this kind of constant reminder.

Info

There is information on volunteering in a gap year in Chapter 12 and you can also look for voluntary work at your local Volunteering England. You will find the contact details in the Yellow Pages. *Alternatively, visit www.do-it.org.uk or www.volunteering.org.uk.*

It is not necessary to commit to a full working week of voluntary work. Often there is the chance to do as much or as little as you like. You may want to fit volunteering around other commitments.

Don't forget the Community Service Volunteers website, www.csv.org.uk.

Transferable skills

Spending time working in any organisation, whether paid or otherwise, will teach you skills that can be transferred to other jobs or placements.

These skills are known as transferable skills. Some people believe that being able to identify the transferable skills that you have is one of the most important things that you can do when you are thinking about applying for jobs or courses.

Transferable skills can be divided into different categories. These categories can include communication skills, interpersonal skills (relating to other people), organisation skills and general work skills. Take a look at the lists below for examples of all of these.

Communication skills include:

- speaking effectively to others;
- listening with attention;
- being able to express your ideas;
- being able to take part in group discussions;
- conveying information;
- being able to negotiate;
- being able to 'read' the non-verbal communication of others (such as body language);
- writing effectively and concisely;
- summarising and editing;
- handling electronic communication such as e-mails;
- being able to communicate effectively on the telephone;
- skills of self-expression.

Interpersonal skills include:

- being sensitive to the needs of others;
- being able to express your own needs assertively;
- getting on with people and developing rapport;
- supporting others;
- motivating others;
- being able to cooperate;
- managing conflict;
- having skills of perception.

Organisation skills include:

- being able to pace and organise your workload;
- noticing details;
- coordinating the tasks that you have to do;
- making decisions;
- solving problems;
- handling information and data;
- working to deadlines;
- leadership skills;
- goal-setting skills;
- goal-realisation skills;
- being able to cope with change.

General work skills include:

- literacy and numeracy skills;
- being able to follow instructions;
- accepting responsibility;
- being able to implement decisions;
- punctuality;
- time-management skills;
- skills of self-motivation;
- creativity;
- commercial understanding;
- research and information-gathering skills;
- skills of analysis and evaluation.

The list is virtually endless; there are many more that could be added here. There is no way that a single employer or course admissions tutor would expect you to have all of these skills under your belt, but you will almost certainly be very good at a few of them, reasonably good at others, have just a little knowledge of some and be ready to learn the rest. That's fine; as long as you can identify some of these skills in yourself, you will have an excellent base on which to build in the future.

The thing to remember with transferable skills is that it is not necessarily what you are doing in a job or placement that matters. You might be washing glasses in a restaurant and may never again do that in your working life, but the experience will still have taught you how to take instructions, how to work in a team and how to work safely, to name just a few. These are all skills that will be useful in future jobs.

Transferable skills

First of all, add any transferable skills that you can think of that have been left off the lists above.

Now go through each one and think about what situations in your life may have taught you each skill. For example, you may have learned about teamwork through playing in a sports team or you may have learned some commercial understanding from your Saturday job in a clothes shop. Aim to think as widely as you can about it. Do not worry if there are some skills there that you just cannot account for; that does not matter. What you are aiming for is as long a list as possible of your own personal transferable skills (with examples of how and where you learned them) that you can refer to when you make your job applications.

Action

You have probably realised by now that simply identifying transferable skills is not enough. A potential employer or course admissions tutor does not want to read that you have an array of transferable skills unless they are related directly to the job or course that you want to do. Being able to facilitate group discussions is not necessarily going to help you in your application for a holiday job in a call centre! However, being able to negotiate and listen attentively will. Transferable skills have to be applicable to the job, placement or course that you want to transfer them to. For every transferable skill, ask yourself: how will this help to support my application or future life direction?

Action

Look at Table 14.1. It shows possible interview questions and the responses of two imaginary candidates. Which one would you rather employ, A or B? Think about why you made that decision.

Table 14.1

Interview question	Response from candidate A	Response from candidate B
You left school six months ago. What have you been doing since then?	Applying for jobs.	As well as applying for jobs I've been working as a volunteer in my local library.
Do you work well with other people?	I prefer to work on my own.	Yes, I really enjoy working with others. I'm on the children's homework team at the library and we help them with their homework and coursework problems. It's good fun.
Have you had experiences of working with the general public?	No, but I can learn.	Yes, working at the library has given me lots of experience of working with the public, especially when it's really busy at the weekend and we have to deal with one question after another.
Are you confident dealing with telephone and e-mail enquiries?	Yes, I've got my own mobile phone and computer, so I know how they work.	Yes, I was trained at the library, so I can take telephone enquiries, and I help my Dad out answering the e-mails he gets for his business.

Summary

The key points from this chapter include the following:

- Being a volunteer can give you many benefits such as useful experience, developing skills and knowledge of exactly what it is like to do a certain job or activity.
- The voluntary sector in the United Kingdom is huge and covers just about every area of society.
- There are many places to find information on volunteering.
- Volunteering gives you valuable transferable skills.
- Transferable skills can be very useful to add depth to job and course applications.
- Being aware of what skills you are learning, and how and when you are learning them, is crucial.

15
Being unemployed

This chapter looks at:

- unemployment statistics;
- what happens when you visit your local Jobcentre Plus office;
- the Jobseeker Direct telephone service;
- Income Support;
- Jobseeker's Allowance;
- New Deal;
- Work Trial and Employment on Trial.

Unemployment statistics

Being unemployed literally means not having a job. The latest unemployment figures (March 2010) showed that there were 715,000 18- to 24-year-olds classified as unemployed. This figure is substantially higher than the one for the year before. If you are facing unemployment for whatever reason, you are not alone. Sadly, it does seem that young people aged 16–25 are twice as likely to be unemployed compared to those in older age groups in the labour market (which is defined as men aged 16–64 and women aged 16–59).

There is a link to qualifications here. Surveys in the past have found that someone with no qualifications is 1.8 times more likely to be unemployed than someone with GCSEs (grades A*–C) and 4.6 times more likely to be unemployed than someone with A levels. For this reason alone it is best to stay on in FE if you possibly can.

Jobcentre Plus

If you are looking for work, you will be familiar with your local Jobcentre Plus office. When you first visit one of these offices you will meet a personal adviser who will need to take some personal details and will probably want you to prove your identity, so it is worth taking some documents with you, such as your passport. You will be told about the vacancies that suit you and arrangements will be made for you to be sent the relevant claim forms for any benefits that you are entitled to (see below).

Jobcentre Plus is part of the Department for Work and Pensions. It provides services to people who are of 'working age'. This means people between the ages of 16 and 65. The aims of Jobcentre Plus include:

- *helping to get more people into paid work;*
- *helping employers to fill their vacancies;*
- *giving people support if they cannot work.*

You can find out all about Jobcentre Plus by visiting www.direct.gov.uk and www.dwp.uk.

Visiting your local Jobcentre Plus office

When you meet the personal adviser, he or she will want to talk to you about the following:

- The work experience that you have so far. This could be paid work in the form of previous jobs, including part-time ones, or unpaid in the form of work experience you did at school or college or have arranged for yourself.
- Your skills. This is why it is really important to have thought about what you have to offer. See the chapters on looking for a job in Part Three for more information.

- Any training and qualifications that you have. Your working file (if you are using Progress File) will be useful here as you will already have gathered all the relevant information together.
- The education and training opportunities that you are interested in taking up.
- The support that you might need in order to do a job or take part in further training and education (such as childcare, or special help if you have a disability).

You will also get the chance to discuss what kind of jobs might suit you, the amount of money you can expect to earn and the support that Jobcentre Plus may be able to give you once you have started work.

Jobseeker Direct is a telephone service that can help you find a job. When you ring up, the advisers will be able to tell you about the vacancies that exist in your area. You can telephone Jobseeker Direct on 0845 6060 234. Lines are open between 8.00 am and 6.00 pm Monday to Friday and 9.00 am and 1.00 pm on Saturday. It is helpful if you have your full address, your National Insurance number, your date of birth and the vacancy job reference ready when you call.

Benefits

There are two main benefits that young unemployed people can claim: Income Support and Jobseeker's Allowance. There may be other benefits that you are entitled to, and when you go to your local Connexions office or Jobcentre Plus office the advisers there will be able to go through exactly what you can claim.

For further information and a rough guide as to how much you may be able to claim, contact your local Jobcentre Plus or visit the Connexions website, www.connexions.gov.uk. The Direct Gov website has useful information too: www.direct.gov.uk.

Flexible New Deal

Flexible New Deal is designed to help unemployed people who have been getting Jobseeker's Allowance for 12 months (six months in some cases). It is delivered for Jobcentre Plus by 'providers' who will discuss with you the help you may need to get work and help you draw up a plan of action to improve your chances of success among other things. Flexible New Deal can last for a year and during that time you would do some work experience. You can find out if you are eligible to take part by contacting your local Jobcentre Plus.

> *You can find out more about Flexible New Deal by visiting www. direct.gov.uk and putting 'Flexible New Deal' in the search facility on the site.*
>
> **Info**

> **Young Person's Guarantee**
> *At the time of writing, if you are aged between 18–24 and have been on Jobseeker's Allowance for six months or more you are guaranteed an offer of a job, training or work experience. You can find out more from your local Jobcentre Plus.*
>
> **Info**

Work Trial and Employment on Trial

The Jobcentre Plus Network runs several schemes to help people find jobs. One such scheme is Work Trial. This is usually open to people who are aged 25 years or over and who have been out of work for six months or more. However, there are exceptions to this rule, so it is well worth checking with your local Jobcentre Plus office or Jobcentre to see whether you could benefit from this scheme.

Employment on Trial gives you the opportunity to try out a job if you are not certain whether it is the right one for you. To be eligible for the scheme (which basically means that if the job does not work out, you will not jeopardise any benefits you may be entitled to) you have to stay in the job for over 4 weeks but not more than 13, working at least 16 hours in each week. The scheme is only open to those who have been out of work or full-time education for 13 weeks before the job starts.

> *For more information on these schemes, visit www.direct.gov.uk.*

If you are unemployed, it goes without saying that you should be doing everything you can to get a job. See Part Three of this book for all the information you need.

> *Don't forget that Jobseeker Direct can help you to find a job if you are aged 18 or over. You can telephone Jobseeker Direct on 0845 6060 234. Lines are open between 8.00 am and 6.00 pm Monday to Friday and between 9.00 am and 1.00 pm on Saturdays.*

Being unemployed... View from Chris

Having been unemployed and now working, I think I'm in a good position to say what's best. I thought that if I was unemployed I'd get loads of benefits and wouldn't have to bother working, but it's not like that at all. You have to show all the time that you're actively seeking work, and that's like a full-time job itself. I also got really bored because most of my mates got jobs really easily and all I was doing was looking for work (not very well) and getting more and more depressed about always being skint. I started to feel like I was wasting my life. Not having to get up in the mornings isn't fun for long when you know that other people are all going to work, having a laugh with their mates and earning money. That's what I wanted.

I was lucky that I got a job that gave me one day a week to go to college. I'm working towards an NVQ now and I'm earning money too (although I wish it was more!). I'm much happier now than I was this time last year.

The advisers I saw at the Jobcentre Plus office were good for me. They weren't really pushy – I hate that. But they do keep you thinking about what you want to do and the kinds of jobs you might be good at. I think that's important – to try to get something you're good at. After being unemployed you need something that will make you feel good about yourself. I'm really glad I've got that now.

Summary

The key points from this chapter include the following:

- Young people aged 16–25 are twice as likely to be unemployed as those in older age groups.
- Not having any qualifications further increases the likelihood of being unemployed.
- If you are aged 16 or over, your local Jobcentre Plus office is the place to go for help if you are unemployed.
- If you are aged between 16 and 18 then you can also call in to your local Connexions office if you are unemployed.
- Jobseeker Direct is a telephone service that can help you to find a job.
- The two main benefits that you may be able to claim if you are unemployed are Income Support and Jobseeker's Allowance.
- New Deal and Flexible New Deal offers 18- to 25-year-olds the chance to work in the voluntary sector, the Environment Task Force or full-time education and training, among others.
- Work Trial is a scheme that is usually open to people who are aged 25 years or over and who have been out of work for six months or more.
- Employment on Trial gives you the opportunity to try out a job if you are not certain whether it is the right one for you.

Part Six
Practical issues

16
Moving away from home

This chapter looks at:

- living away from home;
- going to university;
- finding accommodation;
- moving away for work;
- making new friends.

Living away from home

Whatever you decide to do when you leave school, there is a possibility that you will have to live away from home, for at least part of the time, to do it.

Going to university

Going to university is an amazing experience for many students. It is exciting and challenging, new and yet daunting all at once. There is a lot to think about, though. For most students this is their first time away from home and the thought of being responsible for all the things you have had help with up until now can be scary! If you are leaving home, there will be no one to do your washing and ironing, no one to do the food shopping, no free taxi service and no one to remind you to get on with your work. But on the positive side, you will be leaving home in a relatively gentle and safe way, and will probably still go home for the holidays!

Although increasing numbers of students are choosing to live at home while they study at university (usually to save money), you may be one of those who decide to leave home. If this is the case, the first thing you will need to do is to find somewhere to live.

Finding accommodation

You should be given advice from your university on how to go about getting accommodation. You will probably be faced with two choices: living in a university-owned hall of residence; or renting a room in a house or a flat close to where you will be studying. This house or flat may be university owned or leased, or it may be on the private rental market.

As soon as you have your place confirmed, get in touch with the university's accommodation office. They will be able to give you all the information you need. If you want to apply for university accommodation, make sure that you get your forms in on time. You may want to visit the university again to look round some of the accommodation options open to you. If you do this, be sure to talk to as many students as you can for some first-hand opinions.

If you apply for university accommodation but do not get a place, ask to go on a waiting list. There are bound to be would-be students dropping out before the first term starts, so you never know, you may be lucky!

> **Info** Take a look at your university's website for more information about finding somewhere to live. The site might include some students' experiences to help you decide what you want to go for.

Making new friends

When you start at university it is really important to make new friends. You will be taking part in new experiences, and so many opportunities will be open to you (not just related to studying, either!). Unless you are happy to integrate with others you could be in for a lonely and isolated time. Sure, it is wise to remember that you are at university to study, but being there also gives you a chance to take part in non-academic activities, even if that is just a prolonged chat over coffee with your mates.

Friendships are often made early on in the term – even in the first week. You will probably find that those you befriend in your first few days will stay friends throughout your course. It goes without saying that you need to trust your instincts when making friends at university. Make sure that the people you befriend want you purely for your friendship and that they have no ulterior motives (such as getting you to join a club or organisation that you are simply not interested in).

If you are living at home and going to university, as increasing numbers of students are choosing to do now, be sure to make friends with other students who are doing the same. Perhaps there is someone you can travel in with or share lifts with? Your experience of university will be slightly different from that of students who are living in halls of residence or house and flat shares around campus, so it will be important to make friends with those who are having a similar experience as you as well as other students.

Making new friends... View from Al

When I first went to university I lived in a hall of residence. It's fairly easy to make friends as you're all together, all in the same circumstances. You naturally have quite a bit in common with each other. I found that the older students were pretty good at making sure that all the freshers were looked after, and within no time at all, people had formed friendship groups. Certain corridors got certain reputations, too! There were some people who seemed to prefer to be on their own rather than part of a big group. In a strange way, these people kind of found each other, too.

I was really surprised when one girl along my corridor suddenly left hall. Apparently she hadn't been happy living like that and wanted to live in a family group. So she left and rented a room in a local family's house. I guess hall isn't for everyone.

Even though being in hall means that you have loads of people around you really close by, it's still important to make friends with people on your course and from other halls. Join societies and get out there so you don't just rely on your mates from hall. It can get pretty intense living and socialising with the same people, so you need to be willing to take part in other activities. I joined the countryside conservers, so we often went out on Sundays to do conservation work. I was also in the rowing club, and that took up quite a bit of time but I did make great friends through it.

I think making friends at uni is just like anything else: the more you put into it, the more you get out of it.

The friends that you make at university could well be friends you keep for life. They will certainly be an important dimension of your enjoyment while studying, so it is worth putting as much into your friendships as you can (provided you have the time, that is!).

Not making friends can leave you feeling isolated and lonely and may even have an impact on the way in which you settle into your course. Some people even leave because they have not managed to settle in. If you are having trouble settling in, there will be help available. All universities have student welfare counsellors who can talk things through with you and help you to see a way forward. Whatever you do, don't attempt to get through these feelings alone; you don't have to. There will always be help out there for you. It is usually a good idea to find out where you can get this help should you ever need it. There will probably be posters up in the student union building or contact numbers in the information that you are given.

Insuring your possessions

Some universities suffer from more crime than others, but it is worth being aware that as a first-year student you may be slightly more vulnerable to theft than other people. Some estimates suggest that one in four students is a victim of crime. Taking out insurance for your possessions is one way of guarding against the misery and inconvenience that theft can cause.

Info

Endsleigh Insurance specialises in student packages. For further information, visit www.endsleigh.co.uk or telephone 0800 028 3571.

There are other companies that offer policies to students, so do ask around for ideas.

Personal safety at university

Although campuses can be relatively safe places to be, you do need to make sure that you are aware of any potential risk situations that you are putting yourself in. You will almost certainly be given advice on your personal safety when you arrive at university. If you are not, find out for yourself what measures the university has taken to ensure your safety as you live and study there. Never walk alone after dark, or in isolated places even with friends, and get into the habit of telling each other what you are doing each day and roughly when you will be back. If a friend is later than you expect, ring his or her mobile or just be aware of watching out for them. In short, look out for each other.

There are specialist books about going to university that will give you more detailed guidance on personal safety. Above all, never takes risks, and trust your instincts. It may be a cliché, but it's better to be safe than sorry.

> *You can find out more about keeping safe from the Suzy Lamplugh Trust website, www.suzylamplugh.org.*
>
> **Info**

Staying healthy at university

Going to university is a great experience, not least because of the relative freedom you have to start living your life in your own way. For many, this can mean making some choices that aren't exactly supportive of great health! Mostly this doesn't matter, and within reason your body can cope with what you throw at it, but it's always worth taking care of your physical body. That can sometimes mean taking additional food supplements or making certain food and lifestyle choices when you're feeling shattered or facing difficult deadlines.

Interestingly, when you're at rest, your brain uses about 20 per cent of your body's energy, and if you're really exerting yourself mentally, this energy consumption will increase. That's why you need to make sure you're putting in good enough fuel to keep everything going so you don't waste valuable socialising time because you've been too sluggish to get your work done!

There are many ways of boosting your brain power through food and drink. These ideas may help:

● Believe it or not, your brain is over 60 per cent fat, so it's really important to make sure that you take in the right amounts of essential fatty acids such as those found in oily fish like salmon and mackerel as well as nuts and seeds. Omega 3 in particular will help to keep your brain healthy.

- Ever been dehydrated and tried to concentrate? It's virtually impossible! Your brain really needs to be properly hydrated in order to operate to its full potential, so make sure you drink plenty of water, especially if you have been drinking alcohol, which can dehydrate you. If you want to feel the difference, try drinking at least 2 litres of water a day.

- Eat breakfast! Skipping this all-important meal has been shown so many times to be a bad thing, so however busy you are, make time for it. Your performance will improve and you'll have more energy through the day, too. Eating a healthy breakfast is even thought to help maintain a healthy weight, so don't ever be tempted to skip it.

- Move more. Exercise is great for getting blood pumping and sending oxygen to the brain, and that's what's going to make it work more efficiently, so take every opportunity to get moving. Choose a sport or activity that you know you'll enjoy so that you actually do it. Also, try to incorporate walking into your daily life as much as possible. You'll save money and stay fit at the same time.

- Top up the healthy bacteria in your gut with a serving of probiotics.

- Keep your iron levels topped up. Foods such as dark-green leafy vegetables, red meat (make sure it's lean), liver (if that's your thing!) and tuna are good sources.

- Protein is great for brain health. Go for beans or poached eggs on toast. Chicken or fish are good choices, too.

- Carbohydrates provide the body with glucose, which is vital for brain health as it cannot store energy. In order to make sure it has a steady supply, go for slow-release carbohydrates such as whole grains and unrefined cereals. Wholewheat pasta is a great choice, and go for brown bread rather than white. And in order for your body to make good use of the carbohydrates you give it, it needs vitamin B1, also found in wholegrains as well as nuts and seeds, among others.

- Don't forget to relax. There will be loads going on when you get to university and it's easy to get caught up in it all without appreciating that you do need to recharge every now and then. Don't wait until you get struck down with a cold or flu before giving yourself some rest time.

- If you know you're going to be drinking, eat a big meal before you go out. If this is a starchy one (containing bread, potatoes or pasta, for example), even better. Always be mindful of the number of units of alcohol you are consuming. It's easy to get totally carried away, but alcohol affects your health and possibly your life, and when you're drunk, your judgement is seriously impaired. Take care of your liver (you only get one, and you need it to function for life) by choosing to drink in moderation. More than 3–4 units a day for men and 2–3 units for women and you just might be developing a problem. If you think this might apply to you, your university's health centre will have advice on sensible drinking and how you might best cut back. Just about every aspect of your life will be adversely affected by excessive alcohol consumption, particularly your love life, so it is definitely a trap worth avoiding. Find out more at www.units.nhs.uk. If you know you'll be drinking through the evening, make sure you have plenty of water, too, and try not to mix alcoholic drinks, as this will give your liver twice as much work to do.

If you're unsure exactly how many units you are drinking, the Drink Aware website has a useful unit calculator as well as other information on the hows and whys of being alcohol-aware. Visit the website at: www.drinkaware.co.uk.

If ever you binge drink, or drink heavily, it is important to give your body at least 48 hours without alcohol so that it can recover.

Info

Moving away for work

If your new job requires you to be mobile, or it is simply too far away for you to continue living at home, you will have to move. This means finding suitable accommodation that is safe, comfortable and affordable. It is probably wise to do this only if there are no other alternatives. Staying at home with your parents for a while can help you to save some money and decide what you want to do: get your own place (if you can afford it), lodge in someone's house, share a house or flat with friends or stay put where you are.

If you will be moving away from home, here are the options open to you:

- Privately rented flats, houses and an array of other possibilities such as mobile homes and houseboats. These could be either furnished or unfurnished.
- Housing association properties.
- Lodging in a spare room in someone's house. Some meals may be provided, too.

- Hostel or hotel/B&B accommodation.
- Buying your own home (although unless you have a very good salary and pretty big deposit, or the assistance of a member of your family, for example, you are unlikely to be able to afford to do this in most parts of the country).

Living anywhere other than your parents' house is going to feel expensive. The first thing you need to do when deciding where to live is to work out what you can realistically afford to pay. Once you have done this, here are some other factors that you will need to take into consideration:

- How will you get to work? (Will you go by foot, use public transport, or go by car or bike?)
- How close you realistically need to live to your place of work. (You can save money by being within walking distance.)
- The additional bills you will have to pay on top of rent. (You can ask to see recent bills, and be sure to find out what is included in the cost.)
- Any hidden costs there may be. Always ask for the full details of what you would be financially responsible for so that there are no hidden shocks!
- If the place is furnished, is there an inventory of what items of furniture, kitchen equipment, etc are there? There should be, and only when you have been through it to check that what should be there really is there should you sign it.
- How is rent to be paid? The usual arrangement is payment one month in advance with a month's rent as a deposit. You should get the deposit back unless you have caused any damage that needs to be repaired. Find out about rent deposit schemes at www.communities.gov.uk.
- How much notice of leaving would you have to give? Do not get locked into lengthy contracts in case you need to get out fairly quickly. A month's notice is common.
- You may be asked by the landlord or landlady for a reference. Don't forget, though, that the rental contract is a two-way thing. Are you happy with the landlord or landlady? Always trust your gut instincts and get advice from your family or friends if you are at all unsure. Landlords are bound by various laws and should provide a good standard of housing. They are providing a service, and if it isn't good enough for you, find somewhere else.

- If you are lodging in someone's house, find out what they do and who else lives in the house. How much of the house would you have access to? Would your room be secure and private? Would you be able to use the washing machine? Would you get a shelf in the fridge?
- Make sure that the place is clean and dry. Are there any telltale signs of damp? Does it smell musty? Are the windows secure?
- Consider the location of the property. Is it in a safe part of town? Is it near a busy main road? Is it somewhere you could envisage living?
- It may feel more like home if you can give it a fresh coat of paint and add your own personal touch to it. Do, however, check with the landlord or landlady before doing anything!

You may have to resort to living somewhere that does not match your ideal, but the chances are that you will be able to make a go of it.

Always ask your boss to be if he or she knows of any accommodation that you could rent. There may be someone who works at the organisation that you are about to join who has a spare room or flat to rent out, or you may be able to share a house with some of the other people starting at the same time as you. There is absolutely no harm in asking, and your new place of work is likely to be a great source of contacts. Other places to look for accommodation are:

- *local lettings agencies;*
- *the Yellow Pages;*
- *the local paper and local radio stations;*
- *newsagents' and post office windows;*
- *the human resources department at the organisation you are going to join.*

Lodging in a house... View from Anna

When I first left home, I lodged in a house owned by an elderly lady. She took lodgers so she didn't get lonely. I had to leave really early for work but she always got up even earlier than me to make my breakfast! When I got in from work she always wanted to know what sort of day I'd had and really took an interest in me.

Although I really appreciated all that she did for me, it did get a bit claustrophobic after a while. I wanted to move to be nearer some of the friends I'd made, so I left and rented a room in a big family house. I'd really hoped that it would be a better situation, but the family rowed all the time and sometimes the dad was in such a bad mood that everyone had to get out of his way. I'd have to wait until they were all out of the way before I could use the kitchen, and when I was home I spent most of the time in my room regretting that I'd ever left my first place!

In the end I joined a house share with my mates, which was best of all. We had a real laugh and if I hadn't changed my job I'd still be there. I guess the lesson I learned is that you don't know what you like and don't like until you give it a go.

If you do leave home, make sure that you stay in touch with the friends and family that you leave behind. They will be a great source of support for you and will almost certainly appreciate your letters, phone calls and e-mails home. If you do write regularly, ask the recipient to keep the correspondence (especially if it is to your parents) as this could become your diary or record of this time in your life.

Making friends

If you have just left school or college and started work for the first time, it may seem a little strange having to start out making friends again. However, it is likely that there will be other people starting at the company at the same time, and even if they are not exactly your type, you can support each other through the first few months as you all find your feet. And they may turn out to be good friends anyway!

You can also make friends by joining local clubs and societies or by doing some voluntary work in your spare time. Your local Citizens' Advice Bureau may have some contact details for you, as might the local Connexions office or local paper. Many towns have their own websites, too, listing details of what's on. The local library will also be a great source of information.

Making friends at work... View from Nikki

I found it really hard to make friends when I first started work. They were all older than me and it felt so different from when I was at college. I got quite down about it, especially as I'd chosen not to go to university, but a lot of my friends had gone and I was getting e-mails from them about what great times they were having.

I knew I had to do something about it, and when I overheard a couple of the others talking about going to the local gym I actually asked if I could go, too. They were fine about it! I felt really embarrassed about butting in like that but I just thought I'd got nothing to lose. We go out quite a lot now and I invited some of them round to my house and cooked a meal. It was a laugh and I think I'm quite accepted now.

I'd always found it really easy to make friends at school but starting out at work is completely different. You really have to make an effort and not expect everything to come to you. I've also joined my local Green Drinks group and that's been a great way to meet people. At least all my friends aren't from work!

Nikki joined her local Green Drinks group. These are set up for people who are interested in the environment, sustainability and all things 'green'. To find out if there is one run in your town, take a look at www.greendrinks.org.

Info

If you are finding it difficult to make friends, make a pact with yourself to do at least one thing a week that will help you to meet new people. Take a deep breath and go for it. Sometimes all it takes is a smile and you've broken the ice.

Action

Summary

The key points from this chapter include the following:

- Going to university is an amazing experience for many students. It is exciting and challenging, new and yet daunting all at once.
- You should be given advice from your university on how to go about getting accommodation.
- When you start at university it is really important to make new friends.
- Taking out insurance for your possessions is one way of guarding against the misery and inconvenience that theft can cause.
- Living anywhere other than your parents' house is going to feel expensive.
- There are many sources of information about finding accommodation, so it is important to look at as many of those as possible.
- Even if making friends and joining clubs and societies might seem daunting when you are in a new location, it is worth the effort and will help you to settle in.

17
Money

This chapter looks at:

- what money means to you;
- money management;
- opening a bank account;
- budgeting;
- 'cheap money';
- getting into debt;
- FE and money;
- HE and money;
- your first job and money.

Whether you are starting work or going to university, money is about to gain a whole new significance! Money means different things to different people, and this greatly affects the way they use it, so it is well worth taking a moment to think about what money means to you.

What does money mean to you? Are you a spender or a saver? A risk taker or someone who always likes to play it safe? Can you stick to a budget or do you always overspend? Is money a means to take part in the world or a hindrance? Are you in control of your money or do you need people to bale you out? Do you see yourself as someone who

Action

wants enough money or as someone who wants to be rich? Take some time to think about your answers to these questions. There is no real need to write your answers down, but do think hard about what your conclusions are.

Money management

It is essential that you manage your money, otherwise the consequences of debt and all the problems that brings could rule your life for decades to come. That may sound gloomy, but the importance of sound money management cannot be overstressed.

Opening a bank account

The easiest way of getting in control of your finances is to have a bank account. If you have not opened one already, these ideas may help:

- Do you have any strong feelings over whether your money should be with a so-called ethical bank? If so, your choices are slightly more limited (see the Information point below).
- Forget the freebies, gimmicks and promotions. For each bank, look closely at the charges you would pay, what would happen if you went overdrawn (took more money out of your account than there was in it) or over your agreed overdraft limit, interest rates, and whether so-called interest-free loans or overdrafts really are that (ask what happens in the long term).
- Think about where you will be able to get cash out. Most banks have cash machines (check that you will not be charged for using another bank's cash machine), and you can often get 'cash back' in many shops, as well as the Post Office. Will there be opportunities near you? Does it matter if there are not? Does the bank offer telephone and internet banking?
- What banking services, exactly, would you have to pay for?
- Shop around and make sure you open an account with the bank that will serve your needs best. Always ask them direct questions about the level of support and understanding they would be prepared to give you in your circumstances.

Your bank will send you a statement of your account showing all incoming money and all outgoing expenditure. Banks usually send these out once a month, although some banks are making statements available to view anytime online. Make sure that you read these statements and check every item. It is a good idea to keep all your receipts at least until the item appears on the statement. Do not throw these statements away when you have checked every item. Always file them away in case you need to refer to them at a later date. Ask your bank about anything on your statement that you do not understand or that you want to question. Never leave statements unopened for weeks on end! Open them as soon as you receive them. Get into this habit and money problems are unlikely to get on top of you before you have a chance to realise what is happening.

It is extremely important to remember that the financial advice you get from a bank is not independent advice. It will be geared towards 'selling' you one of their products, so always be hyper-vigilant.

Independent financial advice is quite hard to come by, and you should be aware that some so-called financial advisers are simply promoting the financial products (such as accounts and pensions) of one particular company. If you need financial advice, ask at your Connexions office to see what they suggest for your area.

Two banks that work to strict ethical codes are The Co-operative Bank and Triodos Bank. Neither have as many branches as some of the other banks, but that is not a problem with telephone, internet and postal banking. If you would like to find out more, visit www.co-operative bank.co.uk and www.triodos.co.uk.

Info

Budgeting

All but the filthy rich have to budget! In fact, it is the only way to get on top of your money. This means planning for your known and expected expenditure (such as rent, bills and food) and whatever is left over for your spending money.

The most essential thing to remember when budgeting is: do not spend, or plan to spend, money that you do not actually have. In order to draw up a budget, you first need to work out exactly how much money is available to you each week and exactly how much you spend. For example, if you are working and your take-home pay (that is, what is left after tax and National Insurance) is £300 a week, then that is the amount available to you.

Next, write down a list of everything that you spend money on over a week. The following suggestions will help:

- rent or board and lodging (if you are at your parents' home, you include any contribution to the housekeeping);
- food;
- utility bills such as gas and electricity;
- travel and transport costs (particularly if you own a car);
- laundry;
- insurance;
- mobile phone;
- hobbies;
- clothing;
- union or professional association fees;
- going out;
- presents and cards;
- books, magazines and newspapers;
- stationery, photocopying;
- equipment;
- other.

Next to each item, write down as accurately as possible what you have to spend on it. Remember that essential items (such as rent and food) have to be paid for first.

If there is any money left over, you can put that towards some savings. OK, it is not always that simple, but you get the general gist!

When budgeting, do not forget these golden rules:

- Write yourself a budget sheet that shows your sources of income (for example, job, student loan and so on), your expenditure (for example, rent, bills and food), your budget for each item of expenditure and what you actually spend. Get in the habit of keeping an eye on what comes in and what goes out, and you will almost certainly not get in a financial mess.
- Never go over your agreed overdraft limit. Always get in touch with the bank in good time to make sure that you can extend your overdraft; it

is only polite! If you do not, you may be hit with astronomical charges or a refusal for an extension (but remember, they are allowed to do that). This could be right at the worst time – when your rent is due and you have no money left to buy food.

- Economise whenever you can. Before you buy anything, always ask yourself: do I really need it? If you think you do, try going without it for a week (not food, obviously!) and seeing whether you still think you need the item then. The chances are that you won't, and you will have saved yourself some money.

- Think about where you can cut back if you are consistently spending more than you have. For example, do you need to buy magazines or can you club together with a friend and share the cost? Can you buy anything in bulk with others and benefit from lower prices? Can you recycle anything that you might once have thrown away?

- If you are thinking of getting a job as a student to make ends meet (and about 75 per cent of students do), remember that your studies should come first, so do not do anything that will take hours out of your study time or mean that you cannot have time off when you need it. Agency work might be best, as you can usually choose your hours and decline work when you need to focus on your studies.

- Remember that every pound you overspend has to come from some-where. Where is that? Blagging from your parents? Your overdraft? A student loan? Your credit card? Are you getting that money from the cheapest place possible?

Getting cheap money

The cheapest money you can get is an interest-free loan. If this is from a bank (in the form of a free overdraft), you will have to repay it, but if it is from your parents or a member of your family, there is a chance that you won't, or you will at least be able to arrange a way of paying it back that suits you all.

If you borrow money and have to pay interest on the loan, it is essential to shop around so that you get the best deal. The things to look out for are the length of the loan and the annual percentage rate of charge (APR). Table 17.1 shows you how much you would have to pay back on a £1,000 loan over various lengths and at different APR rates. It is quite shocking when you see the figures in black and white!

Table 17.1

APR	1 year	3 years	5 years	10 years
5%	£1,027	£1,077	£1,129	£1,266
10%	£1,053	£1,154	£1,262	£1,557
15%	£1,078	£1,231	£1,398	£1,867
20%	£1,102	£1,308	£1,536	£2,191
25%	£1,126	£1,385	£1,675	£2,523
30%	£1,149	£1,461	£1,815	£2,860

If you need to borrow money, always ask your bank about what it can offer you. Don't be tempted to run up large credit card debts, as the chances are you will be paying far more interest than you need to. Make sure that you fully understand the implications of borrowing money. If there is an interest rate attached to the loan, you will pay back more than you borrow – considerably more in some cases. Personal debt is becoming an immense problem in the United Kingdom. The latest figures available show that consumer credit lending now stands at £225bn (Jan 2010). Total UK personal debt stood at £1,463bn at the end of Jan 2010. Keeping debt under control is crucial.

> **Info**
>
> *BBC Radio 1's The Surgery section is packed with useful information. It is well worth spending some time browsing www.bbc.co.uk/switch/ surgery/advice/your_world/world/money. You can find out more about debt from the Credit Action website, www.creditaction.org.uk.*

Professional and Career Development Loans

If you are aged 18 or over and want to further your career by doing a vocational course, you may be eligible for a Professional and Career Development Loan. You can only apply for these loans if you do not have reasonable or adequate funds to pay for the course yourself. If eligible, you can borrow between £300 and £10,000 to help you to fund up to two years' learning (plus one year's practical work).

For further information about Professional and Career Development Loans, visit www.direct.gov.uk or telephone 0800 585 505.

Info

What if it all goes wrong?

The one thing to remember about getting into financial difficulties is that the sooner you seek help, the less likely you are to get into serious debt. Don't put your head in the sand about it. The problem will not go away, and procrastination could land you in serious trouble. The sooner you get advice, the sooner you will be able to sort out a sensible budget and plan for the future. Do not borrow more money from potentially unscrupulous sources or simply increase your overdraft. Go straight to your bank or to your parents or another trusted relative or friend and be honest about the situation you are in. Gather all your bank statements and (if you have a credit card) credit card statements together and ask for help in getting straight for the future.

Don't feel that you are alone if you get into debt. Most people do at some stage of their lives and it is pretty hard to find a student who does not owe money! Just make sure that you face up to the reality of debt as soon as it happens and you will be able to keep it under control.

FE and money

You do not have to pay course fees for FE courses (post-16 education up to the age of 19). You may also be entitled to a little help with travelling expenses and living costs if you are suffering severe hardship.

However, it is wise to get information on this as early as possible before starting the course, as you will need to complete claim forms and some of these have to be in months before courses start. Your local Connexions office can help you to find out what you are entitled to, but do ask their advice as early as possible.

Info *To find out more about funding for your FE courses, contact your local authority (LA). Contact details will be in your telephone book, usually under the county or borough name, or listed in the front pages.*

Education Maintenance Allowance (EMA)

The EMA is a weekly payment of up to £30 that is intended to help you to cover the day-to-day costs of studying at the ages of 16, 17 and 18. For example, it`could help towards the cost of books, equipment, travelling and so on.

The EMA is dependent on the amount of income your household receives, so if this is below £30,810 a year, you will be eligible to apply. However, this is not money for nothing! Once you enrol on a course you must sign an EMA contract and attend all of your course sessions. There are also expectations of you in terms of course work and progress.

For more information about EMA, you can ask at your local Connexions office or visit http://ema.direct.gov.uk. You can also call the freephone helpline on 0800 121 8989. For details relating to Scotland, visit www.emascotland.com; for information relating to Wales, visit www.studentfinancewales.co.uk; and for Northern Ireland, go to www.delni.gov.uk.

You may well be entitled to other forms of support to help you to stay on for FE, so make sure that you ask your local Connexions or careers office all about what is available.

HE and money

If you are planning to go into HE, you will almost certainly have given money some thought. HE is not just about having the qualifications to get on to the course you want; it is also about having a sensible idea about how you are going to fund your time at university.

Funding for students is often in the news and has been the subject of much debate and a few protests recently. It is important that you know exactly what you would be responsible for paying for as a student (fees and maintenance – in other words, living expenses) and what help you can legitimately claim. Most of this information will come either from your LA (the one where you live, not where you plan to study if it is different) or from the university itself.

Read the Information point below and visit the appropriate website for you. Make a list of what you think you are entitled to claim and the forms that you need to fill in. Now contact your LA to double-check that you have all the relevant information. Remember to mention the fact if you are a student with a child or with a disability.

Then, write out a timetable of what you need to do next. Pay special attention to the fact that most forms will need to be in by certain times. If you miss key deadlines, you will probably end up having to deal with disruptions to the start of your course or late payments of money you are entitled to.

There is a lot of information on higher education student support on the Department for Business, Innovation and Skills website: http://bis. gov.uk./

See also www.direct.gov.uk and put 'student finance' in the search box.

If you are in Scotland, visit www.student-support-saas.gov.uk.

For information about financial support in Wales, visit www. studentfinancewales.co.uk, and for Northern Ireland go to www.delni. gov.uk (Student Support branch).

Other sites to explore are:
www.nusonline.co.uk – the National Union of Students
www.funderfinder.org.uk – if you are looking for charity support
www.scholarship-search.org.uk – for funding sources.

Student loans

At the time of writing, there are different types of student loan including tuition fee loans and maintenance loans. On top of any contributions you will be making towards tuition fees, you will be paying for accommodation, books, travel, clothes, going out and so on. All of this can add up, and unless you are lucky enough to have parents who can give you money to pay for it all, or large sums of money of your own saved from work that you have done during a gap year, you are likely to need to take out a student loan. Student loans are not unlimited. It is worth keeping in mind that the amount that you can borrow in student loans is almost certainly not going to be enough to live on. Think about how you can boost this through your own earnings, an agreed overdraft (make sure you know exactly what costs are involved in this) or borrowings from family members if possible.

Student loans, as the name implies, do have to be paid back, but only when you have left university. Even then, you only start to repay them when you start earning at a particular rate (at current rates you would start repaying when your income hits above £15,000).

Many student advisers feel that students should take out maximum student loans regardless of whether they think they will need them. If you find that you do have some money left over (this is not exactly likely, but possible if your budgeting skills are on top form), put it into a savings account, quickly, and make sure that it is earning at an interest rate that is higher than inflation. That way, you will make yourself some money – more than you need to pay back!

Don't delay in sending in your forms for a student loan; you need to make sure that you make all the deadlines, otherwise you could face a delay in the money actually reaching your bank account.

Info

All you need to know about student loans can be found on the Student Loans Company website, www.slc.co.uk.

A word about debt

It would be neglectful not to mention a word about student debt here. While there are definitely significant social and academic benefits of going to university and studying for a degree, it is a big financial commitment. Unless you are fortunate enough to receive substantial sums of money from your parents or family to see you through university, or you work like crazy every spare second to earn as much money as possible while studying (not advised!), it is likely that you will get into some degree of debt. You will see stories in the media about student debt levels and how they are rising. Some studies have also found that leaving university with debt that takes time to pay off prevents some students from even thinking about buying a home.

It would be a shame if fears of debt put you off studying for a degree. Do at least sit down and prepare a detailed budget, taking into account any money you have saved, any you can rely on from family members, any grants, loans and bursaries you have access to and any earnings you can expect from jobs you take while studying.

Be as realistic as possible and aim to think about any potential debt as an investment in your future. Yes, the prospect of debt needs to be taken seriously, but don't let it put you off studying without finding out all you can about the support available.

Sponsorship

It is possible for some students to be sponsored to complete a course. This is not as common as it used to be but there are still some sponsorships to be had, particularly if you want to enter the armed forces or have an NHS-funded place. The NHS Business Services Authority administers the NHS Bursary Scheme for eligible NHS and social work students. Visit www.nhsbsa.nhs.uk/Students.aspx for further information.

Some universities offer sponsorships and bursaries too, but these will have fairly strict criteria attached to them and will probably be snapped up early. Do your homework and get in touch with your university as early as possible to find out whether there is anything you could apply for. It is best to do this before you get an offer of a place, so that you have all the relevant information needed to apply for sponsorship as soon as you know you will be going to that university. Again, watch out for any deadlines, as late applications probably will not be considered.

Don't ever depend on receiving sponsorship or bursaries. They are pretty few and far between and there may be a catch involved (read all the small print!).

Info

www.scholarship-search.org.uk/ is a comprehensive guide to all you need to know when planning and organising your finances as a student. Check it out!

Funding available for Scottish students studying in Scotland

This section gives an overview of the funding available for **Scottish students** from August 2009. Whatever your age, abilities or family responsibilities, you can apply to get help, as there are many sources of funding available. One or more of them may well apply to you, whether you want to:

● stay on at school;
● go to college or university;
● study full-time or part-time.

What's on offer?

The financial support you get will depend on different factors such as:

● what course you want to study;
● your income and family circumstances;
● how old you are;
● where you want to study;
● whether you want to study full-time, part-time or by distance learning.

Some funding comes as a grant, some as a loan and some in the form of free course fees. Most is income assessed and there is different support depending on the type of course you want to do.

Do I qualify?

To be eligible to apply for some funding you must meet certain residence conditions. These are complicated, and we advise you to contact your local college (for further education courses) or the Student Awards Agency for Scotland (SAAS) (for higher education courses) if you are in any doubt about your residence status.

See the Quick Guide presented in Table 17.2 for a breakdown of what's available.

Table 17.2

		Full-time		**Part-time**		**Distance Learning**	
Type of Funding	Staying at School	Further Education	Higher Education	Further Education	Higher Education	FE	HE
Course Fees							
Tuition Fee		✓	✓	✓	✓	✓	✓
ILA Scotland		✓		✓	✓	✓	✓
Career Development Loan		✓	✓	✓	✓	✓	✓
Living Costs							
Education Maintenance Allowances	✓	✓					
Student Loans			✓		✓		✓
NHS Bursaries			✓				
HE Young Student Bursary			✓				
HE Young Student Outside Scotland Bursary			✓				
FE Maintenance Bursary		✓					

Table 17.2 continued...

Type of Funding	Staying at School	Full-time		Part-time		Distance Learning	
		Further Education	Higher Education	Further Education	Higher Education	FE	HE
Living Costs							
Travel Costs		✓	✓	✓		✓	
Study Costs		✓		✓		✓	
Help for Dependants							
Adult Dependant Grant		✓	✓				
Child Tax Credit		✓	✓	✓	✓	✓	✓
Lone Parents Grant			✓				
Lone Parents Childcare Grant			✓				
Childcare Funds		✓	✓	✓		✓	
Other Support							
Disabled Students Allowance			✓		✓		✓
Additional Support Needs for Learning Allowance		✓		✓			
Discretionary Funds		✓	✓	✓	✓	✓	✓
Vacation Grant for Care Leavers			✓				
Charities		✓	✓	✓	✓		

NB: This is a general guide and only indicates the funding that you may receive.

Full-time

Staying at school

If you wish to stay on at school after your school leaving date, you may receive an **Education Maintenance Allowance** (EMA).

- This gives you up to £30 a week during term time, depending on your household income
- plus two bonuses of £150 if you remain on your course and make good progress.
- Find out more from www.emascotland.com.

Further education students

Generally, full-time students do not pay fees. Check with your chosen college if you are in any doubt.

If you are a school leaver going to college, you may also be eligible for an EMA (as above), or you could receive a non-repayable bursary of up to £89.07 per week, but this depends on age, family circumstances and income.

Some of the other financial help you may get is:

- **travel expenses** – if you are under 18, this allowance is not means-tested;
- **Additional Support Needs for Learning Allowance** – this offers additional travel and study help to students with disabilities, on top of other disability grants and benefits, and is not means-tested;
- also, every college operates a **Discretionary Fund**, and students with particular financial difficulties or emergency needs can apply for assistance.

Contact your college bursary officer for advice on what support you may be eligible for.

Higher education students

The Student Awards Agency for Scotland (SAAS) pays the tuition fees for eligible students studying at publicly funded institutions in Scotland.

- The main source of help with living expenses is through an income-assessed **student loan**. The maximum loan is £4,625 for students living away from home and £3,665 for those living at home. An **additional loan** of £605 is available to young students from families with an income of up to £21,760.
- Some young students may qualify for a **Young Student Bursary** (a means-tested non-repayable grant) of up to £2,640 a year instead of part of the loan, so it reduces the amount of loan you need to take out.

Talk to SAAS about the additional funding that is available; this includes:

- **travel costs**;
- **Disabled Students' Allowance** (DSA) for those students who have additional expenditure while undertaking their course because of their disability;
- students who are experiencing particular financial difficulty can apply for assistance from their institution's **Discretionary Fund**;
- a **Vacation Grant for Care Leavers** of up to £105 a week to help students who were previously in care with accommodation costs.

> **Info**
>
> *Find out more from the Student Awards Agency for Scotland (SAAS) at www.saas.gov.uk or on 0845 111 1711.*

Part-time

Further education

Most students studying part-time and on distance learning courses will have to pay tuition fees. However, if you are in receipt of certain benefits, on a low income or are disabled, you may be eligible for free tuition.

- You may also be eligible for the **Individual Learning Account (ILA) Scotland** scheme (see below).
- You may also be eligible for support towards appropriate **study and travel expenses**, as well as the **Additional Support Needs for Learning Allowance**.

Higher education

Most students studying part-time and on distance learning courses will have to pay tuition fees. However, a '**fee waiver**' scheme can provide you with fee support if you are unemployed or on a low income.

- You may also be eligible for the **ILA Scotland** scheme (see below).
- You may also be eligible for the **Disabled Students' Allowance** (DSA), which is not income-assessed.

Other sources of funding

ILA Scotland

ILA Scotland can help pay for a wide range of learning with a variety of approved learning providers. If you are aged 16 or over and live in Scotland and your income is £22,000 or less per year or are on benefit, then you may qualify for up to £500 each year towards the cost of learning.

> *For information on ILA Scotland and to request an application pack, call the free ILA Scotland helpline phone on 0808 100 1090 or visit the website at www.ilascotland.org.uk for advice about what learning is available.*
>
> **Info**

Career Development Loans (CDLs)

CDLs are deferred repayment commercial bank loans available to cover a wide range of vocational training or education for adults. The Government supports these loans by paying the interest on the loan while the individual is undertaking his or her training. You can borrow between £300 and £10,000 to support any course of learning that will help you in your career.

> *Further information about the CDL scheme can be obtained on freephone 0800 585 505.*
>
> **Info**

Info

Further information
To find out more about the various financial help available, contact:

Learndirect Scotland

If you want to get into learning but aren't sure where to start, contact Learndirect Scotland on their free helpline number, 0808 100 9000. Alternatively, browse around for ideas on their website, www.learndirect scotland.com.

Student Awards Agency for Scotland (SAAS)

For more information on higher education student finance, contact SAAS at saas.geu@scotland.gov.uk or telephone 0845 111 1711 or visit their website, www.saas.gov.uk.

Your local college

For more information on further education student finance, contact your local college. Contact Learndirect Scotland for a list of bursary offices.

Careers Scotland

Careers Scotland gives guidance to anyone in Scotland about work or learning. The aim is to increase participation in learning, employment and provide guidance. Find out more on their website, www.careersscotland. org.uk.

Scottish Government

You can visit their website, www.scotland.gov.uk/fundingforlearners.

Your first job and money

Starting your first full-time job is incredibly exciting. It is probably your first taste of the adult world outside of education and your first experience of earning a wage.

Before you start work, you should be told exactly what your conditions of employment are. This includes how many days of paid holiday a year you are entitled to and what benefits and bonuses you may be entitled to. You will also be given details of what is expected of you and what happens if you do not keep your side of the contract (usually called 'disciplinary procedures'). You will be asked to sign the contract. If none of this happens, it is important that you ask what the terms of your employment are. There may be a union or professional association that you can join, and it is usually a good idea to do this. They can offer advice and protection as well as numerous other benefits. You usually have to pay a small amount each month to be a member.

There is a minimum wage which is the very least you should be paid. The rates since October 2009 are as follows:

- *16- to 17-year-olds: £3.57 per hour;*
- *18- to 21-year-olds (the development rate): £4.83 per hour;*
- *22 and over (the adult rate): £5.80 per hour.*

You can find out all you need to know about the National Minimum Wage either from your local Connexions office or from www.direct. gov.uk.

The chances are that your earnings will be paid directly into your bank account on a monthly basis. Alternatives include being given a cheque to pay into your account yourself or an envelope stuffed with money (although the latter is highly unusual now). The amount that you are paid will almost certainly be out of your control, although as you gain experience over the coming years you may be in a position to negotiate your salary upwards. As well as pay, you should also receive a pay slip.

If you think that you are being underpaid and want to make a complaint, you can telephone 0845 6000 678 or visit www.hmrc.gov.uk/nmw/ help.htm.

When you get your pay slip, you will notice that what you receive is less than your salary because tax and National Insurance will already have been deducted. If these contributions have not been deducted, it could be that you are not earning enough. Don't forget that you don't pay tax on the first £6,475 of your earnings.

> **Info**
>
> *If you have any questions at all about tax and National Insurance, your local tax office will be able to help you. Find the contact details in your local* Yellow Pages. *You might also like to look at the HM Revenue & Customs website: www.hmrc.gov.uk.*
>
> *To find out about the National Minimum Wage and how it applies to you, telephone 0845 600 0678. For information relating to Northern Ireland, telephone 0845 6500 207.*

Wages are usually paid at the end of the month for work done that month. This might mean that for the first month you have very little, if any, money. If this is a problem to you, you could ask your employer if your first month's wages could be paid weekly to help you to budget.

Summary

The key points from this chapter include the following:

- Part of understanding money is knowing what it means to you.
- It is important to open a bank account.
- Budgeting keeps you on top of your money. Do not spend, or plan to spend, money that you have not got.
- The cheapest form of money is an interest-free loan. Be very careful about any money that you borrow, and check the rate of interest that you will be charged.
- If you start sinking into debt, ask for help. There are several places you can go.
- There is financial help available for FE and HE students.

- There is a minimum wage that school leavers wanting to find work should be aware of.
- Your earnings above a certain level will be subject to tax and National Insurance.

18

Advice: working with parents and advisers

This chapter looks at:

- careers advice – where can you get it?;
- working with advisers;
- the Connexions service;
- special needs and equal opportunities in FE;
- special needs and equal opportunities in HE;
- special needs and equal opportunities when starting work;
- discrimination.

There probably is not a person alive on the planet today who has not received advice at some stage of his or her life. We all need it to help us make potentially difficult decisions and you are fortunate in that there are many sources of help and advice out there for you as you make your decisions.

Careers advice

There are several sources of careers advice that luckily are usually free of charge for 16-year-olds (unless you choose to see an independent adviser, who may make a charge). Just remember that the more involved you are in this whole process, the more likely it is that you will get something out of it. Don't be a passive recipient of advice! Be clear in your head exactly what it is you want to know and ask plenty of questions.

The Connexions service

There will be a Connexions office in your nearest town that is your point of contact for the Government's support service for all young people aged between 13 and 19 in England. Connexions offers a huge range of services and advice on just about everything you could ever want to make the transition between school and adult life as smooth as possible. It basically joins Government services together with private and voluntary organisations to ensure that young people have access to the best advice possible.

The support that Connexions offers is practical as well as informative. To get an idea of the full scope and range of what is on offer, do take a while to browse the Connexions website, and remember to check this website every time you have an issue you need help with. The topics covered are about not just work and studying, but also health, housing, drugs and more. Most Connexions offices also have a careers library that you can browse, as well as computers that you can use for careers-related work.

> *You will find your nearest Connexions office either through the website www.connexions.gov.uk or by looking in your* Yellow Pages. *Connexions offices are staffed by qualified personnel, advisers and their support staff. You may well have already come across Connexions staff, as they visit schools a lot.*

Info

The careers teacher and library

Your school or college careers teacher and library are likely to be great sources of help and advice. The careers teacher can help you in many ways, but in particular he or she is likely to:

● organise visits from local employers, careers advisers, and colleges and universities;

- allow you to use computer guidance programs that can help you to iden-tify careers paths and the qualifications that you need to follow them;
- help you to progress through the decision-making process – some careers teachers encourage students to keep careers logs or diaries documenting the process;
- run careers fairs;
- organise work-experience placements;
- keep the careers library well stocked with the latest information;
- tell you about useful websites to look at.

It is a good idea to talk to your careers teacher about any careers matter that you need help with or advice about. He or she is there to help you. If there is anything you particularly want to know about that has not been covered, you could ask whether an outside speaker could come in to talk to you about it. Or better still, ask if you can organise this yourself!

Independent consultants

Independent careers consultants charge for their services, which are likely to be very good, but it should be remembered that there is such a huge amount of excellent advice that is free of charge (in books, on the internet and via the Connexions service, to name but a few) that it would be surprising if you needed to use the services of an independent careers adviser at this stage.

> *It goes without saying that if you want to use an independent consultant, try to get one on personal recommendation rather than picking one 'blind' from the telephone book. You need to know a little about the consultant, his or her business and his or her specialist areas of knowledge.*

Parents and carers

Your parents or other adults who act as parents are bound to be able to offer you practical advice, and it is usually a good idea to enlist their help. You are facing a period of change in your life, and this can make you and those who care for you feel apprehensive. Get them on board and involved, and you will be able to gain from their experience and ideas at the same time as helping to reduce their anxiety!

However, don't forget that the decisions you make must ultimately be yours. You are the one who will need to follow them through, and if you choose a course or job simply to please someone else, you are likely to end up feeling resentful. That's no good for anyone! Use the help and advice of others, let them help you to research options and provide resources and perhaps some useful contacts, but make sure that the decision you make is yours. This will ensure that you are as motivated as possible about the coming years. And the chances are, your parents will be in agreement with you.

Just remember that although you are in the middle of a really busy time, what with applications to write, coursework to complete and exams to revise for, showing your appreciation for all your family has done for you will go a long way in keeping them on your side, even if this is only a simple 'thank you'.

Special needs and equal opportunities

Everyone has needs. Often these can be met within the usual framework of education and training available to all, but sometimes additional arrangements have to be made to ensure that we all have as equal an opportunity to succeed as possible.

If you have particular needs that are not 'mainstream', you will probably already be used to additional arrangements being made to ensure that you are being supported. Other people, such as your parents or your teachers at school, will have had the responsibility to arrange this support for you. However, now you will be responsible for it yourself, although of course you can expect to be helped through this process.

Laws that came into effect in October 2004 may have an impact on you if you are disabled. For further information, visit the Equality and Human Rights Commission website, www.equalityhumanrights.com.

Info

Special needs and equal opportunities in FE

If you find that you cannot pursue the FE courses that you want at your local college because of your particular needs, there are some possibilities:

- Some colleges of FE are able to offer courses for specific groups of people.
- Live-in facilities are available at some FE colleges to enable you to attend your courses either alone or with help.
- Some colleges of FE are fully residential and adapted specifically for the needs of their students.

> **Info**
>
> *Your local Connexions service or local authority should be able to help you to find out about FE colleges to suit your needs. The National Bureau for Students with Disabilities (SKILL) can give you up-to-date information, too, in particular on funding issues. Find out more at www.skill.org.uk (and see also Part Six of this book).*

If you are disabled, it is worth keeping in mind that you must not, by law, be treated any less favourably by your FE college than non-disabled students are. You should not be placed at a 'substantial disadvantage', so your college should make reasonable adjustments to avoid this.

Once you have chosen a college of FE to continue your studies in, it is a good idea to make an appointment to speak to the Student Welfare Adviser or the equivalent to discuss exactly what support you might be entitled to and how you go about claiming it. It can be complicated to navigate your way through this, as different funds come from different 'purses' (some will come from the college itself, some from the local authority, and you may be entitled to claim some form of benefit, too), probably meaning that you have to make several applications (more forms!). If you can get someone to take you through this process, it will be very much easier than attempting it without advice and help.

After 16 – what's new?

www.after16.org.uk is a website for teenagers and young people who have an impairment or disability and need to know about what opportunities there are for them when they leave school.

Info

Special needs and equal opportunities in HE

Depending on the nature of your particular needs, you should research suitable potential universities very carefully. The Connexions service may be able to help with this, as will SKILL and your current school or college. Contact your LA as soon as you know that you are applying for HE and ask to be told about the full range of allowances and grants that might be available to you.

The Student Loans Company can give you the latest details about how much you can borrow and how it will be calculated. You may be given longer to pay your loan off if you have extra costs because of your disability.

Info

Starting work

Fortunately, there is plenty of help out there for you if you have particular needs and plan to start work. Your local Connexions office will be up to date on what you need to know, and your local Jobcentre Plus will have specialist advisers you can consult. They have a Disability and Financial Services team as well as Disability Employment Advisers. There may also be local groups and organisations that could offer you support. Ask at your local Citizens' Advice Bureau or look in your telephone book under 'Disability'.

Since October 2004 it has been unlawful for any employer to discriminate against a disabled person when choosing someone for a job or considering people for promotion, dismissal or redundancy. Check out the Equality and Human Rights Commission website for further information (see below).

Discrimination

Discrimination is illegal on many grounds, and it is wise to be aware of exactly what your rights are when it comes to disability discrimination, sexual discrimination, racial discrimination and religious discrimination. There are laws to protect you, so if you suspect you are being discriminated against or treated unfairly in any way, do seek help and advice.

Info

The Equality and Human Rights Commission is a new organisation designed to promote equality and human rights for all. Its main work is centred on reducing inequality, eliminating discrimination, protecting human rights and helping to make sure that everyone has a fair chance to participate in society. You can find out more by visiting the Equality and Human Rights Commission website, www.equalityhumanrights.com.

Summary

The key points in this chapter include the following:

- Sometimes we all need advice to help us to make the right decisions.
- Careers advice can come from many sources.
- Connexions is the place to go to for information and advice about how to make the transition to adult life as smooth as possible.
- Your school or college careers teacher or library will be able to go through your career options with you.
- There are independent careers consultants but there is usually no need for teenagers to use their services.
- If you have particular needs that are not met within what is known as the 'mainstream', you will need to be responsible for making sure that you get the help that you need once you leave school.
- The student welfare adviser at your college or university will be able to help you to claim all the support that you are entitled to.
- Your local Jobcentre Plus office will be able to help you to look after your particular needs when you start work.

- Discrimination is illegal on several grounds, but unfortunately it does still happen sometimes. If you think that you are being discriminated against, there are organisations you can go to for specialist help.

19
Dealing with problems

This chapter looks at:

- feeling down or depressed;
- getting help;
- the meaning of stress;
- the symptoms of stress;
- dealing with stress.

Feeling down or depressed

It is a sad fact of life that there will be times when we feel that life is against us and it all seems too much. This can happen to everyone, and if anyone tells you that it does not happen to them, the chances are that they are not being completely honest!

It is not always possible to detect our personal warning signs that things are getting on top of us until it feels too late. If you can be alert to changes in your mood, feelings and attitudes, you may be able to ask for help sooner rather than later.

Telltale signs that we may be struggling with our emotions are:

- general feelings of discontent;
- disturbed sleep;
- mood swings;

- inability to concentrate;
- feelings of isolation;
- getting frequent infections;
- not wanting to socialise with friends;
- feeling tired all the time;
- feeling tearful;
- feeling aggressive;
- being drawn to caffeine, alcohol, drugs, smoking.

If you find that you are experiencing any of these feelings, it is really important that you talk to someone about it as soon as possible. Even if only one or two of these apply to you, don't struggle on alone. Take action sooner rather than later.

Get a piece of paper and write at the top of the page the words: I feel…

Then write down everything that comes to mind. If it takes a while for your thoughts to flow, don't worry.

Underneath that, write the words: Things I would like to change are…

Then write down all the feelings and situations that you would like to change. If there is anything in your list that you know you need help with, underline it.

Choose the item on your list that is giving you the most grief right now and make a promise to yourself to get help to resolve the situation.

Action

Getting help

There are many sources of help that you can go to if you feel in need. Even if you can objectively understand why you feel bad (for example, you have just failed your A levels and will have to resit them), you are still entitled to help to get through this time and start to feel better. The following ideas may help.

Friends and family

Our friends and family usually know us best of all and can detect even the smallest of changes in our mood. If you have a good relationship with your family, they are likely to be a great source of support for getting through problems. That said, you may feel that you want to talk to someone who does not know you so well, in which case there are other places to turn to.

Your GP

Your GP will be able to point you in the right direction of appropriate support. You do not just have to have a physical problem to consult your GP; he or she can help with emotional issues too. You do not have to agree to what your GP suggests, but you can at least find out what suggestions he or she has. While you are at the surgery for your appointment, have a good look at the notice board and leaflets that will be on display there. If you are not happy with the way in which your GP has dealt with you, ask to see a different GP.

Your school or college

There will be someone at your school or college who has responsibilities for student welfare. Not only will he or she be able to offer practical advice and guidance, but he or she may also be able to make allowances for you if necessary.

Counselling

Counselling is open to anyone. You can either go to a private practitioner (see your *Yellow Pages* for further details) or ask to be referred to a counsellor by your GP (this will be free of charge). There are different types of counselling, so if you find that it does not work very well for you, it could just mean that you need to try a different kind of counselling, or a different counsellor. Some counsellors use tools such as artwork and creative writing to help their clients to work through their problems.

Finding a counsellor can be difficult if you do not know someone who could personally recommend one. If this is the case, visit the website of the British Association for Counselling and Psychotherapy (www.bacp. co.uk) for information on how to find an accredited counsellor in your area. Most reputable private counsellors will have a sliding scale of fees for students, young people and those on low incomes.

The Samaritans

The Samaritans are a telephone listening service for those who need to talk. You do not need to be suicidal to call; the Samaritans are there to help all sorts of people with a huge range of problems. If they can direct you to a more appropriate service, they will (for example, if you think you are pregnant and feel terrified, they will give you the contact details of a local clinic to go to). You can telephone anonymously so that no one will know you have made the call.

> *You can telephone the Samaritans 24 hours a day, 7 days a week on 08457 909090.*
>
> *For more information on what the Samaritans can do for you, visit www.samaritans.org.uk.*

Info

Youth agencies

There will almost certainly be a drop-in centre in your town specifically for young people. It will also have loads of information on services for young people in the area and could be a good place to go if you need some confidential advice from someone you do not know. Check out your *Yellow Pages* or local library for more information.

Self-help organisations

There are hundreds of self-help organisations that may be able to help you with any problems or issues you have. Either contact your local Citizens' Advice Bureau or search the internet to see what you can come up with.

Solving problems... View from Steve

I really didn't see my depression coming. I thought I was on top of things and didn't see any of my mates suffering, so I didn't have anything to compare myself with. My family kept asking me if I was OK; they obviously thought something was wrong. I just felt worse and worse as the weeks went by. I'd taken my A levels and wasn't that worried about the results. I'd decided to take a year out but didn't yet know exactly what I was going to do with my time.

As I started looking around for ideas, it just kind of hit me that I wasn't that interested in anything. I was really worried about how I was going to pay for my time at university as I don't like being in debt, but I just couldn't drum up any enthusiasm for anything. I started staying in and watching TV in my room rather than going out, and days started to fly by. Some of my friends left for uni and I started wondering if I'd done the right thing. My parents kept trying to help but I pushed them away.

Then one day I was at the doctor's for a bad cough I couldn't shake off and he asked me if I felt depressed. Just as he said it I started to cry. I felt stupid but I knew that he'd hit on exactly how I'd been feeling for the last six months if I'm honest with myself.

I had a great GP. He encouraged me to talk to my family about how I felt and said he didn't want to prescribe any drugs until I'd tried some counselling. I was so nervous before my first appointment; I had no idea what would happen for a whole hour. But it's not that bad at all. In fact, I really enjoyed the sessions in the end and got so much better that I didn't ever need to take any prescribed drugs.

The one thing that still worries me about what happened to me is the nagging question: what would have happened if I hadn't gone to the doctor for that cough? How much worse would I have got without realising? My counsellor told me that one in four British men suffer from depression. It's so common, but how many could be helped if they only knew they needed to get advice?

In a funny way the whole experience has been great. I've learned a lot about myself and I'm sure I'd know the signs and symptoms in the future. It might sound crazy but I think I'm actually grateful for that! It's made me more aware of others' feelings, too. You have to face up to it when life isn't going right, even if you don't know why, and then you have to deal with it and move on. I did tell a few of my friends and one had actually had counselling too and I didn't know! So, to anyone out there who feels even slightly that things aren't right, don't just get on with it by yourself. Get some help. You won't be the only one it's happening to, and the sooner you deal with it, the sooner you can get on with the rest of your life. Believe me, problems won't go away on their own.

Stress

We all hear people talking about stress all the time. People say that they are 'stressed out' or that something was 'really stressful'. Almost everywhere you look you will see references to stress: on the television, the radio, in books and newspapers – you name it, there will be something about stress and the impact it is having on us all.

Stress in the workplace is now at record levels, with enormous numbers of working days being lost to it. In fact, it is thought to be the number one reason for taking time off work; even more people have time off for stress-related problems than for other common reasons such as backache and colds.

Many people have theories about why we all seem to be more stressed than in the past, but regardless of the reasons for the apparent increase in stress, it is really important to understand exactly what it is and how it can actually help us in certain circumstances.

Positive stress

Believe it or not, there is such a thing as 'positive stress'. It is what motivates us and gives us the kick we need to push forward and get things done. We all need a certain level of drive and enthusiasm in our lives, and positive stress can give this to us. When we are positively stressed, we feel that whatever it is that we have to do is achievable. Positive stress is still demanding and we may well feel exhausted after we've achieved a particular goal, such as taking exams, but it helps us to respond to the challenges in our lives in a positive and creative way.

Negative stress

Negative stress is what makes us feel that we cannot achieve our tasks and goals. Everything seems too much, and life seems like one big race against time. The motivating pressure of positive stress is now the crushing force of pure negative stress that can lead to a wide range of adverse physical and mental symptoms.

In fact, negative stress keeps us in a state of 'fight or flight' for longer than is healthy for us. We start to treat life as one big emergency and lose our perspective on what really matters.

Take a moment to think about what stress means to you. The following questions may help to get you thinking:

- Do you see stress as a good thing or is it a bad thing in your life?
- When you think of stress, do you also think of pressure, worry and fear?

Action

- Does stress affect your sense of self-worth? For the better or the worse?
- What do you think is the opposite of stress? Is that a good thing or a bad thing?
- How do you feel when you are stressed?
- How do you feel when you would describe yourself as 'not stressed'?

If you think it will help you in the future, jot your responses down. What conclusions can you reach about the thoughts you have had? Do you have a good understanding of what stress means to you?

Stress... View from James

I hate it when I hear people saying stuff like 'I'm totally stressed out' or that life's so stressful. Mostly it isn't. There's bound to be stuff that winds us up and I think young people today do have to put up with a lot. Many of us haven't got a hope of ever buying our own house while prices are so high, and we have to get into a lot of debt to go to university. There is stuff that could happen that would be really stressful, so going on about all the small stuff isn't worth it.

I have been through a time when I felt totally stressed out. I was in the middle of doing my A levels and my Mum was diagnosed with cancer. They didn't want to tell me about it but I knew what was going on, and she went for treatment almost straight away, so I had to know. It felt like everything was crushing in around me. Like real pressure. I came so close to walking out of a couple of my exams but managed to get it together enough to stay and finish them. Sometimes I felt really panicky and I told one of Mum's nurses when she asked me how I was. She said that was normal under the circumstances but that I should try not to do too much for a while. As soon as my exams were finished, I had some time off. I had planned to get a job for the summer before going to university but couldn't cope with anything new at that time.

Sometimes you just have to start cutting stuff out of your life for a while and just focus on one or two of the important things. As soon as you start to feel less stressed you can start to do more. I found that as long as I made changes to what I had to do, I could cope better.

My Mum had surgery and is much healthier now. It really taught me that sometimes you do just have to drop everything to deal with the big stuff, and when you do, everything can seem more manageable than it did.

Symptoms of stress

There are some symptoms that you may experience if you are suffering from negative stress. You will not suffer from all of them – perhaps only one or two – but they are a signal that your body and mind may be suffering and that you should seek some support and advice (see the Information point on page 224).

Being self-aware (taking notice of your feelings, whether they are physical or mental) is crucial. Ignore the way that you are feeling, and you are likely to be ignoring important messages from your body and mind that all is not well.

Here are just some of the changes that can take place in your body as a result of suffering from too much negative stress:

- the blood supply to the muscles increases;
- the adrenal glands produce more adrenaline;
- the pupils become dilated;
- the heart rate increases;
- blood pressure may rise;
- the sweat glands produce more sweat;
- breathing becomes more rapid or troubled;
- swallowing may become difficult;
- muscles may become tense;
- more headaches and migraines are experienced;
- the digestive system may become upset;
- the immune system becomes less effective, leading to frequent infections such as coughs and colds;
- fatigue and exhaustion may develop;
- skin problems such as acne may develop.

Here are just some of the changes that can take place in your mind as a result of suffering from too much negative stress. You may:

- become more anxious and nervous;
- get depressed and moody;
- feel lonely and isolated;
- have emotional outbursts;
- find concentration and decision making difficult;
- get excessively self-critical;
- start to avoid certain situations;
- feel lethargic or 'lazier' than usual;
- feel over-dependent on stimulants such as alcohol.

There are many more symptoms and feelings that could be added to this list, but if you find yourself experiencing even just one or two of them, do make sure that you seek help sooner rather than later.

Dealing with stress

The symptoms that your body gives you are not for you to ignore. If you think that stress is a problem for you, the first thing you should do is talk to someone. There is a lot of advice out there for you (see the Information point below) and self-help techniques that you can learn, but it is essential to get the advice of someone who is not on the 'inside' of your stress so that you can get valuable perspectives and insights.

Never feel that a problem cannot be tackled or alleviated. Everything can be. Even if an issue cannot be removed entirely, you can certainly be helped to feel better about a particular situation or about your life in general. Don't suffer in silence!

Info

If you suspect that negative stress is an issue for you, or you would like to talk to someone about the way that you are feeling, there are many sources of help for you.

In person
- *Your tutor at school or college may be able to help, especially if you get on well together.*
- *If you are at university, there will be a student welfare office with staff who you can talk to.*
- *Your GP will be able to talk to you and may be able to arrange some counselling for you.*

- *Your family and friends may be a sound source of support.*
- *Your town may have a drop-in centre for young people to get advice on the way that they are feeling.*
- *Your local Connexions office will have staff who know where you can get good-quality support.*

On the internet
Connexions Direct has loads of advice for you on stress management www.connexions-direct.com.

On the telephone
The Samaritans are always there for you day and night. You can telephone confidentially and anonymously on 08457 909090 or e-mail jo@samaritans.org.

You can telephone Connexions on 080 800 13 2 19.

According to the website www.beatingaddictions.co.uk the most common addictions seen in young people include smoking, alcohol, solvents, cannabis and even self-harm, cocaine and heroine.

There are some factors which make certain people more likely to suffer an addiction, for example, some genetic factors, or growing up under the influence of certain behaviours that can become addictive. But it's important to remember that addictions can develop as a result of peer pressure to try something to 'fit in'.

If you think that you may be becoming physically or psychologically dependent on something, seek help as soon as possible (see the info box below). The quicker you do this, the easier it will be to manage the situation and start to explore the feelings that led you to this point. Gaining that kind of self-understanding is so valuable in life, and there is support out there should you ever need it. Above all else, never think that you have to struggle on alone, as this can only really make things worse. It will always be possible to take steps to recovery so that you can regain your enjoyment of life.

Info

If you suspect that you may be becoming dependent on, or addicted to, something, that's a great starting point for recovery. See your GP as soon as possible for advice and take a look at the following websites:

- *www.beatingaddictions.co.uk*
- *www.actiononaddiction.org.uk*
- *www.talktofrank.com*
- *www.mind.org.uk*

Summary

The key points in this chapter include the following:

- There are times in our lives when all of us can feel that life is against us and everything seems too much.
- You have to be self-aware to make sure that nasty symptoms do not creep up on you without your realising.
- If you feel depressed or are struggling with your emotions, it is essential to talk to someone about how you are feeling. There are many places that you can go for help.
- Stress can be divided into positive stress and negative stress.
- Positive stress can be inspiring and motivating.
- Negative stress can tip us into excessive anxiety and a whole host of physical and mental symptoms.
- It is essential to deal with negative stress sooner rather than later, and there are many sources of help out there for you.

Part Seven
Spotlight on key professions

In looking at career options after school, there is a wealth of information available on all sectors of UK business. *A–Z of Careers and Jobs*, published in 2009 by Kogan Page, provides detailed information for more than 300 different occupations and job types. We have taken six of those job sectors – accountancy, actuarial work, advertising, law, medical and healthcare science and retailing – and included them here as examples of the detailed material available. Each chapter discusses the various roles involved in that particular sector and includes useful contact details, helpful websites and realistic salary ranges. For further information on this and all other Kogan Page titles, look at our website, www.koganpage.com.

PRICEWATERHOUSECOOPERS

Tom Gee
Joined September 2009
Alcester Grammar School

Why did you choose the HEADstart programme?

I chose the HEADstart programme as I felt it would be a great way of starting my career in Tax, especially as I would be trained within a leading firm such as PwC. The training programme includes the opportunity to gain my Accounting Technician Technicians (ATT) and could lead towards me studying for the Chartered Tax Associate (CTA). I didn't want to go to university as I felt that I could progress my career just as quickly, if not faster, by going straight into employment. The added benefit of this route is that I wouldn't accrue any student debt!

What have you been doing since joining the firm (what does the job involve)?

Since joining PwC my main role has been to prepare tax returns for individuals who come on assignment to work in the UK, or who go on assignment from the UK to work abroad. I like to get involved in additional work to build my knowledge and further my development, which all means I expand my role within my team. As my experience grows I have become involved in training and coaching new members of the team.

How have you found the exams?

I will begin studying for my exams in August 2010, which will be one year into my training with PwC. I expect the exams to offer a further challenge and an opportunity to expand my knowledge within the various areas of Tax. PwC enter me for the exams and cover the costs. I've benefited from lots of support and advice from my team, which is really insightful as they have been through this process.

What have you found most rewarding so far?

The most rewarding aspect about my job is how much I really enjoy it! My work portfolio is busy, so the weeks fly by, and it all helps to further build the foundations of my career. I always feel like I'm aiming for something, whether they are small day-by-day things, or longer term goals. There are fresh opportunities and challenges all the time.

Chelsea Senior
Joined September 2008
Tollbar Business and Enterprise College, Grimsby

Why did you choose the HEADstart programme?

I always had an interest in business, and after starting my accountancy A-level realised this was where my passion was. I did some research and found that a university degree was not essential in order to begin a professional accountancy qualification. Whilst researching my options I learnt more about the HEADstart programme at PwC. To find out more I attended an event and got to meet lots of people from the business, which gave me a feel for the company culture. This was really important as from this I knew I wanted to start my career with PwC.

I was eager to get into the work place and gain that all important work experience, whilst earning a good wage, rather than go to University.

What have you been doing since joining the firm (what does the job involve)?

I work in Assurance, which involves performing client audits. This entails visiting a new client site every couple of weeks, and meeting lots of people and building trust with the clients. The job itself involves reviewing client financial statements, and gaining comfort that they are accurate and then documenting in detail how we have achieved this.

Putting the work element aside, I have also been able to take time out of work to help in my local community, painting school buildings, and other projects the firm are involved in. We have a great social side to the team as well, I have attended many social events ranging from black tie evenings to treasure hunts and visits to the local pubs!

How have you found the exams?

There's no denying the exams are challenging and many hours need to be spent revising. Finding the right work/life/college balance is tough but there are only two exam sittings per year with the Association of Chartered Certified Accountants (ACCA) so you have the rest of the time free to work and study. Our tutors are only an email away if we ever have any queries, they are really accessible. We also have the support of a PwC Professional Qualification Manager. They provide guidance on anything from work related issues to personal ones, which may be affecting our studies. There is so much support available which puts you in the best possible position to pass exams, which are not easy at the best of times.

What have you found most rewarding so far?

The most rewarding thing for me is the variation in the job and meeting new clients all the time. This all means I can clearly see my career develop every year as I progress through the firm. Not forgetting the fact that I am getting a great wage for a person of my age which is always rewarding at the end of the month!

20
Accountancy

Members of the accountancy profession are involved in the financial transactions of businesses, including the preparation and verification of accounts, auditing and analysis.

Accountant

Accountants work with and have expert understanding of a wide range of financial questions, issues and procedures. They work in many different settings, including small high street accounting firms, local and central government departments, management consultants and for the finance departments of commercial and industrial organisations from small businesses to huge multinationals. They deal with such questions as taxation, business forecasting, monitoring financial performance, advising on investments, acquisitions and mergers and good daily financial management. They also audit the paperwork and computer records of organisations to make sure that all financial transactions are accounted for and comply with the law.

Because accountants cover such a wide area of expertise, there are several different specialist branches within the profession. They work in one of the following three areas.

Management accountant

Chartered management accountants, usually referred to as management accountants, work in commerce and industry. They work with a company or organisation monitoring and planning budgets, preparing information for external auditors, overseeing credit control, monitoring financial performance and making suggestions about future business development. They work closely with other members of the management team. They may be qualified Chartered Accountants, Chartered Certified Accountants or Management Accountants.

Accountant in private practice

Accountants working in private practice assess, monitor and advise on the financial status of private businesses. They work for freelancers, for small firms or for large practices offering their services to fee-paying clients.

Practitioners are either qualified as Associate Members of the Institute of Chartered Accountants in England and Wales (ICAEW), the Institute of Chartered Accountants in Scotland (ICAS), the Institute of Chartered Accountants in Ireland (ICAI) , or the Association of Chartered Certified Accountants (ACCA). Members of the Association of International Accountants (AIA) also do private practice work.

One specific role within accountancy is that of the auditor. Auditors are responsible for checking the financial records of every kind of business and organisation and they are not employees of that organisation. External auditors must be qualified Chartered Accountants or international accountants.

Accountant in the public sector

Chartered public finance accountants (public sector accountants) control and assess the efficiency of public spending. Working for example in health trusts, local authorities, universities and central government departments, they examine the cost-effectiveness of policies, manage budgets, conduct internal audits and advise on policy.

Knowing in what kind of environment you would work and what specialist knowledge you wish to apply will help you choose which of the branches of accountancy is most appropriate for you.

Qualifications and training

Each of the professional bodies offering training asks for slightly different entry qualifications. It is, however, possible to offer some general useful guidelines. Trainee accountants are taken on by employers of many kinds, but they also have to fulfil the entry criteria for the appropriate professional body.

With the exception of a few people with three grade As at A level, the vast majority of trainee accounts are graduates. A good honours degree in any subject is fine, although business, mathematics and technical subjects are strongly represented in the profession. If your degree includes a lot of maths, you may be exempt from some of the professional exams. Many employers set numeracy tests as part of their selection process.

You should have five GCSEs grades A or B and two A levels. Many accountancy firms require you to have 280 to 300 UCAS points if you wish to become a Chartered Accountant. All the accounting professional bodies do offer alternative entry routes for mature students and for applicants who are already qualified accounting technicians.

Management accountants do not have to be graduates, but a good honours degree in a mathematical or business subject may offer exemptions from some of the professional examinations.

Accountants qualified with any of the professional accountancy bodies can work in the public sector, but the most relevant organisation is the Chartered Institute of Public Finance and Accountancy (CIPFA). If you don't have another accountancy qualification you must have three GCSEs grades A to C and two A levels and you must have maths and English at either GCSE or A level.

All the accountancy professions offer similar training routes where you have to complete three years' supervised work and take professional exams at two levels.

Personal qualities and skills

Accountants have to be good at working with numbers but they must also be very good communicators. They have to be able to understand complex information and also to explain complicated information to people who don't have detailed financial knowledge. They must be persistent, and assertiveness is as important as tact and discretion.

Salaries

Starting salaries vary considerably, depending on location, size of firm and type of accountancy, but start at around £28,000 for trainees in London and the South East; £16,000 to £23,000 is more typical elsewhere.

RSM Tenon

Refreshingly
different

Are you looking for a career with real responsibility and opportunity? Somewhere you will get noticed? Where you are well rewarded for your hard work? You've come to the right place.

Our focus on being refreshingly different means we need employees with the capability and drive to take our business forward.

We are looking for ambitious and highly motivated school and college leavers who want a career with real opportunities. We will provide you with a positive and motivational environment and ongoing professional support to help you achieve your full potential.

We are an employer of choice who will give you reward and recognition for your work and ongoing professional support. Our RSM Tenon Academy will provide you with a programme of internal courses, external training and on the job mentoring, to help you progress through your career.

RSM Tenon is the UK's 7th largest accounting firm with a fee income of £250m, employing nearly 3,000 people with offices in all major commercial centres across the UK, creating more and exciting opportunities for our employees.

To find out more about our career opportunities, visit our website
www.rsmtenon.com

About RSM Tenon

RSM Tenon is regarded as one of the most progressive and entrepreneurial professional services firms in the UK today, providing business advisory, audit, tax, financial management, recovery and risk management services. We offer intelligent solutions to a national client base that ranges from individuals and entrepreneurially-led owner managed businesses, to large corporations and public sector organisations.

With over 50 offices across the UK, there are a wide range of challenging and diverse career opportunities within the organisation. We have a commitment to invest in our people and combining this with our continuous growth makes RSM Tenon the perfect environment to launch and progress your career.

Opportunities are available in the following disciplines:

- accounting and auditing
- internal audit
- risk management
- tax compliance and planning
- business consultancy
- corporate finance
- fraud solutions
- human resource development
- independent financial advice
- forensic accounting
- IT services and bespoke software development
- outsourcing

We recognise that career development is important and our aim is to work in partnership with you to help identify and progress your chosen career path.

To enhance training, all staff work closely with clients in developing their businesses, providing a variety of learning experiences.

We have a range of training and development activities specifically designed to support trainees in achieving their chosen professional qualification. This includes revision courses and in-house training and coaching. With clients from a vast range of different market sectors, you have the potential for a variety of learning experiences. In addition to this, professional training courses are available according to your chosen discipline, including AAT and ATT. Following successful completion, further qualifications which you may choose to study are ACA, ACCA, IIA or CTA.

For more information about careers or to apply online, please see
www.rsmtenon.com

Jonathan Gascoigne
ATA Semi Senior

Jonathan joined RSM Tenon straight from Sixth Form, where he had gained 4 A-Levels. Jonathan took the decision not to go to university but was very keen to obtain a further qualification and was looking for an employer who would support him through his continued studies. He has recently finished his AAT qualification.

Tell us a bit about your career so far with RSM Tenon

I started with RSM Tenon in September 2008, since then I have taken on a variety of different roles within the Audit, Tax and Advisory department of the firm. I have had opportunities to develop my career and improve my knowledge on a day to day basis and put into practice the experience I gained at college. I am now taking on increased responsibilities at work and with my clients.

What do you enjoy most about your role and the company you work for?

Audit, Tax and Advisory is as much about meeting and talking to clients as it is 'number crunching'. I enjoy the challenge of building a rapport with clients as well as giving the best advice possible.

Working in a firm such as RSM Tenon gives me the opportunity to see a vast array of businesses from small owner-managed companies to large multinationals. This means I can apply the skills I learnt at college to a range of clients. As well as applying these skills I also learn from being 'on the job' about how different businesses are run. This will be of great benefit to me in the future.

What are your future career plans?

I have started my ACA qualification and I am looking forward to qualifying. I plan then to specialise in a particular area such as tax or insolvency. I would also like to work overseas for 12 months or so to experience accounting in a different country and culture. As RSM Tenon are part of the RSM International network of accountancy firms, this is a real opportunity which I am very much looking forward to taking advantage of.

THE RIGHT PATH

If you have a technical and inventive mind and are looking for a variety of work while operating in a constantly changing environment – a career in tax provides an excellent and exciting opportunity to put those qualities to use.

The Chartered Institute of Taxation (CIOT) administers the highest level tax examinations in the UK, the Chartered Tax Adviser (CTA) qualification.

Gaining the CTA sets you on to the right path to a fulfilling career.

THE NEXT STEP

For more information visit the CIOT's website at www.tax.org.uk or call us on 0844 579 6700 or 020 7340 0550

THE
CHARTERED
INSTITUTE OF
TAXATION

A career in tax

A career in tax has an enormous amount to offer graduates, including variety, intellectual stimulation and plenty of early responsibility. If you enjoy working with people, the challenge of problem solving and an ever-changing, dynamic working environment then a career in tax is for you.

What does a tax adviser do?

A tax adviser works with companies and individuals, trying to create the best tax strategies for them. The complex and diverse nature of taxation means that tax advisers rapidly develop areas of specialist knowledge. The main areas of specialisation are corporate, personal, international, inheritance tax, VAT, National Insurance, and trusts and estates.

Benefits

Variety — tax is a mixture of law, administration and accountancy and it draws on a huge range of intellectual, presentational and personal skills.

Competitive salary — the job market in tax has its ups and downs, as all job markets do. But a qualification and experience in tax forms an excellent basis for a secure and well-remunerated career.

Early responsibility and management opportunity — if you are ambitious, tax can lead you to the top, not only in professional practice but also in business and commerce.

Challenging and stimulating work — tax is a complex and ever-changing world where your actions can translate into financial consequences. You have to make professional judgments and be prepared to back them up.

Prospects

Work in practice, commerce or industry — many offer training contract opportunities or the opportunity to start off as a tax trainee

Work for the Government — HM Revenue and Customs have their own training and career structure

How to become a Chartered Tax Adviser

To be eligible to sit the CTA exams you will have a previous professional qualification or equivalent tax experience. Once you pass the exams you can progress to membership of the Institute. For more information on the CTA visit the CIOT's website at **www.tax.org.uk** or call us on 0844 579 6700 or 020 7340 0550.

On qualifying, salaries can increase significantly – £40,000 to £50,000 with a few years' experience. Salary packages can also include benefits such as pay bonuses, share options and pension and private health plans.

The Association of Accounting Technicians (AAT)
154 Clerkenwell Road
London EC1R 5AD
Tel: 020 7415 7500
www.aat.org.uk

Association of Chartered Certified Accountants (ACCA)
ACCA Connect
2 Central Quay
89 Hydepark Street
Glasgow, Scotland G3 8BW
Tel: 0141 582 2000
www.accaglobal.com

Association of International Accountants
Staithes 3, The Watermark
Metro Riverside
Newcastle Upon Tyne NE11 9SN
Tel: 0191 482 0277
www.aia.org.uk

Chartered Institute of Management Accountants (CIMA)
26 Chapter Street
London SW1P 4NP
Tel: 020 8849 2287
www.cimaglobal.com

Chartered Institute of Public Finance and Accountancy (CIPFA)
3 Robert Street
London WC2N 6RL
Tel: 020 7543 5600
www.cipfa.org.uk

Financial Services Skills Council
51 Gresham Street
London EC2V 7HQ
Tel: 0845 257 3772
www.fssc.org.uk

Info

HM Revenue & Customs (HMRC)
www.hmrc.gov.uk

The Insolvency Service
21 Bloomsbury Street
London WC1B 3QW
www.insolvency.gov.uk

Institute of Chartered Accountants in England and Wales (ICAEW)
Chartered Accountants' Hall
PO Box 433
EC2P 2BJ
Tel: 020 7920 8100
www.icaew.co.uk

Institute of Chartered Accountants in Ireland (ICAI)
Burlington House
Burlington Road
Dublin 4
Tel: +3531 637 7200
www.icai.ie

Institute of Chartered Accountants of Scotland (ICAS)
CA House
21 Haymarket Yards
Edinburgh EH12 5BH
Tel: 0131 347 0100
www.icas.org.uk

Institute of Public Finance
No. 1 Croydon
12–16 Addiscombe Road
Croydon CR0 0XT
Tel: 020 8667 1144
www.ipf.co.uk

National Audit Office
151 Buckingham Palace Road
London SW1W 9SS
Tel: 020 7798 7000
www.nao.org.uk

Accounting technician

Accounting technicians work in a variety of roles, often alongside professionally qualified Chartered Accountants. They are involved in the day-to-day practical work of accountancy and finance, including the preparation of information and accounts and the interpretation of computer information, such as audit tax and payroll. Accounting technicians are widely employed in public finance, industry and commerce, and private practice. Their roles range from accounts clerks to finance managers. A growing number of accounting technicians provide a range of services direct to the public and manage their own practice. Many go on to qualify with the senior chartered accountancy bodies.

Qualifications and training

There are no set entry qualifications, but you must be confident with maths. Some employers may prefer you to have GCSEs (A–C) or equivalent in English and maths. Previous experience of office work and good IT skills, especially in creating spreadsheets, are also valuable.

You can start as an accounts clerk doing basic duties, and take work-based training or a part-time college course to qualify as a technician with the Association of Accounting Technicians (AAT) or Association of Chartered Certified Accountants (ACCA). You may not have to do the first stages of accounting technician training if you already have an A level or equivalent in accounting, previous relevant work experience or a basic book keeping qualification. AAT and ACCA qualifications comprise a foundation, an intermediate and a technician stage. The AAT or the ACCA can advise you about where to find a training place. It is also sometimes possible to do an apprenticeship as an accounting technician.

Personal qualities and skills

You must be thorough and methodical and enjoy working with figures. Good IT skills and the ability to work as part of a team are also very important. Some positions involve considerable responsibility and/or the pressure of deadlines.

Salaries

There are often significant differences between salaries in London and the South-East compared to other regions. Starting salaries for trainees range from £15,000 to £19,000. Qualified technicians earn from £18,000 to £25,000. Accounting technicians with other management responsibilities can earn far more than this.

Info

The Association of Accounting Technicians (AAT)
140 Aldersgate Street
London EC1A 4HY
Tel: 0845 863 0800
www.aat.org.uk

Association of Chartered Certified Accountants (ACCA)
ACCA Connect
2 Central Quay
89 Hydepark Street
Glasgow G3 8BW
Tel: 0141 582 2000
www.accaglobal.com

Financial Services Skills Council
51 Gresham Street
London EC2V 7HQ
Tel: 020 7216 7366
www.fssc.org.uk

The Actuarial Profession
making financial sense of the future
Be ready for anything
Whatever the future brings
It's virtually impossible to predict the future. But whatever it may be, it's an actuaries job to help businesses prepare for it. Their highly valued skills and ability to assess risks are instrumental in helping organisations around the world plan for what may be around the corner.
Find us on facebook
www.be-an-actuary.co.uk

The Actuarial Profession
making financial sense of the future

Be ready for anything.
Whatever the future brings.

What an actuary does

Put simply, actuaries help make financial sense of the future. They make long term decisions and forecasts that affect people in all aspects of their everyday life and impact on businesses, financial institutions and even governments. Working in sectors as diverse as pensions, insurance, healthcare, banking and investment, actuaries provide organisations with specialist advice on how best to manage their assets and liabilities. This is a very high profile career: one actuarial decision can have an impact of millions – sometimes billions – of pounds.

What you will need and what you can expect

This is a specialised profession, so that although actuaries come from all sorts of backgrounds, they have certain things in common. They enjoy maths and have the ability to solve problems, analyse data and evaluate financial risks. If you decide to become an actuary, these are all the skills you will develop whilst studying for the professional qualification. Before you can get to that stage you will need to have the following:

A-levels. If you decide the actuarial profession is for you, the first thing you will need is a good grade in A-level Mathematics (or equivalent). It doesn't matter what other subjects you take as long as the grades are good enough to take you to the next stage …

A degree. For the majority of actuaries, a good degree is essential. Any subject is acceptable, although most employers prefer numerate degrees from a university department within a strong reputation. These degrees may offer exemptions from some of the professional exams; actuarial science degrees are likely to give the most exemptions and offer an excellent grounding for any business career.

Achieve all of that and you will be well on the way to a career which offers:

Diverse and varied work. Not only will you have the opportunity to work in diverse sectors, you could find yourself being a consultant, analyst, trouble-shooter, and risk assessor – all in one day.

Professionalism. Actuaries are responsible for upholding the highest professional standards, especially because they are often involved in safeguarding the public's financial interests.

Intellectual satisfaction. Actuaries are problem solvers. They use their training to analyse and interpret data and create models of the future to assess risks and estimate outcomes.

A good work/life balance. With variety comes flexibility. You could have the opportunity to work part-time, from home or even abroad.

Good pay. Salaries and benefits packages are excellent – even for those starting out in their career. In fact it's one of the highest paid professions wherever you go in the world.

Trainee positions

After university, the first step in becoming an actuary involves finding a trainee position – any relevant work experience will be of advantage here. Your school's careers adviser may be able to help you with this and the Actuarial Profession (the UK professional body for actuaries) maintains a list of employers.

Training and qualification

Qualification usually takes three to six years and the exams cover core topics such as statistical modelling, economics and financial and actuarial maths. The exam programme is designed to be flexible so you can study at your own pace whilst working for an actuarial employer – many employers will give you time off to study.

Sounds good?

Once you have qualified, the future is up to you. Actuarial skills are welcomed all over the world and, with such a wide range of actuarial employers, you can find a huge variety of exciting careers.

To find out more visit **www.actuaries.org.uk**

21
Actuarial work

Actuary

Actuaries use their knowledge of mathematics, statistics, economics and business to assess financial risks and probabilities. Traditionally their work is mainly concerned with pensions, life assurance and other types of insurance, but they may also work in investment and other business areas where major financial risks are involved.

They create statistical and mathematical models to analyse past events and predict the financial outcome of different situations. For example, in insurance they may study accident rates or medical data to develop and price new insurance policies, making sure that there are sufficient funds to cover liabilities but allow the company to remain profitable.

Around 45 per cent of actuaries work for consultancies providing specialist actuarial services to businesses of every kind. They advise on business recovery, acquisitions and employee benefit schemes. Central government also has its own actuarial departments which provide actuarial support and information across central government, its agencies and the National Health Service.

Qualifications and training

To qualify as an actuary you must become a student member of one of the professional bodies; either the Faculty or Institute of Actuaries – referred to collectively as the Actuarial Profession. Minimum entry qualifications are three GCSEs grades A–C including English and two A levels, one of which must be maths at grade B. If you have a second class honours degree in any subject A level maths grade C is acceptable. If you have a degree in maths or actuarial science you do not need a maths A level. If your degree is in maths or a highly numerate discipline a third class honours degree is acceptable. In practice, entry to the profession is competitive, so the majority of recruits are graduates.

Once you have completed your professional training, study and examinations you become a Fellow of either the Institute or Faculty.

To qualify as a Fellow of the Faculty or Institute of Actuaries, you must pass 15 professional examinations. After one year's work experience and appropriate examinations you should reach associate membership and after three years' work experience and appropriate exams you should reach fellowship.

If you have a degree or postgraduate qualification in actuarial science, statistics or economics, you may be exempt from some or all of the exams at the Core Technical Stage and some at the next stage. Please contact the Institute of Actuaries for further details of exemptions.

Personal qualities and skills

You must have excellent maths and statistical skills and be able to understand and explain complex information. You should have a thorough understanding of business and economics, be a great communicator and be aware of the bigger picture while paying attention to fine detail.

Salaries

Trainee actuaries start on between £26,000 and £33,000; this rises to between £35,000 and £50,000 for part-qualified associate actuaries. Qualified actuaries with at least five years' experience can earn between £45,000 and £75,000 and some salaries in the profession reach more than £100,000.

Info

The Actuarial Education Company
31 Bath Street
Abingdon
Oxfordshire OX14 3FF
Tel: 01235 550005
www.acted.co.uk

The Actuarial Profession
Napier House
4 Worcester Street
Oxford OX1 2AW
Tel: 020 7632 2111
www.actuaries.org.uk

The Association of Consulting Actuaries
Warnford Court
29 Throgmorton Street
London EC2N 2AT
Tel: 020 7382 4594
www.aca.org.uk

Faculty of Actuaries
Maclaurin House
18 Dublin Street
Edinburgh EH1 3PP
Tel: 020 7632 2111
www.actuaries.org.uk

Financial Services Skills Council
51 Gresham Street
London EC2V 7HQ
Tel: 0845 257 3772
www.fssc.org.uk

Government Actuary's Department (GAD)
Finlaison House
15–17 Furnival Street
London EC4A 1AB
Tel: 020 7211 2601
www.gad.gov.uk

Insurance Careers
www.insurancecareers.org

Computer Economics Limited and Remuneration Economics (CELRE)
Survey House
51 Portland Road
Kingston upon Thames
Surrey KT1 2SH
Tel: 020 8549 8726
www.celre.co.uk/

Royal Statistical Society (RSS)
12 Errol Street
London EC1Y 8LX
Tel: 020 7638 8998
www.rss.org.uk

22
Advertising

Communication is the heart of this complex industry, providing a wide range of openings, many with agencies that plan, organise and run advertising campaigns. Working on behalf of clients, advertising agencies study the product or service to be advertised and its market. They then plan how it should be sold and distributed, and how the media might be used to the best advantage in this process.

Account executive

Account executives are responsible within the agency for a particular client or group of clients. They interpret the client's wishes; coordinate and supervise the work of others within the agency, such as creatives, account planners, copywriters and scriptwriters; seek advice from other experts such as media executives; and then present the ideas most likely to meet with the client's approval.

Account planner

Account planners consider the client's brief and work to identify the ideal audience and optimum method of getting the client's message across. They analyse market research and other data and provide the creative team with the information that will help them develop the most effective campaign. They may also work on forward planning for the agency, identifying likely future clients based on market data they have researched.

Art editor/executive director

This position involves coordinating the work of the creative department, which converts the client's original intentions into a visual form for approval. Others, including copywriters, may elaborate upon this.

Artist

Agency artists prepare initial visual layouts of adverts, posters and displays, and produce final artwork for printing. They need to be competent in using design software.

Copywriter and scriptwriter

The writers in the agency produce headings, text, jingles and copy for articles in journals, and scripts for films and commercials. Copywriters often work closely with the Art Editor and visualisers.

Media executive

Media executives provide expert advice on the advertising medium – for example, television, cinema, posters, newspapers, journals – that will best suit a particular campaign, and negotiate the most economical rates.

Qualifications and training

Advertising is a fiercely competitive sector, especially in the current economic climate. Most entrants to jobs in advertising have either a degree or an HND. Any subject is acceptable, but some employers prefer related subjects including advertising, business studies, marketing, English or consumer science. Smaller agencies may take you without a degree, particularly if you have some relevant work experience. Work experience is extremely valuable, it shows you how agencies work and makes you a stronger applicant, but this experience is hard to come by. You may want to consider doing voluntary work for an agency. Some agencies offer formal work experience schemes and details of these appear on the Institute of Practitioners in Advertising website. There are many courses in marketing, communications and media studies at many levels. These may provide useful background, but they won't necessarily make you more employable. There are a few highly respected postgraduate courses in advertising including a diploma in copywriting at West Herts College and a postgraduate diploma in advertising at Falmouth College of Art and Design.

The majority of training is on the job, learning from colleagues, and you are usually considered to be a trainee for about two years. The IPA offers induction courses and continuing professional development courses and the Chartered Institute of Marketing offers a range of part-time and distance learning courses for those who are already working in the sector.

Since September 2008 a limited number of schools and colleges have introduced new Vocational Diplomas in creative and media studies. These can be taken at foundation, higher or advanced level. These courses combine academic study and training with an employer.

Personal qualities and skills

Excellent communication skills at every level are extremely important. Being able to deal with people, write clearly and work creatively are all essential skills. Many roles require you to be persuasive and tactful, and to be a media planner you need to be highly numerate. Advertising is a highly pressured business so you have to be thick-skinned and keep calm when chasing deadlines.

Info

Account Planning Group
16 Creighton Avenue
London N10 1NU
Tel: 020 8444 3692
www.apg.org.uk

The Advertising Association (AA)
7th Floor North, Artillery House
11–19 Artillery Row
London SW1P 1RT
Tel: 020 7340 1100
www.adassoc.org.uk

British Interactive Media Association (BIMA)
Briarlea House
Southend Road
South Green
Billericay
Essex CM11 2PR
www.bima.co.uk

Chartered Institute of Marketing (CIM)
Moor Hall
Cookham
Maidenhead
Berks SL6 9QH
Tel: 01628 427500
www.cim.co.uk

The Communication Advertising and Marketing Education Foundation
(CAM)
Moor Hall
Cookham
Maidenhead
Berkshire SL6 9QH
Tel: 01628 427 120
www.camfoundation.com

The Creative Circle
22 Poland Street
London W1F 8QQ
Tel: 020 7734 9334
www.creativecircle.co.uk

Creative and Cultural Skills
4th Floor
Lafone House
The Leathermarket Weston St
London SE1 3HN
Tel: 0207 015 1800
www.ccskills.org.uk

Salaries

Starting salaries range from £18,000 to £26,000 depending on your job title and the size of the agency. Many agencies are based in London and the South-East. In the regions, starting salaries range from £15,000 to £20,000. Senior accounts executives can earn £100,000, but averages are closer to £40,000 to £50,000.

23
Law

The legal profession has many occupations within it, but all are based on upholding the laws of the land and dealing with those who contravene the laws. The word 'lawyer' is a blanket term that covers both solicitors and barristers. Solicitors advise clients and operate in the lower courts. Barristers are instructed by solicitors to act for clients, and work in the higher courts. Opportunities for lawyers can be found in the public and private sector as well as within the legal system. The legal profession also offers careers for those who have not trained as lawyers, such as legal clerks and executives.

Advocate/barrister

The services of a barrister are required by solicitors (*see also* Solicitor), who deal with the clients and then 'brief' the barrister. Barristers give specialised advice on the law and plead counsel in the higher courts. They may also appear in the lower courts, where they usually begin their careers. Some are employed in the Army Legal Services, giving advice on all aspects of service and civil law that may affect the Army.

In Scotland, an advocate is the equivalent of a barrister. Advocates may not select their clients. Provided that a reasonable fee is tendered they may not, without good cause, refuse instructions to act in litigation. Advocates also work in the public sector, Crown Prosecution Service, the legal section of a government department or as Parliamentary drafters.

Barristers specialise in arguing a case in court and offer a legal opinion for solicitors when asked to consider a particular question of law. Barristers are instructed by solicitors on behalf of clients and never directly employed by clients.

The majority of barristers work independently through sets of 'chambers' (which are a collective organisation of barristers), and tend to be self-employed. Once established within chambers, barristers can advertise for work.

Qualifications and training

This is a highly competitive, almost exclusively graduate profession. In England and Wales you will either need a good law degree (2.1) or a good degree in another traditional academic subject. If your degree is not in law, you must take a one-year full-time or two-year part-time course – the Common Professional exam (CPE) or Graduate Diploma in Law (GDL). After this, the route is the same for everyone. You must get a place on the Bar Vocational Course (BVC). This is also offered as one-year full-time or two-years part-time and there is a central clearing system for applications. Applicants for the BVC also have to join one of the four Inns of Court before starting the course. At the end of the BVC, hopeful barristers apply for a pupillage in a set of barristers' chambers (their word for offices). After completing a pupillage, the next stage is to get a tenancy to practise in a set of chambers. All stages are exceedingly competitive.

In Scotland advocates need to pass a postgraduate diploma in law and spend two years practising as a solicitor before being called to the bar.

Personal qualities and skills

As it will be necessary to understand and interpret complex legal wording into clear basic English, barristers must have an excellent command of the English language and a meticulous understanding of the use of words. Barristers must understand and talk knowledgeably about technical matters in order to be able to cross-examine the most expert witness, for example, on complex aspects of technology. It is also useful if barristers present a highly confident and self-assured manner and can put on a 'good performance' in court. Since the work is confidential, a barrister needs to be trustworthy and discreet.

Salaries

Barristers' earnings relate to the amount and type of their work, their reputation, and, if they share chambers, the apportionment and value of briefs. Barristers may find it a struggle to make a living at the beginning of their profession, but the rewards for those who succeed can be high.

> *General Council of the Bar*
> *2/3 Cursitor Street*
> *London EC4A 1NE*
> *Tel: 020 7440 4000*
> *www.barcouncil.org.uk*
>
> *Details of education and training at the Bar:*
> *www.legaleducation.org.uk*
>
> *Faculty of Advocates*
> *Advocates Library*
> *Parliament House*
> *11 Parliament Square*
> *Edinburgh EH1 1RF*
> *Tel: 0131 226 5071*
> *www.advocates.org.uk*

Barrister's clerk/advocate's clerk

The barrister's clerk is the administrator or manager of the business chambers, deciding which briefs to accept, which of the barristers in the chamber to give them to, and negotiating the fees with the solicitor. The accounts, the barristers' appointment books and the efficient day-to-day running of the office are all part of the job of an experienced clerk.

Qualifications and training

The minimum qualification is four GCSE pass grades at A, B or C in academic subjects. Training is on the job and juniors can apply through the Institute of Barristers' Clerks to attend a two-year part-time Edexcel (BTEC) national certificate course studying organisation, finance, management, law, marketing and chambers administration. On obtaining the certificate, juniors may apply, after five years' service, for qualified Membership of the Institute of Barristers' Clerks.

The Bar in Scotland is divided into 10 'stables', each of which is served by an advocate's clerk and a deputy clerk employed by Faculty Services Ltd. Training is provided in service. The job of advocate's clerk is very similar to that of barrister's clerk in England and Wales. Their rates of pay are linked to the Civil Service scale on a level that roughly relates to a comparable post within the courts' administration. The 10 advocate clerks have clerical and secretarial staff to provide them with administrative support.

Personal qualities and skills

In order to manage efficient chambers and the barristers who work from them, a barrister's clerk needs good organisational skills, the ability to lead a team as well as be part of a team, and to get on with the general public. A good command of written and spoken English and an appreciation of the necessity for absolute confidentiality at all times are vital to success in this career.

Salaries

Starting salaries are in the region of £10,000. Junior clerks with two or three years' experience receive £13,500–£18,000, going up to £28,000 for very experienced juniors. Senior clerks may earn £60,000–£75,000 plus a performance-related bonus. Senior clerks were traditionally paid a fee which was a percentage of the barrister's own earnings. Some are still paid in this way, and the fee is usually around 5 per cent.

Info

The Bar Council
289–293 High Holborn
London WC1V 7HZ
Tel: 020 7242 0082
www.barcouncil.org.uk/

Institute of Barristers' Clerks (IBC)
289–293 High Holborn
London WC1 7HZ
Tel: 020 7831 7144
www.barristersclerks.com

COURT STAFF
Court administrative officer

Court administrative officers and court administrative assistants ensure the smooth day-to-day running of the courts. They book cases, allocate cases to courtrooms, prepare lists of the day's cases and send out correspondence. They may also be involved in the collection of fines and providing information to members of the public. More senior administrative officers lead teams of assistants, ensuring that all the tasks listed above are carried out efficiently.

Qualifications and training

To work as an administrative assistant you require two GCSEs grades A–C and to be an administrative officer you need five GCSEs grades A–C. If you have other useful administrative experience, you may be considered without these formal qualifications.

Personal qualities and skills

You must be able to deal calmly and politely with people. You should have good organisational skills and be able to stay calm in a busy environment. You should be able to pay attention to detail and work well as part of a team.

Court clerk

Court clerks are legal advisers who give advice to unpaid (non-stipendiary) magistrates who are trying cases in the magistrates' courts. They are qualified lawyers, but they do not take part in the decision making about judgments and sentencing. As magistrates do not have to be legally qualified, it is the court clerks who ensure that magistrates interpret and apply the law correctly.

Qualifications and training

Court clerks have to be either qualified solicitors or barristers, who themselves must have either a law degree or an approved postgraduate legal qualification. Court clerks follow a set training programme and also learn by working with more experienced clerks, finding out about the many different areas of work – road traffic, licensing, fines enforcement, sentencing, etc.

Personal qualities and skills

As well as a real interest in and broad knowledge of the law, court clerks must be logical thinkers, capable of undertaking fairly detailed research. They must be discreet, sensitive and calm, but also able to remain detached when dealing with stressful and upsetting situations.

Court usher

Whether you are a defendant, a witness, a jury member or a lawyer, it is the responsibility of the court usher to ensure that you know where you should be, what you should do and how you should do it. Ushers ensure that the court room is prepared and that everyone is present. They call witnesses and defendants, label evidence and administer the taking of oaths. At Crown Court, where a jury trial is taking place, court ushers escort members of the jury to and from the courtroom. They remain on duty outside the jury room while the jury is in discussion and they take messages between the jury and the judge.

Qualifications and training

You do not necessarily need any formal qualifications to become a court usher, though you would be expected to have a good general level of education. Previous work experience of dealing with the public and handling difficult situations are more important than professional qualifications. Your training will be on the job and you start by shadowing another usher. You will probably be sent on several short in-house courses. Skills for Justice have recently introduced NVQ levels 2 and 3 qualifications in court operations, so you may have the opportunity to work towards one of these.

Personal qualities and skills

These are really important. You have to be trustworthy and truthful and you must have excellent people skills, be able to calm, reassure and explain, but be able to remain confident if people are hostile or difficult. You have to be well organised and pay attention to detail.

Salaries

Court administrative assistants and ushers are paid between £13,000 and £14,500, while court administrative officers earn between £15,500 and £20,000. Trainee court clerks start on £19,000 to £20,500, rising to £26,000 on completion of training.

HM Courts Services
Clive House
Petty France
London SW1H 9HD
Tel: 020 7189 2000
www.hmcourts-service.gov.uk

Skills for Justice
Centre Court
Atlas Way
Sheffield S4 7QQ
www.skillsforjustice.com

Info

Court reporter

Court reporters attend court sittings and take down a complete report of all the evidence, the summing-up or judgment and, on occasions, the speeches of counsel in the various cases. Formerly, the proceedings were taken down in shorthand; now a palantype or stenograph is used. This is a typewriter-like machine that enables the reporter to achieve 200 words per minute. In addition, computers may be used to prepare transcripts, with all the advantages of on-screen editing and speed of preparation. The work sometimes involves travelling to a number of different courts. The majority of verbatim reporters begin their careers in the courts but can also work for Hansard, producing reports of proceedings in the House of Commons and the House of Lords. Television subtitlers also use the skills of verbatim reporting.

Qualifications and training

No specific academic qualifications are demanded for court reporters, although GCSE and A level passes can be an advantage. Applicants need to have proven ability in shorthand or stenotyping (usually over 150 words per minute), good typing speeds, and a thorough knowledge of grammar and punctuation. Legal experience can also be an asset. Details of full-time, part-time and distance-learning courses are available from the British Institute of Verbatim Reporters. In Scotland, there are no college courses but training is provided on the job by working alongside an experienced reporter.

Administrative officers need five GCSE passes (grade C or above), one of which must be English. The Scottish Court Service looks for applicants with Highers. Training lasts for two to three years, during which time trainees work and undertake courses run by the Court Service.

Personal qualities and skills

Anyone concerned with the courts must be discreet, honest and trust-worthy, as most of the work is confidential. Reporters must show a high degree of accuracy.

Salaries

Salaries are between £16,000 and £20,000. Many court reporters work freelance and can earn anything from £60 to £320 a day. What you earn depends very much on how complex and demanding your work is.

HM Courts Service
Clive House
Petty France
London SW1H 9HD
Tel: 020 7189 2000
www.hmcourts-service.gov.uk

Ministry of Justice
Selbourne House
54 Victoria Street
London SW1E 6QW
Tel: 020 7210 8500
www.justice.gov.uk

British Institute of Verbatim Reporters (BIVR)
Cliffords Inn
Fetter Lane
London EC4A 1LD
Tel: 020 8907 8249
www.bivr.org.uk

Legal Services Commission research assistant

The statutory government advisory body on law reform, the Law Commission, is currently working on projects in a variety of fields including common law, company and commercial law, crime and property law, and on general revision of statute law. The work is carried out in small teams, each under the direction of a Commissioner, consisting of qualified lawyers and research assistants. Law graduates and graduates of other disciplines who have completed the Legal Practice Course or the Bar Vocational Course are recruited annually to work as research assistants. The work offers the opportunity to take part in the creation of new legislative measures, as well as the in-depth development of skills in a particular area of law. Extensive consultation and investigation takes place before proposals are formulated; a sizeable proportion result in legislation. Projects range from major investigations of controversial areas of law to the consideration of a specific problem.

Qualifications and training

The minimum academic standard required is a first or high upper second-class (or equivalent) degree achieved in legal studies (based on the law of England and Wales) of at least two years' duration.

Personal qualities and skills

You need a genuine interest in, as well as a thorough knowledge of the law and legal issues. You must have excellent research skills, including the use of databases. You must be able to think and write articulately, be good at solving problems and be able to communicate well.

Salaries

Starting salaries range from £20,000 to £29,000. The highest salaries include London Weighting and are also paid to entrants with good post-graduate qualifications as well as a high class of degree.

Info

Legal Services Commission
Legal Services Research Centre
85 Gray's Inn Road
London WC1X 8TX
Tel: 020 7759 0000
www.legalservices.gov.uk

Asset Skills
2 The Courtyard
48 New North Road
Exeter
Devon EX4 4EP
Tel: 01392 423399
www.assetskills.org

Paralegal

Paralegals work for firms of solicitors, commercial companies and public sector bodies. They are not qualified solicitors or legal executives, but they develop considerable specialist knowledge. They normally specialise in a specific area of the law such as conveyancing, probate or family law. Their work involves researching information, drafting and managing documents, attending client meetings and some general clerical work. Paralegals also have to keep up to date with legal developments in their specialist field.

Qualifications and training

While there are no specific entry qualifications for paralegals, many hope to become solicitors, barristers or legal executives. This means that many applicants for these posts have a law degree. In any case, some firms ask for four or five GCSEs grades A–C or two A levels. Training is on the job and there are City & Guilds courses leading to a certificate level 2 and diploma level 3 available in paralegal studies. The Institute of Legal Executives (ILEX) also offers part-time and distance-learning courses for paralegals.

Personal qualities and skills

You must be very well organised, able to manage your own workload and pay attention to detail. You should have good spoken and written English skills and be interested in legal matters.

Salaries

Salaries for paralegals are between £16,000 and £25,000. For large city law firms salaries can be much higher than this, and some firms pay substantial annual bonuses.

Info

Institute of Legal Executives
Kempston Manor
Kempston
Bedfordshire MK42 7AB
Tel: 01234 841000
www.ilexpp.co.uk

National Association of Licensed Paralegals
9 Unity Street
Bristol BS1 5HH
Tel: 0117 927 7077
www.nationalparalegals.com

Legal executive

A legal executive is a professional lawyer employed in a solicitor's office or in the legal departments of commerce and central and local government. The training and academic requirements in a specified area of law are at the same level as those required of a solicitor. Consequently, with few exceptions, a legal executive is able to carry out tasks that are similar to those undertaken by solicitors. The main areas of specialisation are conveyancing, civil litigation, criminal law, family law and probate. In addition to providing a worthwhile career in its own right, the legal executive qualification provides access to those wishing to qualify as solicitors via the Institute route. In Scotland, the term 'legal executive' is not used, but solicitors engage assistants to do similar work.

Qualifications and training

The minimum entry requirement is four GCSEs to include English, but A level students and graduates are welcome. As an alternative, the Institute accepts a qualification in vocational legal studies, and has special arrangements for students who are over 21. In the main, training is on a part-time basis so that there is potential for trainees to 'learn while they earn'. For those already working in a legal environment, but with no formal legal qualifications, an NVQ (level 4) in Legal Practice is available, and the Institute of Legal Executives (ILEX) is the awarding body.

Personal qualities and skills

An ability to communicate, both verbally and in writing, with people at all levels, absolute discretion and trustworthiness, together with meticulous attention to detail, are essential.

Salaries

Salaries for trainees are between £15,000 and £20,000. Qualified legal executives earn between £25,000 and £50,000. Geographical location and the kinds of work in which your firm specialise affect your salary.

Institute of Legal Executives
Kempston Manor
Kempston
Bedfordshire MK42 7AB
Tel: 01234 841000
www.ilex.org.uk
e-mail: info@ilex.org.uk

Solicitor

The role of the solicitor is to provide clients with skilled legal representation and advice. The clients can be individual people or companies, or any type of organisation or group. A solicitor may work on all kinds of legal matters, from house purchases to defence of people accused of crimes; from selling a corporation to drafting a complicated will or trust. Solicitors may also represent clients in all courts, but will often brief a barrister (*see* Barrister) to represent the client, and then act as a liaison between them.

Scottish solicitors can appear in all courts and tribunals in Scotland up to and including the Sheriff Court. They can also gain rights of audience, enabling them to appear in the higher courts by becoming a solicitor-advocate, or may brief an advocate to represent their clients.

While some solicitors may deal with a variety of legal problems, others specialise in a particular area such as shipping, planning and construction, financial services or social security. Specialisation within the profession is increasing. The majority of solicitors work in private practice, with firms made up of several partners. Many others work as employed solicitors in commerce, industry, local and central government and other organisations.

Solicitors are instructed directly by clients and have a lot of contact with them. They have rights of audience in the magistrates' court and the county court. Unlike barristers, solicitors do not wear wigs but do wear gowns if they appear in county court. Solicitors are governed by a professional body called the Law Society.

Qualifications and training

England and Wales: the Law Society governs the training of solicitors in England and Wales, which takes place in two stages – the academic and the professional. Most, but not all, entrants to the profession are graduates. Fellows of the Institute of Legal Executives over the age of 25 with five years' qualifying experience do not need to complete the academic stage. Non-law graduates take the Common Professional Examination (CPE) or a Postgraduate Diploma in Law; those with the qualifying law degrees are exempt from this. The next stage, the vocational stage, is taken via the legal practice course, available at a number of colleges or universities. It is a one-year full-time or two-year part-time course. The trainee solicitor then has to undertake a two-year training contract with an authorised firm or organisation. During the course of this, a 20-day professional skills course is undertaken, usually on a modular basis.

Scotland: the Law Society of Scotland governs the training of solicitors in Scotland. It is possible to study for a Bachelor of Laws degree at five Scottish universities: Aberdeen, Dundee, Edinburgh, Glasgow and Strathclyde. Alternatively, it is possible to take the Law Society's own examinations by finding employment as a pre-diploma trainee. After completion of the LLB degree or professional examinations, all graduates who would like to become solicitors must take the diploma in legal practice – a 26-week postgraduate course, which also offers training in office and business skills. After successful completion of the degree and the diploma, those who wish to become solicitors then serve a two-year training contract with a Scottish solicitor. Trainees must undertake a further two-week course of study, keep training records, which will be examined and monitored by the Society, and take a test of professional competence. The trainees can then apply to the Law Society of Scotland for a practising certificate. All Scottish solicitors must hold a Law Society of Scotland practising certificate.

Personal qualities and skills

A high level of academic achievement, integrity, good communication skills, patience, discretion, a good command of language and problem-solving skills are all required.

Salaries

The range of starting salaries is very wide in this profession. The Law Society suggests that trainees should be paid around £16,000 in the regions and £18,000 in London. In practice, large city firms pay far more than this, somewhere in the region of £25,000 to £35,000. Another factor affecting earnings is the field of law in which you practise: commercial law tends to offer higher earnings than family or employment law, for example.

Law Society
113 Chancery Lane
London WC2A 1PL
Tel: 020 7242 1222
Fax: 020 7831 0344
Legal Education Line: 0870 606 2555
www.lawsociety.org.uk
e-mail: legaled@lawsociety.org.uk

Law Society of Scotland
26 Drumsheugh Gardens
Edinburgh EH3 7YR
Tel: 0131 226 7411
Fax: 0131 225 2934
www.lawscot.org.uk
e-mail: legaleduc@lawscot.org.uk

So... you want to be a lawyer? *(Kogan Page)*
Careers in the Law *(Kogan Page)*

Info

24
Medical and healthcare science

Many scientific disciplines play a key part in medicine – in the development and testing of drugs and the monitoring of the performance of these drugs. Scientists contribute to the understanding of the processes of disease and damage to tissue, organs and systems, as well as to the development of equipment and techniques to improve diagnosis and treatment. There are very many jobs in medical and healthcare science, and those described here are examples from some of the different areas of science in medicine.

Cardiographer

Cardiographers work in hospitals operating the electrocardiograph (ECG) machines which monitor the functioning of the heart. They reassure patients and explain the procedure to them, before fitting electrodes to the patient's body, ensuring they are correctly connected to the machine. They then take readings which a doctor uses to make decisions about diagnosis and treatment.

Clinical embryologist

This is a rapidly developing field. Clinical embryologists are involved in research and investigation of various aspects of IVF treatment and other programmes of assisted reproduction. This work involves the collection of eggs from patients for examination, checking the fertility levels of individuals and the application of cutting edge and sometimes controversial technologies.

Clinical engineer

Clinical or bio-engineers design equipment for monitoring, diagnosis, treatment and rehabilitation or research. They may design laser equipment or electronic aids for patients with disabilities. They examine the mechanics of the human body to see how to replicate the functions of particular organs or systems. They develop a detailed knowledge of materials and of engineering processes and apply this technical knowledge in a medical environment.

Clinical immunologist

Clinical immunologists use sophisticated laboratory techniques to examine the effects on the immune system of diseases such as AIDS and allergic conditions such as hay fever or asthma. They apply the knowledge they acquire to developing better treatments of these conditions. This is a fast-moving and developing area of medical science.

Clinical microbiologist

Clinical microbiologists work to diagnose all kinds of infections – bacterial, viral, fungal or parasitic. What they discover about which infections a patient has plays an important role in how that patient is treated, for example in choosing which antibiotics they are given. They also work for the Health Protection Agency, helping to prevent the spread of diseases.

Medical laboratory technician

All the scientific research and development work which goes on throughout the health service and in medical schools needs the support of medical laboratory technicians and medical laboratory assistants. Laboratory technicians work in all aspects of medical and clinical sciences, whether it is testing blood, screening cells for disease, or developing new materials to treat burns or wounds. Medical laboratory technicians assist scientists in setting up experiments, monitoring these experiments and recording the results.

Medical physicist

Medical physicists are involved in developing the highly sophisticated equipments for measuring the effects of illnesses and disabilities. Medical physicists have developed X-ray and ultrasound scanning equipment and they use their research skills to refine and improve these techniques and technologies. They often work closely with radiographers in the field of nuclear medicine, treating cancer cells with the correct dose of radiation.

Neurophysiology technologist

Neurophysiology technologists, also referred to as clinical physiologists, work in hospital outpatients departments, in intensive care units and in operating theatres. Their work is concerned with monitoring and measuring activities in the central and peripheral nervous systems. They use highly sophisticated equipment to obtain their readings. They work closely with patients of all ages, a child who has suffered a brain injury, or an older person who has had a stroke, for example. They also have to work closely with other members of the healthcare team.

Perfusionist

Perfusionists (or perfusion scientists) work in operating theatres where patients are undergoing open heart surgery. The term 'perfusion' refers to the movement of liquid through tissue. The perfusionist ensures that oxygen is circulated through the patient's blood even when the action of the heart and lungs is temporarily stopped in order to carry out the surgery. Perfusionists use a range of complex machinery and monitoring equipment to carry out their work. They must alert fellow members of the operating team if they have any cause for concern.

Phlebotomist

Phlebotomists take blood samples from patients, so that these samples can be analysed to diagnose diseases and other disorders. They have to take great care when collecting blood to disturb the patient as little as possible, and ensure that the blood is taken and labelled correctly and that it is taken to the correct laboratory. Phlebotomists also work for the blood donor agency, collecting blood from healthy volunteers.

Qualifications and training

With such a variety of career options there are several different entry levels, so what follows is a guide to some of the main points to bear in mind. To gain employment as a scientist involved in research and development in an area such as pathology, microbiology or biochemistry you will need a relevant degree in that subject, normally at least a 2.1. Many people entering research have a postgraduate degree as well. In some instances you need to ensure that your degree will be accredited by the appropriate professional body – the Institute of Biomedical Science, for example. Useful degrees include biology, microbiology, biochemistry, chemistry, physics, physiology and medicine.

Many of the more patient-focused roles within life science and physiological science require you to have two or three A levels, including sciences. It is important to check the particular requirements for the work that especially interests you.

Laboratory technicians usually need five GCSEs grade A–C including English, maths and at least one science subject. Assistant laboratory technicians may be able to get into laboratory work without formal academic qualifications and work towards relevant NVQs once they are employed.

All roles include training on the job and in many instances you will get a chance to work towards appropriate recognised, professional qualifications.

Personal qualities and skills

If you are engaged in research and development you must have a rigorous and questioning scientific approach to your work and be good at problem solving and coming up with imaginative solutions. If your work involves contact with patients, you must have an understanding and reassuring manner, but you must also be able to avoid becoming too emotionally involved in your work. Many roles require you to have good practical skills, manual dexterity and the ability to be meticulous and highly observant. Many roles will also require you to use complex instruments and take careful recordings of results.

Salaries

Apart from doctors, dentists and a few senior managers, all healthcare workers, including all those working in healthcare science, are paid on a graded scale with pay being linked to qualifications, experience, skills and level of responsibility. It is not possible here to go through all the different levels of pay, but for example, a healthcare science support worker or a phlebotomist would start on Band 2, £13,000 to £16,000, while at the other end of the scale a healthcare scientist who reaches consultant or director level is paid on Bands 8 to 9, £37,000 to £47,000. Most healthcare science professionals start somewhere between £20,000 and £27,000. The NHS Careers website provides detailed information on pay rates for each job. There is also some slight variation between pay rates for different healthcare trusts. Pay rates in the private healthcare sector tend to be a little higher than in the NHS.

Info

NHS Careers
PO Box 376
Bristol BS99 3EY
Tel: 0845 606 0655
www.nhscareers.nhs.uk

Health Professions Council
Park House
184 Kennington Park Road
London SE11 4BU
Tel: 020 7582 0866
www.hpc-uk.org

Institute of Biomedical Science
12 Coldbath Square
London EC1R 5HL
Tel: 020 7713 0214
www.ibms.org

Association of Clinical Scientists
c/o Association of Clinical Biochemists
130–132 Tooley Street
London SE1 2TU
Tel: 020 7940 8960
www.assclinsci.org

Health Learning and Skills Advice Line
Tel: 0800 015 0850
www.learndirect-advice.co.uk/campaigns/nhs/

Institute of Physics and Engineering in Medicine (IPEM)
Fairmount House
230 Tadcaster Road
York YO24 1ES
Tel: 01904 610821
www.ipem.ac.uk

Association of Clinical Biochemists
130–132 Tooley Street
London SE1 2TU
Tel: 020 7403 8001
www.acb.org.uk

Association of Clinical Cytogeneticists
www.cytogenetics.org.uk

Society for General Microbiology
www.socgenmicrobiol.org.uk

British Society for Immunology
www.immunology.org

Association of Clinical Embryologists
www.ivf.net/ace

Recruitment Centre for Clinical Scientists
Tel: 020 7582 0866
www.nhsclinicalscientists.info

Association for Science Education (ASE)
College Lane
Hatfield
Hertfordshire AL10 9AA
Tel: 01707 283000
www.ase.org.uk

CLEAPSS Schools Science Service
Brunel University
Uxbridge UB8 3PH
Tel: 01895 251496
www.cleapss.org.uk

SEMTA (Science, Engineering and Manufacturing Technologies Alliance)
14 Upton Road
Watford
Hertfordshire WD18 0JT
Tel: 0800 282167
www.semta.org.uk

Association of Medical Laboratory Assistants
12 Coldbath Square
London EC1R 5HL
Tel: 020 7713 8050
www.amlauk.org

Medical illustrator

Medical illustrators employ a range of artistic and technical skills to produce photographs, drawings, videos and other digital images in health-care settings. They produce material to help assess the effectiveness of treatment regimes by photographing patients at different stages of their treatment. They may produce material for medical textbooks, websites, lectures and other training and teaching activities. Some specialise in forensic work, taking pictures of non-accidental injuries or copying evidence from X-rays and slides.

Because medical illustrators use a combination of photography, video and drawing skills, there may be some opportunities to take work which allows you to develop special expertise in one or other of these areas. You are likely to spend your time working in hospital wards, operating theatres and clinics, as well as studios and technical laboratories.

Qualifications and training

While it is not always necessary to have formal qualifications, it is now very difficult to get into this work without a foundation degree, HND or degree in a relevant subject. The most useful subjects are graphic design and photography. It is likely that in the near future medical illustrators will only be able to practise if they are state registered. The exact date for this has not been finalised. However, when this does happen all new entrants to this profession will have to have a relevant degree which meets the standards for registration. It is very useful if you can gain some relevant work experience with an NHS trust medical photography department. You should also be able to produce a portfolio of your work at interview.

Personal qualities and skills

This work demands a wide range of qualities and skills. You should have artistic and photographic ability and be competent working with technical equipment. You must have an interest in and some knowledge of biology, physiology and diseases and medical conditions. You have to have excellent interpersonal skills, and be sensitive and empathic when dealing with people who are anxious or vulnerable. You should be good at working as part of a team, but be able to get on with your own work unsupervised.

Salaries

Salaries start at between £20,500 and £26,500. Senior medical illustrators earn between £31,000 and £37,000. Large teaching hospitals have much bigger medical illustration departments so these offer more scope for management jobs with consequently higher pay.

Info

British Institute of Professional Photography
Fox Talbot House
2 Amwell End
Ware
Hertfordshire SG12 9HN
Tel: 01920 464011
www.bipp.com

Health Learning and Skills Advice Line
Tel: 0800 015 0850
www.learndirect-advice.co.uk/campaigns/nhs

Medical Artists' Association
www.maa.org.uk

Institute of Medical Illustrators
29 Arboretum Street
Nottingham NG1 4JA
www.imi.org.uk

NHS Careers
PO Box 376
Bristol BS99 3EY
Tel: 0845 606 0655
www.nhscareers.nhs.uk

25
Retailing

Retailing is a sector offering many different career opportunities. As well as the careers outlined in this section, retailing offers opportunities in distribution management and warehouse work, in finance, in marketing and in human resource management. There are openings at school leaver level through to graduate and senior management opportunities. Retail outlets include small shops, specialising in a particular type of product: shoes, car spares or quality foods, for example. Supermarkets, department stores and discount stores are just some of the other examples of retail outlets.

Checkout operator

Checkout operators work at the tills in supermarkets and other large retail stores. They scan the prices of all the items customers have purchased, process payments whether by cash, cheque or card, and they may also offer some assistance with packing, eg wrapping delicate items or putting frozen foods into separate bags.

Qualifications and training

No specific qualifications are necessary, though individual stores may request a good standard of education. Training is provided on the job and it is possible to obtain NVQ level 1 in Checkout Operations and NVQ levels 2 and 3 in Customer Service and Sales. Career progression is to supervisory roles.

We're DSG International but you may know us as our big brands such **Currys, Currys.Digital, Dixons.co.uk, Dixons Travel, PC World, PIXmania.com and The TechGuys**. As one of Europe's largest electrical retailers with stores in 28 countries, you can imagine the different career paths we could offer you. With our tailored training you could thrive in a range of careers from Retail Management to Distribution and from Buying to Finance.

Take control of your future at **www.dsgiplc.com/careers**

Personal qualities and skills

You must be polite and friendly and able to talk to people without losing your concentration or slowing down. You need good numeracy skills in order to spot errors. You must have good stamina and be able to work under pressure in a hectic environment.

Salaries

New checkout staff earn around £11,500, rising to £13,000 to £14,000 with some experience. Supervisors earn around £17,000 to £19,000. A few stores include all staff members in profit-sharing schemes.

Skillsmart Retail
Fourth Floor
93 Newman Street
London W1T 3EZ
Tel: 0800 093 5001
www.skillsmartretail.com

Wholesale and Retail Training Council (WRTC)
10 Hydepark Road
Mallusk
Newtonabbey BT36 4PY
Tel: 028 9084 5830
www.wrtc.co.uk

Info

Display designer/visual merchandiser

Display designers are responsible for shop windows and displays inside stores. These may be to attract customers into a shop, promote a new product or reinforce a company image. Displays are often seasonal or themed. Some designers work to instructions from head office, others create their own designs. The work may include making props, arranging lighting and general care of the display areas. Some shops also employ visual merchandisers who arrange products according to an organisation's display policy.

Qualifications and training

While there are no standard, formal entry qualifications, in practice most entrants have a relevant qualification. There are several three- or four-year degree courses in Design Merchandising Management and Exhibition and Retail Design. There are also some two-year foundation degrees available in display design or visual merchandising. Other art-based qualifications may be accepted by some employers. A great deal of training is on the job.

Personal qualities and skills

You need real artistic flair and to be good at working with colour and with three-dimensional design. You should be imaginative and practical, able to work as part of a team and able to relate design ideas to commercial impact. You also need good IT skills and preferably be able to use CAD (computer assisted design).

Salaries

Trainees earn between £11,000 and £14,000, while experienced display designers earn up to £22,000. It is possible for a display manager with a large store to earn more than £35,000.

Info

British Display Society
146 Welling Way
Welling
Kent DA16 2RS
Tel: 020 8856 2030
www.britishdisplaysociety.co.uk

Skillsmart Retail
Fourth Floor
93 Newman Street
London W1T 3EZ
Tel: 0800 093 5001
www.skillsmartretail.com

Retail store manager

Retail store managers work in department stores, in supermarkets and in small, individually owned stores. In a small store they will run the whole operation. In a supermarket they may be responsible for one area, fresh produce or the checkouts, for example. In a department store they may run one or several departments. Managers are responsible for ensuring that everything runs smoothly. They have to organise work rosters, ensure that sales targets are met, that customer service is of a high standard and that sales staff are fully trained.

Qualifications and training

There are several ways to become a retail store manager. Large stores or chains may run graduate management training programmes or programmes open to school leavers with two or three A levels. Experience, however, is often as important as qualifications, and many managers start out as sales assistants and work their way up to management positions.

Sales assistant

There are many opportunities for sales staff in retailing. Your responsibilities and tasks depend on what kind of retail outlet you are working in, as well as your level of experience. In general, sales staff are expected to sort stock, sell goods, ensure these goods are attractively displayed and deal with payments for goods. They also answer customers' queries, give information about products and offer advice. Some sales staff process orders for new stock.

Qualifications and training

While no formal academic qualifications are necessarily needed, GCSEs grades A–C in English and maths are a help as is some experience of working with people. Training is on the job, and large stores or chain stores may offer some structured training programmes. It is possible to work towards several NVQs at levels 2 and 3 in retail, including Sales, Retail Operations and Customer Service. Many people who start as sales assistants become supervisors for a section of a store, or progress to become store managers.

Personal qualities and skills

You must be polite and friendly and enjoy working with people. You need good basic literacy and numeracy skills and must be reasonably physically fit. Being smart and tidy is important, especially in fashion retailing. For anyone interested in supervisory and management responsibility, you have to be very well organised, good at taking decisions and good at leading and motivating other people.

Salaries

Trainee store managers on graduate training schemes start on between £18,500 to £25,000; sometimes starting salaries are a little less than this if you are not on a graduate scheme. As your career progresses there is a huge variation in salary, so managers can earn anything from £23,000 to £60,000. The variation is due mainly to the size and type of store and also whether bonus schemes increase pay. Sales assistants earn between £12,000 and £15,000, but there are often opportunities to move into supervisory or management roles.

Info

The Retail Academy
PO Box 296
York YO1 6WA
Tel: 01904 658 856
www.retailacademy.org

Skillsmart Retail
The Sector Skills Council for Retail
4th Floor
93 Newman Street
London W1T 3EZ
Tel: 020 746 5060
www.skillsmartretail.com

Appendix: Useful information

If you think there is a useful book, website or anything else that should be included in this directory of useful information, you can e-mail the author at eh@elizabethholmes.info and it will be considered for inclusion in the next edition of this book.

Glossary

A level   Advanced level of the General Certificate of Education, a qualification in FE.

academic   As opposed to vocational: a subject or course that is not aimed at a particular profession or career.

accreditation of prior learning   A way of having your skills and knowledge recognised when you have no recognised qualifications for them. You can also get accreditation for prior learning when you have completed some units of a course but have not actually finished it.

admissions tutor   The person at colleges and universities responsible for selecting candidates for courses.

apprenticeship   A training scheme that combines working and studying.

ASL   Additional and Specialist Learning.

AS level   Advanced Supplementary qualification (taken in the first year of sixth form).

awarding body   An organisation that sets and monitors the standards for qualifications.

BA   Bachelor of Arts.

BDS   Bachelor of Dental Surgery.

BEd   Bachelor of Education.

BIS   Department for Business, Innovation and Skills.

BMus   Bachelor of Music.

BNurs   Bachelor of Nursing.

BPharm   Bachelor of Pharmacy.

BSc   Bachelor of Science.

BSocSci   Bachelor of Social Science.

BVetMed   Bachelor of Veterinary Medicine.

CAP   Common Application Process.

C&G (City and Guilds)   An awarding body committed to vocational qualifications.

commune   A group of people living together and sharing responsibilities and/or possessions.

Connexions   The Government's service to help young people aged between 13 and 19.

day release   Time off work to attend educational courses.

DEAs   Disability Employment Advisers.

DfE   Department for Education.

degree   A qualification gained at university after three or more years of study.

DipHE   Diploma of Higher Education.

E2E   Entry to Employment.

ECCTIS   Educational Counselling and Credit Transfer Information Service, which is a database for university and college courses.

Edexcel   One of the largest awarding bodies in the United Kingdom.

EMA   Education Maintenance Allowance.

European Employment Service (EURES)   The European Job Mobility portal on the Europa website. EURES is a network to help workers move around Europe.

FD   Foundation degree.

FDA   Foundation degree (Arts).

FDSc   Foundation degree (Science).

FE   Further education (study usually between the ages of 16 to 18 or 19).

freelance   A person working for different companies at different times or at the same time; not employed by one company.

gap year   A year off, usually taken after FE or HE but sometimes later in life.

GCSE   General Certificate of Education (usually taken at school at the age of 16).

HE   Higher education.

Highers   Exams taken in Scotland instead of A levels.

HNC   Higher National Certificate.

HND   Higher National Diploma.

IAG   Information, Advice and Guidance.

IGCSE   International GCSE

induction   An introduction to a new job or course.

ITT   Initial Teacher Training.

Jobcentre Plus   Local drop-in agencies run by the Jobcentre Plus Network to get people who are 18+ into work.

kibbutz   A communal settlement in Israel, usually a farm.

LAs   Local authorities (which are part of the county or borough council), responsible for state-maintained primary and secondary education in the area. They also administer awards for HE, among other things.

Learning and Skills Council   The organisation responsible for all post-16 education and training in England.

LLB   Bachelor of Law.

LSIS   Learning and Skills Improvement Service.

MB/BS   Bachelor of Medicine and Bachelor of Surgery.

modular   Refers to a course that can be built from separate units and modules.

moshav   A cooperative Israeli village or settlement.

NEET   Not in Education, Employment or Training.

NVQ   National Vocation Qualification (SVQ in Scotland).

OCR   One of the three largest awarding bodies.

outsourcing   Contracting goods and services from outside a company rather than having them made or provided by employees.

PLTS   Personal Learning and Thinking Skills.

profession   Usually described as an occupation that involves prolonged training.

prospectus   A printed or online 'booklet' that advertises a university or college.

QCDA   Qualifications and Curriculum Development Authority.

QCF   Qualifications and Credit Framework.

recruiter   Someone who selects applicants for interview and then decides who gets the job.

referee   Someone who testifies orally or in writing about someone's skills and character.

SEN   Special Educational Needs.

S grade   Standard Grade in Scotland, the equivalent of the GCSE.

SQA   Scottish Qualifications Authority.

SVQ   Scottish Vocational Qualification (National Vocational Qualification, or NVQ, elsewhere in the United Kingdom).

TEFL   Teaching English as a Foreign Language.

UCAS   Universities and Colleges Admissions Service, which handles admissions to most undergraduate courses in the United Kingdom.

vocational education or training   Education or training targeted at a particular occupation or career.

WBL   Work-based learning.

Further reading

There is a huge amount of reading material out there for young people; everything from books about writing CVs to cookery books for students on a budget is available. It is well worth spending time browsing in your local library or good-quality bookshop to see whether there is anything that looks interesting to you. Don't feel restricted by what is suggested below; this is just the tip of the iceberg!

The internet

It is probably fair to say that just about all you need to know for your post-16 decisions can be found on the internet. The trouble is that it is not all in one place on the world wide web, which is why this book has gathered together URLs for all the websites you are likely to find of value and included them in the relevant place in each chapter. If you want to write to any of the organisations you visit online, you will find contact postal and e-mail addresses on the relevant websites. The websites listed below are useful starting points for further information. This is not a definitive list by any means, but it is worth bookmarking these sites and dropping in to see what is new as often as possible. All these sites have lots of suggested links for you to follow. Have fun!

www.bbc.co.uk/learning/ – study, work, money and travel advice for 16- to 24 year-olds

www.connexions.gov.uk – packed with all kinds of advice for 13- to 19-year-olds www.direct.gov.uk – information on the road to HE and university (Use the search box to find what you need)

www.hobsons.com/europe/ – for information on HE

http://careersadvice.direct.gov.uk – for advice on learning and working

www.niace.org.uk – information on improving skills, such as reading and numeracy

www.prospects.ac.uk – graduate careers website

www.thebigchoice.com – for careers ideas and choices

www.thesite.org.uk – packed with information including lots on careers and education

www.universityoptions.co.uk – for impartial advice on HE

www.yourcareerguide.co.uk – for careers suggestions

Books

This is just a starting point from which to launch your search for useful books. Don't forget that many good books have further reading sections at the back, so you will get more ideas by going through those, too.

General careers information and advice

The A–Z of Careers and Jobs (2010) 17th edn, Hodgson, S, Kogan Page, London

British Qualifications: A complete guide to educational, technical, professional and academic qualifications in Britain (2010) 40th edn, Kogan Page, London

Careers In... series, Kogan Page, London

Choosing Your Career: Work out what you really want to do with your life (2004) 2nd edn, Longson, S, Kogan Page, London

Disaster-Proof Your Career (2010) Forsyth, P, Kogan Page, London
The Sustainable Careers Handbook (2000) Shepherd, A and Rowe, F,
    Centre for Alternative Technology, Machynlleth, Powys
What Can I Do With... series, Trotman Publishing, Richmond, Surrey

Going abroad

Browse through the Kogan Page online catalogue at www.koganpage.
com as there is plenty to be found on this topic – in particular:

Working Abroad (2010) 31st edn, Reuvid, J, Kogan Page, London
Living and Working in France: Chez vous en France (2008) 4th edn, Brame,
    G, Kogan Page, London

Applications and interviews

Great Answers to Tough Interview Questions (2008) 7th edn, Yate, M J,
    Kogan Page, London
Knockout Job Interview Presentations (2010) Corfield, R, Kogan Page, London
*Preparing the Perfect CV: How to improve your chances of getting the job
    you want* (2009) 5th edn, Corfield, R, Kogan Page, London
Preparing the Perfect Job Application (2009) 5th edn, Corfield, R, Kogan
    Page, London
Readymade CVs (2008) 4th edn, Williams, L, Kogan Page, London
Readymade Job Search Letters (2008) 4th edn, Williams, L, Kogan Page,
    London
Successful Interview Skills (2009) Corfield, R, Kogan Page, London
Ultimate ... series, Kogan Page, London
Your Job Search Made Easy (2002) 3rd edn, Parkinson, M, Kogan Page,
    London

Taking a gap year

It is well worth spending some time browsing your local bookshop for
inspiration for your gap year. These books may also be of interest:

The Gap Year Guidebook, annual, Withers, A, John Catt

Making the Most of Your Gap Year (2002) Flynn, M, Trotman, Richmond, Surrey

Summer Jobs Worldwide (2010) Griffith, S, Crimson, London

The Backpacker's Bible (2008) King, S and Robertson, E, Anova, London

The Rough Guide to First Time Around the World (2010) Lansky, D, Rough Guides, London

Work Your Way Around the World (2009) Griffith, S, Vacation Work, Crimson, London

FE and HE

There are hundreds of books and guides that could be included here, but as that would not be as useful as it might sound, here is a selection for you to browse. Your local library and Connexions office are likely to have a copy of many of these.

The Art and Design Directory 2010 (2004) Widmer, J, Inspiring Futures Foundation, Camberley, Surrey

Big Guide 2010 (2008) UCAS

Choosing Your Degree Course and University (2010) Heap, B, Trotman, Richmond, Surrey

How to Complete Your UCAS Application 2010 entry (2010) Dixon, B/UCAS, Trotman, Richmond, Surrey

The Times Good University Guide 2010 (2010) O'Leary, J, Times Books, London

The Virgin Alternative Guide to British Universities (2010) Dudgeon, P, Virgin Books, London

Magazines and newspapers

You will find copies of local and national newspapers in your local reference library, but it is also worth talking to the librarian about any other newspapers or magazines that he or she buys that you may not have thought of looking at. The national broadsheet newspapers (just to confuse matters, some former broadsheets are now published in a compact size) cover different themes (such as media, secretarial, technology, education and so on) on different days, so find out on which days you should not miss reading them. It is a good idea to browse the education and HE supplements of these newspapers, too.

Local papers nearly always carry job advertisements. Some will be published weekly and some daily, so make sure that you know when yours comes out. There may well be a local glossy monthly magazine, too, so check that out as well.

Another good source of information on magazines and newspapers is your local large newsagent. Staff there will know exactly what is available and will be able to tell you if there is a specialist publication that you might like to order (make sure that these are not in your local library before paying for your own copies).

Your careers library at school may have some free magazines, so it is worth checking and picking copies up when you see them.

Money

Balancing Your Books: The CRAC guide to student finance (2004) Warrior, J, Trotman, Richmond, Surrey

Guide to Student Money 2010: How to manage your funds, fees and finances at university and college (2010) Thomas, G, Trotman (with the *Daily Telegraph*), Richmond, Surrey

Directory of Grant Making Trusts (2010/11) Directory of Social Change

Students' Money Matters 2008 (2008) Thomas, G, Trotman, Richmond, Surrey

The Essential Guide to Paying for University: Effective funding strategies for parents and students (2009) Dawson, C, Kogan Page (with *The Times*), London

University Scholarships and Bursaries Awards (2009) Heap, B, Trotman, Richmond, Surrey

Self-employment

Going Self-Employed: How to start out in business on your own Right Way, USA

Start Up and Run Your Own Business (2008) 7th edn, Reuvid, J, Kogan Page, London

Software

There are several software packages that you may be able to use either at school or college or at your local Connexions office. Look out for the following:

Higher Ideas Careersoft (database of HE courses)
Kudos CASCAiD (to help you find job ideas)
Pathfinder HE VT Career Progressions (careers guidance as well as suggestions for possible HE courses)
SkillCheck VT Career Progressions (helps you to identify key skills as well as work-related skills)

Tests

Career, Aptitude and Selection Tests (2009) 3rd edn, Barrett, J, Kogan Page, London
How to Succeed at an Assessment Centre (2009) 3rd edn, Tolley, H and Wood, R, Kogan Page, London
IQ Testing (2009) Carter, P and Russell, K, Kogan Page, London
Test Your IQ (2009) 2nd edn, Russell, K and Carter, P, Kogan Page, London
Test Your Own Aptitude (2003) 3rd edn, Williams, G and Barrett, J, Kogan Page, London
The Brain Fitness Workout (2010) Carter, P, Kogan Page, London
Ultimate IQ Tests (2008) Carter, P and Russell, K, Kogan Page, London

Index

NB: page numbers in *italic* indicate tables

Index of advertisers